Propertius

Propertius, Sextus, Butler, Harold Edgeworth, 1878-1951

Nabu Public Domain Reprints:

You are holding a reproduction of an original work published before 1923 that is in the public domain in the United States of America, and possibly other countries. You may freely copy and distribute this work as no entity (individual or corporate) has a copyright on the body of the work. This book may contain prior copyright references, and library stamps (as most of these works were scanned from library copies). These have been scanned and retained as part of the historical artifact.

This book may have occasional imperfections such as missing or blurred pages, poor pictures, errant marks, etc. that were either part of the original artifact, or were introduced by the scanning process. We believe this work is culturally important, and despite the imperfections, have elected to bring it back into print as part of our continuing commitment to the preservation of printed works worldwide. We appreciate your understanding of the imperfections in the preservation process, and hope you enjoy this valuable book.

THE LOEB CLASSICAL LIBRARY

A WORD ABOUT ITS PURPOSE AND ITS SCOPE

THE idea of arranging for the issue of this Library was suggested to me by my friend Mr. Salomon Reinach, the French savant. It appealed to me at once, and my imagination was deeply stirred by the thought that here might be found a practical and attractive way to revive the lagging interest in ancient literature which has for more than a generation been a matter of so much concern to educators. In an age when the Humanities are being neglected more perhaps than at any time since the Middle Ages, and when men's minds are turning more than ever before to the practical and the material, it does not suffice to make pleas, however eloquent and convincing, for the safeguarding and further enjoyment of our greatest heritage from the past.

Means must be found to place these treasures within the reach of all who care for the finer things of life. The mechanical and social achievements of our day must not blind our eyes to the fact that, in all that relates to man, his nature and aspirations, we have added little or nothing to what has been so finely said by the great men of old.

It has always seemed to me a pity that the young people of our generation should grow up with such scant knowledge of Greek and Latin literature, its wealth and variety, its freshness and its imperishable quality. The day is past when schools could afford to give sufficient time and attention to the teaching of the ancient languages to enable the student to get that enjoyment out of classical literature that made the lives of our grandfathers so rich. The demand for something "more practical," the large variety of subjects that *must* be taught, are crowding hard upon the Humanities. To make the beauty and learning, the philosophy and wit of the great writers of ancient Greece and Rome once more accessible by means of translations that are in themselves real pieces of literature, a thing to be read for the pure joy of it, and not dull transcripts of ideas that suggest in every line the existence of a finer original from which the average reader is shut out, and to place side by side with these translations the best critical texts of the original works, is the task I have set myself.

In France more than in any country the need has been felt of supplying readers who are not in a technical sense "scholars" with editions of the classics, giving text and translation, either in Latin or French, on opposite pages. Almost all the Latin authors and many Greek authors have been published in this way by the well-known firms, Panckoucke, Firmin-Didot, Hachette, and Garnier. In Germany only a handful of Greek authors were issued in this form during the first half of the nineteenth century. No collection of this kind exists in English-speaking countries.

Before venturing on so large an undertaking as is involved in the task I had set myself I consulted a number of distinguished scholars as to the desirability of such a series. My correspondence ranged from St. Petersburg to San Francisco, and the replies to my inquiry conveyed an almost unanimous and unqualified approval. I was also encouraged by the opinion of several experienced publishers, who agreed that the time is ripe for the execution of such a project. I therefore set to work, and after two and a half years of not inconsiderable labour I now have the privilege and the satisfaction of accompanying the early volumes of the series with this preface.

The following eminent scholars, representing Great Britain, the United States, Germany, and France, kindly consented to serve on the Advisory Board:

EDWARD CAPPS, Ph.D., of Princeton University.

MAURICE CROISET, Member of the Institut de France.

OTTO CRUSIUS, Ph.D., Litt.D., of the University of Munich, Member of the Royal Bavarian Academy of Science.

HERMANN DIELS, Ph.D., of the University of Berlin, Secretary of the Royal Academy of Science, Berlin.

J. G. FRAZER, D.C.L., LL.D., Litt.D., of Cambridge University.

A. D. GODLEY, M.A., Public Orator of the University of Oxford.

WILLIAM G. HALE, Ph.D., of Chicago University.

SALOMON REINACH, Member of the Institut de France.

Sir J. E. Sandys, Litt.D., Public Orator of Cambridge University.

John Williams White, Ph.D., Professor Emeritus of Harvard University.

I was also fortunate in securing as Editors Mr. T. E. Page, M.A., until recently a Master at the Charterhouse School, and Dr. W. H. D. Rouse, Litt.D., Head Master of the Perse Grammar School, in Cambridge, England. Their critical judgment, their thorough scholarship and wide acquaintance with ancient and modern literature, are the best guarantee that the translations will combine accuracy with sound English idiom.

Wherever modern translations of marked excellence were already in existence efforts were made to secure them for the Library, but in a number of instances copyright could not be obtained. I mention this because I anticipate that we may be criticised for issuing new translations in certain cases where they might perhaps not seem to be required. But as the Series is to include all that is of value and of interest in Greek and Latin literature, from the time of Homer to the Fall of Constantinople, no other course was possible. On the other hand, many readers will be glad to see that we have included several of those stately and inimitable translations made in the sixteenth, seventeenth, and eighteenth centuries, which are counted among the classics of the English language. Most of the translations will, however, be wholly new, and many of the best scholars in Great Britain, the United States, and Canada have already promised their assistance and are now engaged upon the work. As a general rule, the best available critical texts will be used, but in quite a number of cases the texts will be especially prepared for this Library.

The announcement of this new Series has been greeted with so many cordial expressions of good-will from so many quarters that I am led to believe that it will fill a long-felt want, and that it will prove acceptable to a wide circle of readers, not only to-day, but also in the future.

These books will appeal not only to scholars who care for a uniform series of the *best* texts, and to college graduates who wish to renew and enlarge their knowledge with the help of text and translation, but also to those who know neither Greek nor Latin, and yet desire to reap the fruits of ancient genius and wisdom. Some readers, too, may be enticed by the text printed opposite the translation to gather an elementary knowledge of Greek and Latin, thus greatly enhancing the interest of their reading; while the teacher of *modern* literature will, I trust, find these books useful in the effort to make his students acquainted with the prototypes of practically every style of modern literary composition.

It is my pleasant duty to express my sincere thanks to all those on both sides of the Atlantic whose hearty co-operation and help have made my task at once easy and agreeable. Nor can I find a happier way of commending this new Classical Series to the public than by quoting Goethe's words:

"Man studiere nicht die Mitgeborenen und Mitstrebenden, sondern grosse Menschen der Vorzeit, deren Werke seit Jahrhunderten gleichen Wert und gleiches Ansehen behalten haben. . . . Man studiere Molière, man studiere Shakespeare, aber vor allen Dingen, die alten Griechen, und immer die alten Griechen."

JAMES LOEB

MUNICH
September 1, 1912

THE LOEB CLASSICAL LIBRARY
EDITED BY
T. E. PAGE, M.A., AND W. H. D. ROUSE, Litt.D.

PROPERTIUS

PROPERTIUS

WITH AN ENGLISH TRANSLATION BY
H. E. BUTLER, M.A.
PROFESSOR OF LATIN IN THE UNIVERSITY
OF LONDON

LONDON : WILLIAM HEINEMANN
NEW YORK : THE MACMILLAN CO.
MCMXII

9446

PREFACE

A FEW words are necessary in connection with the text contained in this volume. There are a number of passages in Propertius where it cannot be said that any certain emendation has been made. In such cases I have inserted the most plausible correction in the text, in order not to confuse readers of the translation. I do not wish it to be supposed that I regard such corrections as certain. In some cases they are only a *pis aller*. Propertius presents such difficulties to the translator that an apology for its deficiencies is perhaps unnecessary. No one is more sensible of them than myself. I have attempted, as far as possible, to keep close to the Latin, even in cases—and they are not a few—where from the point of view of style a free paraphrase would have been in many ways preferable.

H. E. BUTLER

LONDON, 1912

THE LIFE OF PROPERTIUS

WE know little of Propertius, save for what we can gather from his own poems and a few references to him in later Latin writers. His name was Sextus Propertius. The majority of the MSS., with the important exception of the *Codex Neapolitanus*, style him Sextus Aurelius Propertius Nauta. *Nauta* is demonstrably absurd. Propertius expresses the liveliest terror of the sea in his poems, and the name is accounted for by the absurd reading of the MSS. in II. xxiv. 38, *quamvis navita dives eras*. *Aurelius* is equally impossible. Both Aurelius and Propertius are *nomina gentilicia*, and such names were not doubled at this period.

His birthplace was Assisi. The position of that town suits the indications given in I. xxii. and IV. i. 61–66 and 121–126. The name Asis in the two latter passages (where some, following Lachmann, read *Asisi*), though not found elsewhere, seems pretty conclusive, while in the "Umbrian lake" mentioned in IV. i. 124 we have a reference to a shallow lake in the plain below Assisi, which existed till the Middle Ages. Finally, Pliny the Younger in two of his letters (vi. 15 and ix. 22) mentions a certain Passennus Paullus, a descendant of Propertius and a citizen of the same town. An inscription bearing his name has been found at Assisi.

Propertius was born in all probability between

THE LIFE OF PROPERTIUS

54 B.C. (the earliest possible date for Tibullus' birth) and 43 B.C. (the date of Ovid's birth). This is indicated by Ovid (*Tristia*, IV. x. 51-54), who gives a catalogue of the elegiac poets in the following chronological order: Gallus, Tibullus, Propertius, Ovid. Further, in IV. i. 127-140 Propertius implies that he lost his father while very young, and entered on his diminished inheritance shortly after the distribution of land among the veterans of Octavian and Antony in 41 B.C. Further, I. xxi. shows that he was old enough to be impressed by the death of a relative or neighbour in the Perusine war of 40 B.C. His birth may therefore be conjecturally placed between 50 and 48 B.C. The mention of his having worn the *aurea bulla* (IV. i 131-134) shows him to have been of equestrian rank (see Plin. *N. H.* XXXIII. 10), while from the same passage we learn that he had been destined for the bar, but deserted it for poetry. Soon after his assumption of the *toga virilis* he fell in love with a certain Lycinna (III. xv. 3-6). How long this *liaison* lasted we cannot tell; we only know that his meeting with Cynthia caused him to forget Lycinna but two years after his first acquaintance with love (III. xv. 7, 8). Cynthia was the one deep passion of his life; she was the first woman whom he really loved, and there is nothing to make us think that she was not the last, though in the end, no doubt after many infidelities on both sides, he broke with her (see last two elegies of Book III.). Cynthia's real name was Hostia, a fact which we learn from Apuleius' *Apologia* (c. x.). She was a courtesan, for II. vii. 7 shows that it was impossible for him to marry her: the *lex Papia Poppaea* enacted that no man of free birth might marry a prostitute, and the only possible interpretation of the passage in question is that the unknown law to

THE LIFE OF PROPERTIUS

which Propertius refers contained similar provisions. Further, the same poem shows that he was unmarried and unwilling to marry any one else, while there can be no doubt that Cynthia was unmarried, for among the objects of his jealousy Propertius never makes mention of a husband. It is possible that she may have been descended from Hostius, an epic poet of the second century B.C. (see III. xx. 8, note). We gather from the poems of Propertius that she had a gift for singing, dancing, and poetry, was tall and yellow-haired, with black eyes. We cannot trace the history of the *liaison* with any clearness. Neither party was faithful, and the course of love did not run smooth. On one occasion (see III. xvi. 9) there was a breach which lasted for a whole year. The quarrel was, however, made up, and at the close of the third book, where Propertius finally breaks with her, he claims to have been her faithful slave for five years (III. xxv. 3). In the fourth book Cynthia is mentioned in only two poems (VII. and VIII.), though there is probably a reference to her in the fifth elegy; the seventh tells us that she died neglected and was buried near Tibur.

Propertius left four books of elegies behind him. It is hard to determine the dates of their publication. It is probable that Book I. was published about 26 B.C.,[1] Book II. about 24 or early in 23 B.C., Book III. in 22 or 21 B.C. The fourth book was published not earlier than 16 B.C., as both the fifth and eleventh poems refer to events of that year. As to the latter years of Propertius' life we know nothing. It is perhaps probable that he died not long after the

[1] It was published separately under the title *Cynthia*. Cp. II. III. 4 (also Martial, XIV. 189). In some of the MSS. of Propertius it has the title *Cynthia Monobiblos*.

THE LIFE OF PROPERTIUS

publication of Book IV. But we cannot base any very strong argument on his silence from song. He may even have married and had children. Pliny the Younger (*Ep.* vi. 15) says that the poet Passennus Paullus counted Propertius among his ancestors. All that we can be certain of is that he died before 2 A.D., for Ovid in the *Remedium Amoris* (published about that year) speaks of him in language (I. 764) appropriate only to one already dead. References to Propertius in ancient writers are rare. The only reference of interest (and that an uncertain one) is found in the *Epistles* of Horace (II. ii. 91), where Horace derides a bard who claims to be a second Callimachus (*cp.* Prop. IV. I. 64). Quintilian (x. i. 93) says that some critics ranked Propertius first among Roman elegiac poets, but that he personally prefers Tibullus.

THE MSS. OF PROPERTIUS

N. The best MS. of Propertius is the *Codex Neapolitanus*, now at Wolfenbuttel (Gud. 224). It contains the whole of the poet's works with the exception of IV. ii. 11–76, where four pages have been lost. It dates from the twelfth century.

To supplement *N* we have three MSS. belonging to another family, but on the whole agreeing with *N*. These are:

(1) *A.* The *Codex Vossianus* 38, now at Leyden. This MS. contains Book I. and the first sixty-two lines of II. i. It dates from the early fourteenth century.

(2) *F.* The *Codex Laurentianus*, now at Florence, in the Laurentian Library (plut 36, 49). It contains the whole of Propertius, and dates from the close of the fourteenth or the very beginning of the fifteenth century.

(3) *L.* The *Codex Holkhamicus*, now in the library of the Earl of Leicester at Holkham. It contains Propertius from II. xxi 3 to the end, and is dated 1421.

Two other MSS. may be mentioned. They closely follow *N*, and are useful where *N* fails us in Book IV. They are:

(1) μ. The *Codex Parisinus* (8233), sometimes called *Memmianus*, written in 1465.

(2) v. The *Codex Urbinas* (641), in the Vatican. It likewise dates from the fifteenth century.

THE MSS. OF PROPERTIUS

5. In addition to these MSS. there are a large number of inferior fifteenth-century MSS. Among these are two MSS. which since the edition of Baehrens have appeared in the *apparatus criticus* of modern texts. They are (1) the *Codex Daventriensis* (1792), now at Deventer, and the *Codex Ottoboniano-Vaticanus* (1514), now in the Vatican. Both are late-fifteenth-century MSS. Mr. O. L. Richmond (*Journal of Philology*, xxxi. 161) has shown that they do not deserve the position assigned to them by Baehrens, and that they must be ranked among the inferior MSS. as possessing no independent value.

Where MSS. other than N, A, F, L, μ, v are mentioned their catalogue reference is given.

The text of Propertius is undoubtedly very corrupt. The sequence of thought is at times so broken that the reader necessarily concludes that one of two things has happened: (*a*) couplets have been lost, or (*b*) the order of the lines has been dislocated. While the second alternative is possible, and while various scholars (the best example is Professor Postgate in the new *Corpus Poetarum Latinorum*) have attempted to save the situation by wholesale transposition, as yet no scientific system of transposition has been discovered, and no satisfactory theory has been put forward to account for the dislocation. The first is therefore the safer course.

NOTE ON THE DIVISION INTO BOOKS

LACHMANN held that Propertius' poems should be divided into five books, not, as the MSS. divide them, into four. His main argument is based on II. XIII *a* 25, *sat mea sit magno, si tres sint pompa libelli.* He argues that the words *tres libelli* show that the poem in question must have formed part of the third book. He therefore made the third book begin with II. x., and treated the third and fourth books as recorded in the MSS. as fourth and fifth. But it does not seem necessary to give the words *tres libelli* so literal a meaning, and it is worth noting that the grammarian Nonius, p. 169, quotes III. XXI. 14 as coming from the third book. The division as given in our MSS. would seem, therefore, to be as old as Nonius. Lachmann's division is followed in some texts (*e.g.*, Haupt-Vahlen and L Muller), and much confusion has been caused as regards references to Propertius. Lachmann's theory has, however, been abandoned by all other editors. If the argument as to *tres libelli* is to be used again, it will have to be used on different lines, and associated with some theory of the dislocation of the text.

BIBLIOGRAPHICAL NOTE

The first edition of Propertius was published in 1487 (ed. Beroaldus). Baehrens (Leipzig, 1880) was the first to put the text on a scientific basis. His text is much marred by arbitrary and tasteless conjectures, but the preface is important. Since then texts have been edited by Palmer (London, 1880), Postgate (in *Corpus Poetarum Latinorum*, London, 1894), Phillimore (Oxford, 1901, and Riccardi Press, London, 1911), Hosius (Teubner Series, 1912). Of these Postgate's text alone is other than conservative in tendency. The only modern commentaries are by Rothstein (Berlin, 1898) and Butler (London, 1905). Of the older commentaries those of Passerat (Paris, 1608), Lachmann (Leipzig, 1816, and Berlin, 1829), and Hertzberg (Halle, 1843-45) will on the whole be found most useful. There are also good editions of selected elegies by Postgate (London, 1881) and Ramsay (Oxford, 1900, 3rd ed.). The sixth edition of Haupt's recension (1904, Leipzig), revised by Vahlen, and accompanied by texts of Catullus and Tibullus, is an elegant volume, which follows Lachmann's division into five books, and contains no *apparatus criticus*.

For literary estimates of Propertius the reader may go to Sellar, *Roman Poetry under Augustus: Elegiac Poets* (Oxford), and Ribbeck's well-known *History of Roman Poetry*.

BIBLIOGRAPHICAL NOTE

The most important separate treatises on the MSS. are Solbisky, *De Codd. Propertii* (Weimar, 1882); Housman, *Journal of Philology*, vols. XXI., XXII., Nos. 41–43; Postgate, *Some MSS. of Propertius* (*Trans. Cambridge Philol. Soc.* IV. 1); while O. L. Richmond, *Towards a Recension of Propertius* (*Journal of Philology*, vol. XXXI.), is also worth consulting. For a general discussion of questions connected with Propertius see Plessis, *Études sur Properce* (Paris, 1886), and more especially Schanz, *Geschichte der Römischen Litteratur*, Part 2, § 285 *sqq.* Teuffel's *History of Latin Literature* (English trans.) contains much of the same information, but is an older book and less thorough.

SIGLA

N = Codex Neapolitanus.
A = Codex Vossianus.
F = Codex Laurentianus.
L = Codex Holkhamicus.
μ = Codex Parisinus or Memmianus.
v = Codex Urbinas.
ς = Codices deteriores.

PROPERTIUS

BOOK I

SEXTI PROPERTI ELEGIARVM

LIBER PRIMVS

I

Cynthia prima suis miserum me cepit ocellis,
 contactum nullis ante cupidinibus.
tum mihi constantis deiecit lumina fastus
 et caput impositis pressit Amor pedibus,
donec me docuit castas odisse puellas
 improbus, et nullo vivere consilio.
et mihi iam toto furor hic non deficit anno,
 cum tamen adversos cogor habere deos.
Milanion nullos fugiendo, Tulle, labores
 saevitiam durae contudit Iasidos   10
nam modo Partheniis amens errabat in antris,
 ibat et hirsutas ille videre feras;
ille etiam Hylaei percussus verbere[1] rami
 saucius Arcadiis rupibus ingemuit.
ergo velocem potuit domuisse puellam:
 tantum in amore preces et benefacta valent.
in me tardus Amor non ullas cogitat artes,
 nec meminit notas, ut prius, ire vias.

[1] verbere *Baehrens*   vulnere *N:* arbore *AF.*

PROPERTIUS
THE ELEGIES

THE FIRST BOOK

I

Ah! woe is me! 'twas Cynthia first ensnared me with her eyes; till then my heart had felt no passion's fire. But then Love made me lower my glance of pride unbending, and with implanted feet bowed down my head, till of his cruelty he taught me to spurn all honest maids, and to live a life of recklessness.

[7] A year has passed and my madness is not stayed, though my suit perforce endures the frown of heaven. Yet Milanion shrank not, Tullus, from any toils, howsoe'er hard, and so subdued the cruel heart of the unrelenting daughter of Iasus. For now he wandered love-distraught in the Parthenian caverns, and went to face the shaggy creatures of the wild. Nay, more, hardstricken once by the club of Hylaeus, he groaned in agony on the rocks of Arcady. So at last was he able to conquer the swift-footed maid; such is the reward that prayers and loyal service win for love. But for me, slow-witted Love hath lost his craft and forgets to tread the paths that once he trod.

SEXTI PROPERTI ELEGIARVM LIBER I

at vos, deductae quibus est fallacia lunae
  et labor in magicis sacra piare focis, 20
en agedum dominae mentem convertite nostrae,
  et facite illa meo palleat ore magis!
tunc ego crediderim vobis et sidera et amnes
  posse Cytaeines[1] ducere carminibus.
aut[2] vos, qui sero lapsum revocatis, amici,
  quaerite non sani pectoris auxilia.
fortiter et ferrum saevos patiemur et ignes,
  sit modo libertas quae velit ira loqui.
ferte per extremas gentes et ferte per undas,
  qua non ulla meum femina norit iter: 30
vos remanete, quibus facili deus annuit aure,
  sitis et in tuto semper amore pares.
in me nostra Venus noctes exercet amaras,
  et nullo vacuus tempore defit Amor.
hoc, moneo, vitate malum: sua quemque moretur
  cura, neque assueto mutet amore locum.
quod si quis monitis tardas adverterit aures,
  heu referet quanto verba dolore mea!

II

Qvid iuvat ornato procedere, vita, capillo
  et tenues Coa veste movere sinus?
aut quid Orontea crines perfundere murra,
  teque peregrinis vendere muneribus;

[1] Cytaeines *Hertzberg*: cythalinis *etc. NAF.*
[2] aut *Hemsterhuys*: et *NAF.*

[19] But ye who beguile men's hearts by luring the moon from heaven, and toil to solemnise dread rites on magic altars, go change my mistress' heart and make her cheeks grow paler than mine own. Then will I trust your claims to have power over stars and rivers to lead them whithersoever ye will by Colchian charms.

[25] Or else do ye, my friends, that would recall me all too late from the downward slope, seek all the remedies for a heart diseased. Bravely will I bear the cruel cautery and the knife, if only I may win liberty to speak the words mine anger prompts. Ah! bear me far thro' nations and seas at the world's end, where never a woman may trace my path. Do ye abide at home, to whose prayer the god gives easy audience and answers "Yea," and either to other make equal response of love unperilous. Against me Venus, our common mistress, plies nights of bitterness, and Love that hath no respite faileth never.

[35] Lovers, I warn ye all. Fly the woe that now is mine: cling each one to his own beloved, and never change when love has found its home But if any all too late give ear to these my warnings, ah! with what agony will he recall my words!

II

What boots it, light of my life, to go forth with locks adorned, and to rustle in slender folds of Coan silk? Or avails it aught to steep thy tresses in the myrrh of Orontes, to parade thyself in the gifts that aliens bring, to spoil the grace of nature by the

SEXTI PROPERTI ELEGIARVM LIBER I

naturaeque decus mercato perdere cultu,
   nec sinere in propriis membra nitere bonis?
crede mihi, non ulla tua est medicina figurae:
   nudus Amor formae non amat artificem.
aspice quos summittat humus formosa colores;
   ut veniant hederae sponte sua melius,   10
surgat et in solis formosius arbutus antris,
   et sciat indociles currere lympha vias.
litora nativis persuadent picta lapillis,
   et volucres nulla dulcius arte canunt.
non sic Leucippis succendit Castora Phoebe,
   Pollucem cultu non Hilaira soror;
non, Idae et cupido quondam discordia Phoebo,
   Eueni patriis filia litoribus;
nec Phrygium falso traxit candore maritum
   avecta externis Hippodamia rotis: 20
sed facies aderat nullis obnoxia gemmis,
   qualis Apelleis est color in tabulis.
non illis studium vulgo conquirere amantes:
   illis ampla satis forma pudicitia.
non ego nunc verear? ne[1] sim tibi vilior istis:
   uni si qua placet, culta puella sat est;
cum tibi praesertim Phoebus sua carmina donet
   Aoniamque libens Calliopea lyram,
unica nec desit iucundis gratia verbis,
   omnia quaeque Venus, quaeque Minerva probat. 30
his tu semper eris nostrae gratissima vitae,
   taedia dum miserae sint tibi luxuriae.

[1] verear? ne *Jacob*: vereor ne *NAF*.

charms that gold can buy nor allow thy limbs to shine in the glory that is their own? Believe me, thou hast no art can make thy form more fair; Love himself goes naked and hates those that make a craft of beauty. See what hues lovely earth sends forth; 'tis the wild ivy springs fairest ever; loveliest the arbutus that grows in the caverns of the wilderness, and all untaught are the channels where the waters run. Begemmed with native pebbles the shores beguile our eyes, and birds sing sweetlier from their lack of art.

15 'Twas not by art that Phoebe, Leucippus' child, fired the heart of Castor, nor by adornments that Hilaira her sister won the love of Pollux. Not so did Euenus' daughter become a bride, for whom of old Idas and passionate Phoebus strove; by no false brilliance did Hippodamia lure to her side her Phrygian spouse, and was whirled away on alien chariot-wheels. Unto no jewels their faces were beholden, pure as the hues that shine in Apelles' pictures. They never craved to gather lovers through all the land; enough for them, if their beauty was clothed with chastity. Have I not then good cause for fear? Ah! count me not cheaper than those vile wretches that seek thy love! With one true lover a maid hath enough of honour; so most of all, if Phoebus grant, as to thee, his boon of song and Calliope, nothing loth, bestow Aonia's lyre, and every merry word is graced with wondrous charm, even by all that Venus and all that Minerva loves. All these things shall make thee dearest to my heart, if thou wilt but cast aside thy hateful luxury.

SEXTI PROPERTI ELEGIARVM LIBER I

III

Qvalis Thesea iacuit cedente carina
  languida desertis Gnosia litoribus;
qualis et accubuit primo Cepheia somno
  libera iam duris cotibus Andromede;
nec minus assiduis Edonis fessa choreis
  qualis in herboso concidit Apidano:
talis visa mihi mollem spirare quietem
  Cynthia non certis nixa caput manibus,
ebria cum multo traherem vestigia Baccho,
  et quaterent sera nocte facem pueri.   10
hanc ego, nondum etiam sensus deperditus omnes,
  molliter impresso conor adire toro;
et quamvis duplici correptum ardore iuberent
  hac Amor hac Liber, durus uterque deus,
subiecto leviter positam temptare lacerto
  osculaque admota sumere avara[1] manu,
non tamen ausus eram dominae turbare quietem,
  expertae metuens iurgia saevitiae;
sed sic intentis haerebam fixus ocellis,
  Argus ut ignotis cornibus Inachidos.   20
et modo solvebam nostra de fronte corollas
  ponebamque tuis, Cynthia, temporibus;
et modo gaudebam lapsos formare capillos;
  nunc furtiva cavis poma dabam manibus;
omniaque ingrato largibar munera somno,
  munera de prono saepe voluta sinu;

[1] avara *Baehrens :* et arma *NAF.*

THE ELEGIES OF PROPERTIUS BOOK I

III

Like as the maid of Cnossus lay swooning on the desert strand whilst the bark of Theseus sped swift away, or as Andromeda, child of Cepheus, sank into her first sleep, freed at last from her hard couch of rock, or as the Thracian maenad, no less foredone by the unending dance, lies sunk in slumber on the grassy banks of Apidanus, even so, meseemed, did Cynthia breathe the spirit of gentle rest, her head propped on faltering hands, when I came dragging home my reeling feet, drunken with deep draughts of wine, and the slaves were shaking their dying torches in the gloom of night far-spent.

[11] Not yet were all my senses drowned, and I strove to approach her where she lay, and lightly pressed against her couch. And although a twofold frenzy had laid hold upon me, and the two inexorable gods of wine and love urged on this side and on that, with gentle touch I tried to pass mine arm about her where she lay, and with outstretched hand take passionate toll of kisses; yet I had not dared to break in upon my mistress' rest (for I feared the bitter chidings of that cruel tongue, so oft endured by me), but fixed my gaze upon her with tireless eyes, even as Argus glared on the strange hornèd brow of the daughter of Inachus. And now I loosed the chaplets from my brow and placed them, Cynthia, about thy head, and now rejoiced to compose thy straying locks; and stealthily with hollowed hands gave thee apples, and on thy thankless slumbers lavished every gift, gifts poured abundantly from my bosom as I bowed above thee. And if at times thou didst move and

SEXTI PROPERTI ELEGIARVM LIBER I

et quotiens raro duxti[1] suspiria motu,
   obstupui vano credulus auspicio,
ne qua tibi insolitos portarent visa timores,
   neve quis invitam cogeret esse suam: 30
donec diversas praecurrens luna fenestras,
   luna moraturis sedula luminibus,
compositos levibus radiis patefecit ocellos.
   sic ait in molli fixa toro cubitum:
"tandem te nostro referens iniuria lecto
   alterius clausis expulit e foribus?
namque ubi longa meae consumpsti tempora noctis,
   languidus exactis, ei mihi, sideribus?
o utinam tales perducas, improbe, noctes,
   me miseram quales semper habere iubes!   40
nam modo purpureo fallebam stamine somnum,
   rursus et Orpheae carmine, fessa, lyrae;
interdum leviter mecum deserta querebar
   externo longas saepe in amore moras.
dum me iucundis lapsam sopor impulit alis.
   illa fuit lacrimis ultima cura meis."

IV

Qvid mihi tam multas laudando, Basse, puellas
   mutatum domina cogis abire mea?
quid me non pateris vitae quodcumque sequetur
   hoc magis assueto ducere servitio?
tu licet Antiopae formam Nycteidos, et tu
   Spartanae referas laudibus Hermionae,

---
[1] duxti ς: duxit *NAF*.

THE ELEGIES OF PROPERTIUS BOOK I

sigh, I started for fear (though vain was the presage which won my belief) that visions of the night brought thee strange terrors or that some phantom-lover constrained thee to be his against thy will.

31 But at last the moon gliding past the windows over against her couch, the officious moon with lingering light, opened her fast-closed eyes with its gentle beams. Then with elbow propped on the soft couch she cried:

35 "At length another's scorn has driven thee forth and closed the doors against thee and brought thee home to my bed once more. For where hast thou passed the long hours of the night, that was plighted to me, thou that comest to me outworn when the stars—ah, me!—are driven from the sky? Mayst thou, cruel heart, endure the long agony of nights such as ever thou bidst me broken-hearted keep. For but now I was beguiling mine eyes from slumber with purple broidery, and then, work-wearied, with the music of Orpheus' lyre. And ever and anon, left thus forlorn, I made gentle moan unto myself, that oft thou lingerest locked in another's arms, till at the last I sank down and sleep fanned my limbs with kindly wings. That was my last-thought amid my tears."

IV

Why, Bassus, by praising the beauty of so many fair ones dost thou urge me to change my course and leave my mistress? Why sufferest thou me not to spend in her fetters, to which my heart grows ever more enured, whate'er of life the future has in store? Thou mayest praise the beauty of Antiopa, the child of Nycteus, the charms of Spartan Hermione and all

SEXTI PROPERTI ELEGIARVM LIBER I

et quascumque tulit formosi temporis aetas;
    Cynthia non illas nomen habere sinat:
nedum, si levibus fuerit collata figuris,
    inferior duro iudice turpis eat.   10
haec sed forma mei pars est extrema furoris;
    sunt maiora, quibus, Basse, perire iuvat:
ingenuus color et multis decus artibus, et quae
    gaudia sub tacita dicere veste libet.
quo magis et nostros contendis solvere amores,
    hoc magis accepta fallit uterque fide.
non impune feres: sciet haec insana puella
    et tibi non tacitis vocibus hostis erit;
nec tibi me post haec committet Cynthia nec te
    quaeret; erit tanti criminis illa memor,   20
et te circum omnes alias irata puellas
    differet: heu nullo limine carus eris.
nullas illa suis contemnet fletibus aras,
    et quicumque sacer, qualis ubique, lapis.
non ullo gravius temptatur Cynthia damno,
    quam sibi cum rapto cessat amore deus:
praecipue nostri. maneat sic semper, adoro,
    nec quicquam ex illa quod querar inveniam!

V

INVIDE, tu tandem voces compesce molestas
    et sine nos cursu, quo sumus, ire pares!
quid tibi vis, insane? meos sentire furores?
    infelix, properas ultima nosse mala,

the maids the age of beauty bore; yet Cynthia would make their glory pale; still less, were she compared with meaner beauties, would the harshest judge declare her the less fair. Yet even her shapely form is but the least part of that which frenzies me. Yet greater charms are there, for which, Bassus, to die with passion is my joy. A natural colour, grace sprung from skill in many an art, and joys whereof her couch keeps the secret.

15 The more thou strivest to dissolve our love, the more doth either of us cheat thy craft with unshaken loyalty. Nor shalt thou go scatheless for this; the frenzied maid shall know what thou hast done, and by no gentle outcry shall prove thy foe, nor will Cynthia henceforth entrust me to thy care nor seek thy company; such crime as thine she will remember ever, and in her wrath will defame thee in every beauty's ear; henceforth, alas! no threshold shall give thee welcome. No altar shall be too humble a witness for her tears, no sacred effigy, whate'er its sanctity, shall fail to know her grief. No loss touches Cynthia so deeply as when a lover's heart is stolen from her and Cupid spreads his wings; deepest of all her grief if 'tis my love she loses. Ah! may she ever, I pray, abide thus, and may I never find aught in her to cause me to lament.

V

ENVIOUS, hush now at length thy unwelcome prayers, and let us go hand in hand along the path that now we tread. What wouldst thou, madman? Wouldst thou suffer frenzies such as mine? Poor wretch, thou hastest to acquaint thyself with the

SEXTI PROPERTI ELEGIARVM LIBER I

et miser ignotos vestigia ferre per ignes,
    et bibere e tota toxica Thessalia.
non est illa vagis similis collata puellis:
    molliter irasci non solet illa tibi.
quod si forte tuis non est contraria votis,
    at tibi curarum milia quanta dabit!   10
non tibi iam somnos, non illa relinquet ocellos:
    illa feros animis alligat una viros.
a, mea contemptus quotiens ad limina curres,
    cum tibi singultu fortia verba cadent,
et tremulus maestis orietur fletibus horror,
    et timor informem ducet in ore notam,
et quaecumque voles fugient tibi verba querenti,
    nec poteris, qui sis aut ubi, nosse miser.
tum grave servitium nostrae cogere puellae
    discere et exclusum quid sit abire domum;   20
nec iam pallorem totiens mirabere nostrum,
    aut cur sim toto corpore nullus ego.
nec tibi nobilitas poterit succurrere amanti:
    nescit Amor priscis cedere imaginibus.
quod si parva tuae dederis vestigia culpae,
    quam cito de tanto nomine rumor eris!
non ego tum potero solacia ferre roganti,
    cum mihi nulla mei sit medicina mali;
sed pariter miseri socio cogemur amore
    alter in alterius mutua flere sinu.   30
quare, quid possit mea Cynthia, desine, Galle,
    quaerere: non impune illa rogata venit.

worst of ills, to tread on hidden fire to thy sorrow and drink all Thessaly's store of poison. Shouldst thou compare her, she is not like those flighty loves of thine; her anger is no light thing. Nay, even if perchance she frown not wholly on thy prayers, yet what a world of care she will bring thee! No more will she suffer thee to sleep nor thine eyes to range at will; she, as none other, can bind the fierce of heart. Ah, how often wilt thou run to my doors a rejected suitor, when thy brave speech shall fail for sobs, and a chill shuddering and bitter weeping shall come upon thee, when fear shall trace disfiguring lines upon thy face, and the words thou wouldst speak die on thy lips in the midst of thy complaining and thou canst no more tell, poor wretch, who or where thou art!

[19] Then shalt thou be constrained to know how bitter a thing it is to bear my mistress' yoke, and what it means to return homeward when her doors are barred. Not any more shalt thou marvel so oft at the pallor of my face nor wherefore my whole frame is wasted into naught. Nor will thy high birth avail thee in thy love: Love scorns to yield to ancient ancestry. But if thou givest but the least sign of faithlessness, how soon will thy name, so powerful now, be a mere byword! I shall not then be able to console thee when thou comest asking aid, for mine own woe is cureless, but we shall be constrained, comrades in love and woe, to weep tears of sympathy, either on other's breast. Wherefore cease, Gallus, to seek to learn my Cynthia's power. Heavy the toll they pay in answer to whose prayer she comes.

SEXTI PROPERTI ELEGIARVM LIBER I

VI

Non ego nunc Hadriae vereor mare noscere tecum,
    Tulle, neque Aegaeo ducere vela salo,
cum quo Rhipaeos possim conscendere montes
    ulteriusque domos vadere Memnonias;
sed me complexae remorantur verba puellae,
    mutatoque graves saepe colore preces.
illa mihi totis argutat noctibus ignes,
    et queritur nullos esse relicta deos;
illa meam mihi iam se denegat, illa minatur,
    quae solet irato tristis amica viro.   10
his ego non horam possum durare querelis:
    a pereat, si quis lentus amare potest!
an mihi sit tanti doctas cognoscere Athenas
    atque Asiae veteres cernere divitias,
ut mihi deducta faciat convicia puppi
    Cynthia et insanis ora notet manibus,
osculaque opposito dicat sibi debita vento,
    et nihil infido durius esse viro?
tu patrui meritas conare anteire secures,
    et vetera oblitis iura refer sociis.   20
nam tua non aetas umquam cessavit amori,
    semper et armatae cura fuit patriae;
et tibi non umquam nostros puer iste labores
    afferat et lacrimis omnia nota meis!
me sine, quem semper voluit fortuna iacere,
    hanc animam extremae reddere nequitiae.

THE ELEGIES OF PROPERTIUS BOOK I

VI

Tullus, I fear not now to brave the Adrian waves with thee nor to spread my sails on the Aegean main; with thee I could scale the Rhipean heights or pass beyond the home of Memnon. But the words of my mistress as she hangs about my neck, her urgent prayers, her changing colour, all keep me back. All through the night she shrilly protests her love, and laments that she is left forlorn and that the gods are vanished out of heaven. Mine though she be, she will not yield herself, and uses all those threats that an aggrieved mistress will use to an angry lover. Not even an hour can I endure to live amid such complaints as these; perish the man that dares love unpassionately! Is it worth my while to visit learned Athens or to behold the ancient wealth of Asia, that Cynthia may upbraid me when my bark is launched and mar her face[1] with passionate hands, and cry that she owes kisses to the wind that stays my journeying and that there is naught more cruel than a faithless lover?

[19] Do thou strive to outdo thine uncle's well-earned rule[2] and restore to the allies their long-forgotten rights. For thy youth has never yielded to love, and thy care has ever been for thy country's arms. Never may the accursed boy lay sorrows such as mine on thee, nor all the torments that my tears know well! Let me, whom Fortune hath ever willed to lie prostrate, yield up my life obedient to the worst her wantonness can demand. Many have

[1] Or perhaps "scar my face."
[2] Lit., axes of office. His uncle, Volcatius Tullus, must have been proconsul of Asia.

SEXTI PROPERTI ELEGIARVM LIBER I

multi longinquo periere in amore libenter,
   in quorum numero me quoque terra tegat.
non ego sum laudi, non natus idoneus armis:
   hanc me militiam fata subire volunt.   30
at tu seu mollis qua tendit Ionia, seu qua
   Lydia Pactoli tingit arata liquor;
seu pedibus terras seu pontum carpere remis
   ibis, et accepti pars eris imperii:
tum tibi si qua mei veniet non immemor hora,
   vivere me duro sidere certus eris.

VII

Dvm tibi Cadmeae dicuntur, Pontice, Thebae
   armaque fraternae tristia militiae,
atque, ita sim felix, primo contendis Homero,
   (sint modo fata tuis mollia carminibus:)
nos, ut consuemus, nostros agitamus amores,
   atque aliquid duram quaerimus in dominam;
nec tantum ingenio quantum servire dolori
   cogor et aetatis tempora dura queri.
hic mihi conteritur vitae modus, haec mea fama est,
   hinc cupio nomen carminis ire mei.   10
me laudent doctae solum placuisse puellae,
   Pontice, et iniustas saepe tulisse minas;
me legat assidue post haec neglectus amator,
   et prosint illi cognita nostra mala.
te quoque si certo puer hic concusserit arcu,
   (quod nolim nostros evoluisse[1] deos)

---

[1] evoluisse *Beroaldus on alleged MS. authority*: eviolasse *NAF*.

THE ELEGIES OF PROPERTIUS BOOK I

gladly perished in gyves of love, that they have borne so long, and, when earth laps me round, let me be one of these. Nature has not fitted me for glory or for arms; Love's is the only warfare for which the Fates design me.

31 But thou, whether thy steps be cast where soft Ionia spreads its shores, or where Pactolus' stream steeps Lydia's ploughlands, whether thou rangest the land on foot or goest forth to lash the sea with oars, and makest one of those that rule and are loved by them they rule—then shalt thou be sure, if e'er a moment comes with memories of me, that I still live beneath a baleful star.

VII

Whilst thou singest, Ponticus, of Cadmean Thebes, and the bitter warfare of fraternal strife, and—so may heaven smile on me, as I speak truth—dost rival Homer for crown of song (if only the Fates be kind to thy verse), I, as is my wont, still ply my loves, and seek for some device to o'ercome my mistress' cruelty. I am constrained rather to serve my sorrow than wit and to bemoan the hardship that my youth endures.

9 Thus is my whole life passed: this is my glory: this is the title to fame I claim for my song. Let my only praise be this, that I pleased the heart of a learnèd maid, and oft endured her unjust threatenings. Henceforth let neglected lovers read diligently my words, and let it profit them to learn what woes were mine. Thou too, should the boy strike thee with unerring shaft—but may the gods I serve ordain [1] thee other doom—shalt weep in misery

---

[1] *evoluisse*, lit., unroll.

SEXTI PROPERTI ELEGIARVM LIBER I

longe castra tibi, longe miser agmina septem
 flebis in aeterno surda iacere situ;
et frustra cupies mollem componere versum,
 nec tibi subiciet carmina serus Amor. 20
tum me non humilem mirabere saepe poetam,
 tunc ego Romanis praeferar ingeniis;
nec poterunt iuvenes nostro reticere sepulcro
 "Ardoris nostri magne poeta, iaces."
tu cave nostra tuo contemnas carmina fastu:
 saepe venit magno faenore tardus Amor.

VIII

Tvne igitur demens, nec te mea cura moratur?
 an tibi sum gelida vilior Illyria?
et tibi iam tanti, quicumque est, iste videtur,
 ut sine me vento quolibet ire velis?
tune audire potes vesani murmura ponti
 fortis, et in dura nave iacere potes?
tu pedibus teneris positas fulcire pruinas,[1]
 tu potes insolitas, Cynthia, ferre nives?
o utinam hibernae duplicentur tempora brumae,
 et sit iners tardis navita Vergiliis, 10
nec tibi Tyrrhena solvatur funis harena,
 neve inimica meas elevet aura preces!
atque ego non videam tales subsidere ventos,
 cum tibi provectas auferet unda rates,

[1] pruinas ς: ruinas *NAF*.

that thy seven leaguered hosts are cast aside and lie dumb in everlasting neglect, and in vain shalt thou desire to write soft songs of passion; Love come so late shall ne'er inspire thy song.

[21] Then shalt thou marvel at me as no mean singer; then shalt thou rank me above the bards of Rome; and youths perforce will cry above my tomb: "Mighty singer of our passion, dost thou lie so low?" Beware then lest in thy pride thou spurn my song. Love that comes late oft claims a heavy toll.

VIII

Art thou then mad? Does no care for me stay thy going? Am I of less account to thee than chill Illyria?[1] And esteemest thou that wretch, whoe'er he be, so highly that thou art ready to leave me and fly to his arms on any wind that blows? Canst thou bear unmoved the roar of the raging deep? canst thou make thy couch on the hard ship's-bench? or press with tender feet the fallen hoar-frost? or endure, my Cynthia, the unfamiliar snows? Ah, would that the wintry season's storms were doubled, and the Pleiads' rising delayed, that the sailor might tarry idle and the cables ne'er be loosed from the Tyrrhene strand nor the cruel breeze make light of my prayers to thee; and yet may I never see such winds subside, when thy bark puts out to sea and the wave bears it

[1] *Cp.* II. XVI.

SEXTI PROPERTI ELEGIARVM LIBER I

ut [1] me defixum vacua patiatur in ora
   crudelem infesta saepe vocare manu!
sed quocumque modo de me, periura, mereris,
   sit Galatea tuae non aliena viae:
utere [2] felici praevecta Ceraunia remo;
   accipiat placidis Oricos aequoribus.   20
nam me non ullae poterunt corrumpere, de te
   quin ego, vita, tuo limine acerba [3] querar;
nec me deficiet nautas rogitare citatos
   " Dicite, quo portu clausa puella mea est?"
et dicam "Licet Artaciis [4] considat in oris,
   et licet Hylaeis, illa futura mea est."

VIIIA [5]

Hic erat! hic iurata manet! rumpantur iniqui!
   vicimus: assiduas non tulit illa preces.
falsa licet cupidus deponat gaudia livor:
   destitit ire novas Cynthia nostra vias.   30
illi carus ego et per me carissima Roma
   dicitur, et sine me dulcia regna negat.
illa vel angusto mecum requiescere lecto
   et quocumque modo maluit esse mea,
quam sibi dotatae regnum vetus Hippodamiae,
   et quas Elis opes ante pararat equis.

---

1 ut *Rothstein* · et *NAF*.
2 utere *codd. Par. 7989, Voss. 117*   ut te *NAF*.
3 acerba *Scaliger*   verba *NAF*.
4 Artaciis *Palmer*   atracus *et similia O*.
5 *The MSS. mark no break, the separation is due to Lipsius.*

afar, leaving me rooted on the shore, shaking clenched hands and crying out upon thy cruelty.

[17] Yet, faithless one, whate'er thou deserve of me, may Galatea smile upon thy path. Pass the Ceraunian cliffs with prosperous oarage and may Oricos at last receive thee in its calm haven. For never shall the love of any maid lure me from uttering at thy threshold my bitter complaint against thee, light of my life; nor will I cease to question the mariners as they hurry by: "Tell me in what port has my love found shelter?" and I will cry: "Though she abide on Artacia's shores, or where the Hylaei dwell, yet shall she be mine!"

VIIIa

She never went! She has sworn and she remains! Let those that wish me ill burst for envy! We have conquered! She turned a deaf ear to his persistent prayer! Now let their greedy jealousy lay aside its joy! My Cynthia has ceased to tread new paths and strange. She loves me, and for my sake loves she Rome most of cities, and cries: "Apart from thee a kingdom were not sweet." She has preferred to lie in my embrace, though the couch be poor and narrow, and to be mine, whate'er the cost, rather than enjoy the ancient realm that was Hippodamia's dower and all the wealth that Elis won by its steeds. Great

SEXTI PROPERTI ELEGIARVM LIBER I

quamvis magna daret, quamvis maiora daturus,
   non tamen illa meos fugit avara sinus.
hanc ego non auro, non Indis flectere conchis,
   sed potui blandi carminis obsequio.   40
sunt igitur Musae, neque amanti tardus Apollo,
   quis ego fretus amo: Cynthia rara mea est!
nunc mihi summa licet contingere sidera plantis:
   sive dies seu nox venerit, illa mea est!
nec mihi rivalis firmos[1] subducit amores:
   ista meam norit gloria canitiem.

IX

Dicebam tibi venturos, irrisor, amores,
   nec tibi perpetuo libera verba fore:
ecce iaces supplexque venis ad iura puellae,
   et tibi nunc quaevis imperat empta modo.
non me Chaoniae vincant in amore columbae
   dicere, quos iuvenes quaeque puella domet.
me dolor et lacrimae merito fecere peritum:
   atque utinam posito dicar amore rudis!
quid tibi nunc misero prodest grave dicere carmen
   aut Amphioniae moenia flere lyrae?   10
plus in amore valet Mimnermi versus Homero.
   carmina mansuetus levia quaerit Amor.
i quaeso et tristes istos compone libellos,
   et cane quod quaevis nosse puella velit!
quid si non esset facilis tibi copia? nunc tu
   insanus medio flumine quaeris aquam.

---

[1] firmos *Rossberg*: certos *N*: summos *AF*.

THE ELEGIES OF PROPERTIUS BOOK I

though his gifts were and greater his promises, avarice could not tempt her from my bosom. Not by gold nor by the pearls of Ind did I prevail to win her, but by the homage of beguiling song. The Muses then are maids of might and Apollo is not slow to aid a lover; trusting in their help I pursue my love; and peerless Cynthia is my own. Now is it mine to set my feet upon the highest stars of heaven; come night or day, she is mine own; no rival now shall steal my love; 'tis fixed and sure. The glory of to-day shall crown my head when white with eld.

IX

Mocker, I ever told thee love would find thee out and that thou shouldest not alway be free to speak thy thoughts. Lo! now thou liest low, and goest suppliant at a woman's will, and now some unknown girl, bought by thy gold but yesterday, lords it over thee. Not Chaonia's doves[1] could better divine than I what youths each maiden shall enslave. Sorrow and tears of mine own have given me a just claim to skill. Ah! would that I could lay aside my love and once more be called a novice! What now avails it, poor wretch, to chant thy serious song and to bewail the walls raised by Amphion's lyre? Far more than Homer avails Mimnermus in the realm of love. Smooth are the songs that peaceful love demands.

[13] Go to, prithee, and lay aside thy gloomy books and sing what every maid would wish to hear. What if thou hadst not easy access? Madman, thou seekest for water when plunged in love's mid-stream. Not

---

[1] The dove was the sacred bird of Dodona, but the priestesses also were known as doves, and it may be of them that Propertius speaks.

SEXTI PROPERTI ELEGIARVM LIBER I

necdum etiam palles, vero nec tangeris igni:
    haec est venturi prima favilla mali.
tum magis Armenias cupies accedere tigres
    et magis infernae vincula nosse rotae,   20
quam pueri totiens arcum sentire medullis
    et nihil iratae posse negare tuae.
nullus Amor cuiquam faciles ita praebuit alas,
    ut non alterna presserit ille manu.
nec te decipiat, quod sit satis illa parata:
    acrius illa subit, Pontice, si qua tua est,
quippe ubi non liceat vacuos seducere ocellos,
    nec vigilare alio nomine cedat Amor:
qui non ante patet, donec manus attigit ossa.
    quisquis es, assiduas a fuge[1] blanditias!   30
illis et silices et possint cedere quercus,
    nedum tu possis, spiritus iste levis.
quare, si pudor est, quam primum errata fatere:
    dicere quo pereas saepe in amore levat.

X

O IVCVNDA quies, primo cum testis amori
    affueram vestris conscius in lacrimis!
o noctem meminisse mihi iucunda voluptas,
    o quotiens votis illa vocanda meis,
cum te complexa morientem, Galle, puella
    vidimus et longa ducere verba mora!

[1] a fuge *Bolt :* aufuge *NAF.*

even yet art thou pale, not yet art thou touched by love's true fire: 'tis but the first faint spark of the coming woe. *Then* hadst thou rather approach Armenian tigers, or know the chains that bind unto the wheels of Hell, than feel so oft the arrows of the boy about thy heartstrings, and be powerless to refuse aught that thy angry mistress may demand. To none doth any Love grant freest flight, but ever curbs his wings with tantalising hand.[1] Nor be thou deceived if she is wholly at thy command; possess her, Ponticus, and straightway she steals with keener passion on thy soul. For then thou mayest not turn thine eyes where fancy guides; Love permits thee not to watch in any cause but hers, Love that lies hid until his hand hath pierced thee to the bone.

30 Whoe'er thou art, flee from the charms that urge their suit. To them hard flints and heart of oak might yield; much more must thou, frail breath of air that thou art. Wherefore if thou feelest aught of shame, at once confess thine error. Often in love 'twill bring relief to tell what passion wastes thy soul.

X

O SWEET repose, when I was witness of your first hour of love, and stood by you as you wept together. Ah! what sweet joy to recall that night to memory! Ah! night so oft to be invoked by my prayers, whereon I saw thee, Gallus, languish in thy mistress' arms, and speak love's words amid long-drawn

[1] Lit., now with his right hand, now with his left.

SEXTI PROPERTI ELEGIARVM LIBER I

quamvis labentes premeret mihi somnus ocellos
   et mediis caelo Luna ruberet equis,
non tamen a vestro potui secedere lusu:
   tantus in alternis vocibus ardor erat.   10
sed quoniam non es veritus concedere nobis,
   accipe commissae munera laetitiae:
non solum vestros didici reticere dolores,
   est quiddam in nobis maius, amice, fide.
possum ego diversos iterum coniungere amantes,
   et dominae tardas possum aperire fores;
et possum alterius curas sanare recentes,
   nec levis in verbis est medicina meis.
Cynthia me docuit semper quaecumque petenda
   quaeque cavenda forent: non nihil egit Amor.   20
tu cave ne tristi cupias pugnare puellae,
   neve superba loqui, neve tacere diu;
neu, si quid petiit, ingrata fronte negaris,
   neu tibi pro vano verba benigna cadant.
irritata venit, quando contemnitur illa,
   nec meminit iustas ponere laesa minas:
at quo sis humilis magis et subiectus amori,
   hoc magis effecto saepe fruare bono.
is poterit felix una remanere puella,
   qui numquam vacuo pectore liber erit.   30

THE ELEGIES OF PROPERTIUS BOOK I

silences! Though sleep weighed down my wearied eyes and the glowing moon drove her team in mid-heaven, yet could I not leave the sight of your tender dalliance, such passion rang in the words ye interchanged.

[11] But since thou hast not feared to yield the secret of thy love to me, take thy reward for the joys thou didst confide. Not only have I learnt to say naught of your sorrows; there is in me something yet better than loyal secrecy. I can join parted lovers, and unbar a mistress' reluctant doors; I too can heal another's fresh-smarting griefs; not slight is the remedy my words can bring. Cynthia has ever taught me what things each lover should seek, and what should shun. Love has done something for me.

[21] See that thou seek not to resist thy mistress when she frowns, nor to speak proudly nor be silent long; nor, should she ask thee aught, do thou refuse it with stern countenance, nor let words of kindness fall on thy ears in vain. Spurn her and she comes in wrath to thee; offend her, and she ne'er remembers to lay aside her just threats. But the more thou humblest thyself and yieldest to her love, the more oft thou shalt enjoy the crown of thy desires. He will be able to abide in the enjoyment of one mistress' love who never claims his freedom nor lets her image vanish from his heart.

SEXTI PROPERTI ELEGIARVM LIBER I

XI

Ecquid te mediis cessantem, Cynthia, Bais,
   qua iacet Herculeis semita litoribus,
et modo Thesproti mirantem subdita regno
   et modo [1] Misenis aequora nobilibus,
nostri cura subit memores a! ducere [2] noctes?
   ecquis in extremo restat amore locus?
an te nescio quis simulatis ignibus hostis
   sustulit e nostris, Cynthia, carminibus?
atque utinam mage te remis confisa minutis
   parvula Lucrina cumba moretur aqua,   10
aut teneat clausam tenui Teuthrantis in unda
   alternae facilis cedere lympha manu,
quam vacet alterius blandos audire susurros
   molliter in tacito litore compositam!—
ut solet amota labi custode puella
   perfida, communes nec meminisse deos:
non quia perspecta non es mihi cognita fama,
   sed quod in hac omnis parte timetur amor.
ignosces igitur, si quid tibi triste libelli
   attulerint nostri: culpa timoris erit.   20
nam [3] mihi non maior carae custodia matris,
   aut sine te vitae cura sit ulla meae.
tu mihi sola domus, tu, Cynthia, sola parentes,
   omnia tu nostrae tempora laetitiae.
seu tristis veniam seu contra laetus amicis,
   quicquid ero, dicam "Cynthia causa fuit."

---

[1] et modo ϛ: proxima *NAF*.   [2] a! ducere *Scaliger*. adducere *NAF*.   [3] nam *Keil*. an *NAF*.

THE ELEGIES OF PROPERTIUS BOOK I

XI

Cynthia, while thou tak'st thine ease in Baiae's midst, where the causeway built by Hercules lies stretched along the shore, and now marvellest at the waves that wash Thesprotus' realm, now at those that spread hard by renowned Misenum, dost thou ever think that I, alas! pass weary nights haunted by memories of thee? Hast thou room for me even in the outer borders of thy love? Has some enemy with empty show of passion stolen thee away from thy place in my songs? Would rather that some little boat, trusting in tiny oars, kept thee safe on the Lucrine lake, or that the waters yielding with ease to the swimmer's either hand held thee retired by the shallow waves of Teuthras, than that thou shouldst listen at ease to the fond murmurs of another as thou liest soft reclined on the silent strand; for when there is none to watch her a maid will break her troth and go astray, remembering not the gods of mutual love. Not that I doubt thee, for I know that thy virtue is well tried, but at Baiae all love's advances give cause for fear Pardon me, therefore, if my books have brought thee aught of bitterness; lay all the blame upon my fear. For I watch not over my beloved mother more tenderly than over thee, nor without thee would life be worth a thought.

[23] Thou only, Cynthia, art my home, thou only my parents, thou art each moment of my joy. Be I gay or grave to the friends I meet, whate'er my mood, I will say: "Cynthia was the cause." Only

SEXTI PROPERTI ELEGIARVM LIBER I

tu modo quam primum corruptas desere Baias:
   multis ista dabunt litora discidium,
litora quae fuerant castis inimica puellis:
   a pereant Baiae, crimen amoris, aquae!   30

XII

Qvid mihi desidiae non cessas fingere crimen,
   quod faciat nobis, conscia Roma, moram?
tam multa illa meo divisa est milia lecto,
   quantum Hypanis Veneto dissidet Eridano;
nec mihi consuetos amplexu nutrit amores
   Cynthia, nec nostra dulcis in aure sonat.
olim gratus eram: non illo tempore cuiquam
   contigit ut simili posset amare fide.
invidiae fuimus: num[1] me deus obruit? an quae
   lecta Prometheis dividit herba iugis?   10
non sum ego qui fueram: mutat via longa puellas.
   quantus in exiguo tempore fugit amor!
nunc primum longas solus cognoscere noctes
   cogor et ipse meis auribus esse gravis.
felix, qui potuit praesenti flere puellae;
   non nihil aspersis gaudet Amor lacrimis:
aut si despectus potuit mutare calores,
   sunt quoque translato gaudia servitio.
mi neque amare aliam neque ab hac desciscere[2] fas est:
   Cynthia prima fuit, Cynthia finis erit.   20

---

[1] num ς: non *NAF*.
[2] desciscere *Heinsius:* desistere *F.* dissistere *AN.*

do thou with all speed leave the lewd life of Baiae; to many a loving pair shall those shores bring severance, shores that have aye proved ill for modest maids. Perish the Baian waters, that bring reproach on love!

XII

WHY, Rome, thou witness of my love, ceasest thou never to tax me falsely with sloth, saying 'tis sloth delays my suit? She is parted from my bed by as many leagues as Hypanis is distant from Venetian Eridanus. No more does Cynthia feed my wonted love with her embraces, no longer does her name make music to my ear. Once I pleased her well: then there was none so happy as to love with such true return of devotion. But envy marked us down. Was it a god that overwhelmed me, or some magic herb gathered on Promethean hills for the sundering of lovers?

¹¹ I am not what I was. A distant journey can change a woman's heart! How mighty was that love, and in how brief a space 'tis fled! Now for the first time am I forced to face the long, long hours of night alone and to vex mine own ears with my complaining. Happy the man who can weep before his mistress' eyes; Love has great delight in flooding tears. Or if, once spurned, he hath had power to change his passion, even in change of bondage is there joy. But I may never love another, nor part from her. Cynthia was the beginning, Cynthia shall be the end.

SEXTI PROPERTI ELEGIARVM LIBER I

XIII

Tv, quod saepe soles, nostro laetabere casu,
  Galle, quod abrepto solus amore vacem.
at non ipse tuas imitabor, perfide, voces:
  fallere te numquam, Galle, puella velit.
dum tibi deceptis augetur fama puellis,
  certus et in nullo quaeris amore moram,
perditus in quadam tardis pallescere curis
  incipis, et primo lapsus abire[1] gradu.
haec erit illarum contempti poena doloris:
  multarum miseras exiget una vices.   10
haec tibi vulgares istos compescet amores,
  nec nova quaerendo semper amicus eris.
haec ego non rumore malo, non augure doctus;
  vidi ego: me quaeso teste negare potes?
vidi ego te toto vinctum languescere collo
  et flere iniectis, Galle, diu manibus,
et cupere optatis animam deponere verbis,
  et quae deinde meus celat, amice, pudor.
non ego complexus potui diducere vestros:
  tantus erat demens inter utrosque furor.   20
non sic Haemonio Salmonida mixtus Enipeo
  Taenarius facili pressit amore deus,
nec sic caelestem flagrans amor Herculis Heben
  sensit in Oetaeis gaudia prima iugis.
una dies omnes potuit praecurrere amantes:
  nam tibi non tepidas subdidit illa faces,

[1] abire ς. adire *NAF.*

THE ELEGIES OF PROPERTIUS BOOK I

XIII

Thou, Gallus, as thou oft art wont, wilt rejoice at my misfortunes, because my love has been snatched from me and I am left lonely and forlorn. But, faithless friend, I will never imitate thy taunts. May never fair one have the heart to play thee false. Even now while thy fame for the loves thou hast beguiled increases ever, and self-possessed thou cleavest ne'er for long to one passion, even now late in time thou beginnest to pale with woe, love-frenzied for one girl, and to retire baffled at the first step of thy advance. This shall be thy punishment for thy scorn of their sorrows; one girl shall avenge the wrongs of many, she shall stay thy ranging loves, nor shall thy search for novelty always win thee a welcome.

[13] No spiteful rumour, no soothsayer tells me this; I saw thy love—darest thou deny the truth to me whose eyes were witness? I saw thee languish with her arms fast about thy neck, I saw thee weep lapped in a long embrace, and yearn to breathe forth thy soul in the words of desire; and last, my friend, I saw, what shame bids me hide. I could not part your embraces, such a wild frenzy bound you each to each. Not with such passion did the Taenarian god, made one with Haemonian Enipeus,[1] embrace Salmoneus' child, the willing victim of his love. Hercules burned not with such love for divine Hebe, when on Oeta's heights he tasted the first joys of godhead. One day surpassed the joys of all past lovers; for no faint torch she kindled in thy veins. She suffered not thine old

---

[1] *I.e.*, assuming the form of Haemonian Enipeus.

SEXTI PROPERTI ELEGIARVM LIBER I

nec tibi praeteritos passa est succedere fastus,
    nec sinet abduci: te tuus ardor aget.
nec mirum, cum sit Iove digna et proxima Ledae
    et Ledae partu gratior, una tribus;   30
illa sit Inachiis et blandior heroinis,
    illa suis verbis cogat amare Iovem.
tu vero quoniam semel es periturus amore,
    utere: non alio limine dignus eras.
quae tibi sit felix, quoniam novus incidit error;
    et quodcumque[1] voles, una sit ista tibi.

XIV

Tv licet abiectus Tiberina molliter unda
    Lesbia Mentoreo vina bibas opere,
et modo tam celeres mireris currere lintres
    et modo tam tardas funibus ire rates;
et nemus omne satas intendat vertice silvas,
    urgetur quantis Caucasus arboribus;
non tamen ista meo valeant contendere amori:
    nescit Amor magnis cedere divitiis.
nam sive optatam mecum trahit illa quietem,
    seu facili totum ducit amore diem,   10
tum mihi Pactoli veniunt sub tecta liquores,
    et legitur Rubris gemma sub aequoribus;
tum mihi cessuros spondent mea gaudia reges:
    quae maneant, dum me fata perire volent!
nam quis divitiis adverso gaudet Amore?
    nulla mihi tristi praemia sint Venere!

[1] quodcumque *Volscus:* quocunque *NAF.*

pride to come o'er thee once again, nor will she let thee be taken from her. Thy passion shall drive thee on and always on.

[29] Nor can I marvel since she is worthy Jove, surpassed by Leda only, and fairer herself alone than all three children of Leda. More winsome would she prove than all Inachia's queens; by her sweet words would she force even Jove to love her. Since then in truth thou art doomed once and for all to die of love, use thy chance: thou wert worthy to besiege no other doors than hers. Since madness to which thou art a stranger has seized thee, may she be kind; and may she and she alone be all thy heart's desire.

XIV

THOUGH reclining idly by Tiber's wave thou quaffest Lesbian wine from cups chased by the hand of Mentor, and marvellest now how swiftly the boats run by and now how slowly the towed barges go· though all the woodland round thee spreads its growth of trees along the hill-crest, huge as the forest that weighs upon slopes of Caucasus, yet all these things could not vie with my love; Love will not yield to all the might of wealth.

[9] For if Cynthia lies with me by night in long-desired rest, or spends the day in kindly love, then the waters of Pactolus bring their wealth beneath my roof, and the Red Sea's gems are gathered for my delight; then does my joy assure me that kings must yield to me. And may these joys abide with me till Fate decrees my death. For who may have joy of wealth if Love be not kind? Ne'er be the prize of riches mine if Venus frown! She can bow down the puissant might

SEXTI PROPERTI ELEGIARVM LIBER I

illa potest magnas heroum infringere vires,
　　illa etiam duris mentibus esse dolor:
illa neque Arabium metuit transcendere limen
　　nec timet ostrino, Tulle, subire toro　　　　　　20
et miserum toto iuvenem versare cubili:
　　quid relevant variis serica textilibus?
quae mihi dum placata aderit, non ulla verebor
　　regna vel Alcinoi munera despicere.

XV

Saepe ego multa tuae levitatis dura timebam,
　　hac tamen excepta, Cynthia, perfidia.
aspice me quanto rapiat fortuna periclo!
　　tu tamen in nostro lenta timore venis,
et potes hesternos manibus componere crines
　　et longa faciem quaerere desidia,
nec minus Eois pectus variare lapillis,
　　ut formosa novo quae parat ire viro.
at non sic Ithaci digressu mota Calypso
　　desertis olim fleverat aequoribus:　　　　　　10
multos illa dies incomptis maesta capillis
　　sederat, iniusto multa locuta salo,
et quamvis numquam post haec visura, dolebat
　　illa tamen, longae conscia laetitiae.
nec sic Aesoniden rapientibus anxia ventis　　　17
　　Hypsipyle vacuo constitit in thalamo:　　　　18
Hypsipyle nullos post illos sensit amores,　　　19
　　ut semel Haemonio tabuit hospitio.　　　　　　20

of heroes, she can bring sorrow to the hardest heart. She fears not to o'erpass the threshold of Arabian onyx, she shrinks not, Tullus, to climb into the purple couch, and toss the hapless youth in unrest o'er all his bed. What avail the silken hangings with their weft of varied hue? Ah! while she is kind and aids me in my love I will not fear to scorn the realms of any monarch, nor gifts such as Alcinous might give.

XV

OFT have I dreaded much hardship from thy fickleness, yet never, Cynthia, treachery such as this. See into what perils fortune plunges me! Yet still thou art slow to succour my distress, and hast the heart to raise thine hands to array the yesternight's disorder of thy tresses, to adorn thy face with lingering care, and all unmoved to bestar thy breast with Eastern gems, like some fair maid that goes to meet her bridegroom.

[9] Not so was Calypso moved when the Ithacan left her and she wept of yore to the lonely waste of waves: many a long day she sat moaning his loss, her locks unkempt, and many a plaint she uttered to the cruel sea: and though she never more should see his face, she grieved remembering their long hours of happiness. Not so as the breeze bore afar the son of Aeson did Hypsipyle stand sorrow-laden in the empty nuptial chamber; Hypsipyle tasted of love no more, since once she pined for her lost Haemonian guest. Alphesiboea took vengeance on

SEXTI PROPERTI ELEGIARVM LIBER I

Alphesiboea suos ulta est pro coniuge fratres 15
    sanguinis et cari vincula rupit amor.[1] 16
coniugis Euadne miseros elata per ignes 21
    occidit, Argivae fama pudicitiae.
quarum nulla tuos potuit convertere mores,
    tu quoque uti fieres nobilis historia.
desine iam revocare tuis periuria verbis,
    Cynthia, et oblitos parce movere deos;
audax a nimium nostro dolitura periclo,
    si quid forte tibi durius inciderit!
multa prius:[2] vasto labentur flumina ponto,
    annus et inversas duxerit ante vices, 30
quam tua sub nostro mutetur pectore cura:
    sis quodcumque voles, non aliena tamen.
tam tibi[3] ne viles isti videantur ocelli,
    per quos saepe mihi credita perfidia est!
hos tu iurabas, si quid mentita fuisses,
    ut tibi suppositis exciderent manibus:
et contra magnum potes hos attollere solem,
    nec tremis admissae conscia nequitiae?
quis te cogebat multos pallere colores
    et fletum invitis ducere luminibus? 40
quis ego nunc pereo, similes moniturus amantes
    "O nullis tutum credere blanditiis!"

---

[1] *15, 16, Markland's transposition.*
[2] *I give Rothstein's punctuation. Without it* multa *must be altered to* alta *or the like.*
[3] tam tibi *Palmer.* quam tibi *NAF.*

THE ELEGIES OF PROPERTIUS BOOK I

her own brothers for her husband's sake, and love brake the bonds of kindred blood. Evadne, glory of Argive chastity, perished in the fatal flame and shared her husband's pyre.

[23] Yet none of these has prevailed on thee to change thy fashion of life, that thou too might'st become a glorious memory. Cease at length by thy words to recall thy past faithlessness, nor provoke the gods thou hast so long forgotten. Rash girl, ah! deep, too deep will be thy sorrow for my peril, if aught of woe chance to fall on thee. Ere that shall many marvels be: rivers shall flow upward from the wild sea, and the year reverse its seasons, ere my love for thee shall alter in my breast: be what thou wilt, yet not another's own. Let not those eyes of thine seem of so little worth to thee, those eyes that oft made me believe thy falsehoods true! By them thou swarest, praying that if in aught thou hadst played me false thine own hands might pluck them forth. And canst thou raise them to the mighty sun and tremble not when thou rememberest thy guilty wantonings? Who made thee pale with many a shifting hue, and forced thine eyes to weep unwilling tears?—those eyes for whose sake I die with passion, thus to warn lovers in like plight to mine, "There's never witchery of woman that man may safely trust."

SEXTI PROPERTI ELEGIARVM LIBER I

XVI

Qvae fueram magnis olim patefacta triumphis,
  ianua Tarpeiae nota pudicitiae;
cuius inaurati celebrarunt limina currus,
  captorum lacrimis umida supplicibus;
nunc ego, nocturnis potorum saucia rixis,
  pulsata indignis saepe queror manibus,
et mihi non desunt turpes pendere corollae
  semper et exclusis signa iacere faces.
nec possum infamis dominae defendere noctes
  nobilis obscenis tradita carminibus; 10
nec tamen illa suae revocatur parcere famae
  turpior et saecli vivere luxuria.
has inter gravius cogor deflere querelas,[1]
  supplicis a longis tristior excubiis.
ille meos numquam patitur requiescere postes,
  arguta referens carmina blanditia:
"Ianua vel domina penitus crudelior ipsa,
  quid mihi iam duris clausa taces foribus?
cur numquam reserata meos admittis amores,
  nescia furtivas reddere mota preces? 20
nullane finis erit nostro concessa dolori,
  turpis et in tepido limine somnus erit?
me mediae noctes, me sidera prona[2] iacentem,
  frigidaque Eoo me dolet aura gelu:

---

[1] gravius . . . querelas *Scaliger*. gravibus . . . querelis *NAF*.   [2] prona *ς*. plena *NAF*.

THE ELEGIES OF PROPERTIUS BOOK I

XVI

I that of old was flung wide to welcome mighty triumphs, Tarpeia's portal glorified by her chastity, whose threshold gilded chariots once made renowned and the suppliant tears of captives once bedewed, I to-day am bruised by the nightly brawls of drunkards, and smitten by unworthy hands make moan. Dishonouring wreaths fail not to hang by me, and ever nigh me lie torches that tell their tale to lovers shut out from bliss.

[9] Yet cannot I save my mistress from her nights of shame, but, once so noble, am now the prey of ribald rhymes. Nor yet is she moved to repent and have pity on her fair fame, and to cease from living more vilely than the vileness of a wanton age. And even while thus I make my moan, yet bitterer tears are mine to weep, as the long watches of the suppliant lover deepen my woe. He suffers never my pillars to have peace, with shrill blandishment chanting this refrain:

[17] "Door yet more deeply cruel than even my mistress' heart, why are thy grim portals ever closed and mute for me? Why never dost thou unbar and give entrance to my love, thou that knowest not to relent and bear my secret prayers to my mistress? Wilt thou never grant an ending to my woes? And must a doleful sleep be mine on thy chill threshold? For me the midnight and the stars that turn to their setting and the breeze laden with chill frost of dawn grieve as they behold me prostrate. Thou alone pitiest

SEXTI PROPERTI ELEGIARVM LIBER I

tu sola humanos numquam miserata dolores
   respondes tacitis mutua cardinibus.
o utinam traiecta cava mea vocula rima
   percussas dominae vertat in auriculas!
sit silice [1] et saxo patientior illa Sicano,
   sit licet et ferro durior et chalybe,   30
non tamen illa suos poterit compescere ocellos,
   surget et invitis spiritus in lacrimis.
nunc iacet alterius felici nixa lacerto,
   at mea nocturno verba cadunt Zephyro.
sed tu sola mei, tu maxima causa doloris,
   victa meis numquam, ianua, muneribus.
te non ulla meae laesit petulantia linguae,
   quae solet irato dicere pota ioco,[2]
ut me tam longa raucum patiare querela
   sollicitas trivio pervigilare moras.   40
at tibi saepe novo deduxi carmina versu,
   osculaque impressis nixa dedi gradibus.
ante tuos quotiens verti me, perfida, postes,
   debitaque occultis vota tuli manibus!"
haec ille et si quae miseri novistis amantes,
   et matutinis obstrepit alitibus.
sic ego nunc dominae vitiis et semper amantis
   fletibus aeterna differor invidia.

[1] silice *cod. Voss. 81* licet *NAF.*
[2] pota ioco *Heinsius.* tota loco *NAF.*

never the agony of the heart of men; thy hinges are silent, and thou answerest naught. Would that some whisper of my voice might pass through some hollow rift in thee, and fall upon my mistress' startled ear! Then were she more passionless than flint or Etna's crags, more cruel than iron or steel, yet will she not have power to control her eyes, and mid unwilling tears a sigh shall rise.

[33] "Now she lies propped on another's happy arm and my words fall idly on the breezes of the night. But thou art the sole, the chiefest cause of my grief, unvanquished ever by the gifts I bring. My tongue hath never assailed thee with angry drunken jest, so dear to froward anger, that thou shouldst suffer me to grow hoarse with long complaining and watch all night at the street corner in anguished waiting. But oft for thee have I spun new strains of song and bowed me to print clinging kisses on thy steps. How oft have I turned my back upon thy pillars and with furtive hands bestowed the votive gifts that were thy due."

[45] So cries he with aught else that ye, hapless lovers, have learned to cry, and outclamours the birds of dawn. So by my mistress' vices and her lover's tears am I for aye defamed with ever-during scorn.

SEXTI PROPERTI ELEGIARVM LIBER I

XVII

Et merito, quoniam potui fugisse puellam!
   nunc ego desertas alloquor alcyonas.
nec mihi Cassiope solito visura carinam,
   omniaque ingrato litore vota cadunt.
quin etiam absenti prosunt tibi, Cynthia, venti:
   aspice, quam saevas increpat aura minas.
nullane placatae veniet fortuna procellae?
   haecine parva meum funus harena teget?
tu tamen in melius saevas converte querelas:
   sat tibi sit poenae nox et iniqua vada   10
an poteris siccis mea fata reposcere[1] ocellis,
   ossaque nulla tuo nostra tenere sinu?
a pereat, quicumque rates et vela paravit
   primus et invito gurgite fecit iter!
nonne fuit levius dominae pervincere mores
   (quamvis dura, tamen rara puella fuit),
quam sic ignotis circumdata litora silvis
   cernere et optatos quaerere Tyndaridas?
illic si qua meum sepelissent fata dolorem,
   ultimus et posito staret amore lapis,   20
illa meo caros donasset funere crines,
   molliter et tenera poneret ossa rosa;
illa meum extremo clamasset pulvere nomen,
   ut mihi non ullo pondere terra foret.
at vos, aequoreae formosa Doride natae,
   candida felici solvite vela choro:
si quando vestras labens Amor attigit undas,
   mansuetis socio parcite litoribus.

      [1] reposcere *Baehrens*. reponere *NAF*.

THE ELEGIES OF PROPERTIUS BOOK I

XVII

DESERVEDLY, since I have had the heart to fly from my mistress, do I now cry to the lonely sea-mews, nor shall Cassiope give her wonted welcome to my bark, and all my prayers fall idly on a heartless shore. Nay, more, though thou art far away the winds but aid thy cruelty: lo! what fierce threats the gale howls in my ear! Will Fortune never come to still the tempest? Shall yonder scanty sands hide my bones?

9 Yet do thou but change thy savage complaints to kinder tones; let the dark night and threatening shoals be in thine eyes enough punishment for me. Wilt have the heart dry-eyed to demand my death and ne'er to hold mine ashes to thy bosom? Perish the man, whoe'er he was, that first devised ships and sails, and first voyaged over the unwilling deep! Easier task had it been to overcome my mistress' heart —cruel was she, yet peerless among women!—than thus to gaze on shores fringed with unknown forests and seek in vain for the desired sons of Tyndareus.

19 If some doom had buried all my grief at home, if there my love had ended and at the last the headstone marked its close, then would she have cast those locks I loved so well upon my pyre, and have laid my bones on a soft couch of delicate rose-leaves: she would have cried my name aloud over my last ashes, praying that earth might lie light upon me.

25 But do ye, O sea-born daughters of lovely Doris, give prosperous escort and unfurl our white sails: if ever love has glided down and touched your waves, spare a fellow-bondsman and guide him to a kindly shore.

SEXTI PROPERTI ELEGIARVM LIBER I

XVIII

Haec certe deserta loca et taciturna querenti,
    et vacuum Zephyri possidet aura nemus.
hic licet occultos proferre impune dolores,
    si modo sola queant saxa tenere fidem.
unde tuos primum repetam, mea Cynthia, fastus?
    quod mihi das flendi, Cynthia, principium?
qui modo felices inter numerabar amantes,
    nunc in amore tuo cogor habere notam.
quid tantum merui? quae te mihi carmina mutant?
    an nova tristitiae causa puella tuae?   10
sic mihi te referas, levis, ut non altera nostro
    limine formosos intulit ulla pedes.
quamvis multa tibi dolor hic meus aspera debet,
    non ita saeva tamen venerit ira mea
ut tibi sim merito semper furor, et tua flendo
    lumina deiectis turpia sint lacrimis.
an quia parva damus mutato signa colore?
    et non ulla meo clamat in ore fides?
vos eritis testes, si quos habet arbor amores,
    fagus et Arcadio pinus amica deo.   20
a quotiens teneras resonant mea verba sub umbras,
    scribitur et vestris Cynthia corticibus!
a! tua quot[1] peperit nobis iniuria curas,
    quae solum tacitis cognita sunt foribus?
omnia consuevi timidus perferre superbae
    iussa neque arguto facta dolore queri.

        1 a! tua quot ς : an tua quod *NAF*.

THE ELEGIES OF PROPERTIUS BOOK I

XVIII

Here of a truth is a lonely and a silent place, where I may make my moan, and the breath of the West Wind only rules this deserted grove. Here may I freely utter my secret griefs, if only these lone crags can keep faith.

5 From what first beginning, Cynthia, shall I trace thy scorn? What was the first cause for tears thou gavest me? I that but a short while since was counted among happy lovers am now perforce an outcast from thy love. What woe such as this have I deserved? what spells alter thy love for me? Is jealousy of some new rival the cause of thine anger? So surely mayst thou return to my embrace, fickle maid, as no other woman has ever planted her fair feet within my threshold. Though my grief owes thee much bitterness, yet never shall my wrath fall so fierce upon thee, that I should always give thee just cause for fury and thine eyes be marred with streaming tears.

17 Or is it that I give scant proof of my passion by changing colour, and that no token of my faith cries aloud upon my countenance? Ye shall be my witnesses, if trees know aught of love, beech-tree and pine, beloved of Arcady's god. Ah! how oft do my passionate words echo beneath your delicate shades, how oft is Cynthia's name carved upon your bark!

23 Ah! how oft has thy injustice begotten troubles in my heart, that only thy silent portal knows! I have been wont to bear thy haughty commands with patience, nor ever to bemoan my grief in piercing accents of sorrow. Yet in return for this, ye founts

SEXTI PROPERTI ELEGIARVM LIBER I

pro quo divini [1] fontes et frigida rupes
   et datur inculto tramite dura quies;
et quodcumque meae possunt narrare querelae,
   cogor ad argutas dicere solus aves.   30
sed qualiscumque es resonent mihi "Cynthia" silvae,
   nec deserta tuo nomine saxa vacent.

XIX

Non ego nunc tristes vereor, mea Cynthia, Manes,
   nec moror extremo debita fata rogo;
sed ne forte tuo careat mihi funus amore,
   hic timor est ipsis durior exsequiis.
non adeo leviter noster puer haesit ocellis,
   ut meus oblito pulvis amore vacet.
illic Phylacides iucundae coniugis heros
   non potuit caecis immemor esse locis,
sed cupidus falsis attingere gaudia palmis
   Thessalus antiquam venerat umbra domum.   10
illic quidquid ero, semper tua dicar imago:
   traicit et fati litora magnus amor.
illic formosae veniant chorus heroinae,
   quas dedit Argivis Dardana praeda viris;
quarum nulla tua fuerit mihi, Cynthia, forma
   gratior, et (Tellus hoc ita iusta sinat)
quamvis te longae remorentur fata senectae,
   cara tamen lacrimis ossa futura meis.
quae tu viva mea possis sentire favilla!
   tum mihi non ullo mors sit amara loco.   20

[1] Divini *probably corrupt.* di! nivei *Lachmann.*

divine, lo! this chill couch of rock is mine and broken slumbers on this rugged track: and all that my plaintive cries can tell must be uttered in this waste place to shrill-voiced birds.

[31] But be what thou wilt, still let the woods re-echo "Cynthia," nor these lone crags have rest from the sound of thy name.

XIX

No more now, my Cynthia, fear I the sad world of death; I care not for the doom that at the last must feed the fires of funeral; this fear alone is bitterer than death itself, that I should go down to the grave unloved by thee. Not with such light touch has Love cleaved to mine eyes that my dust should forget thee and lie loveless. Even in the dark underworld the hero son of Phylacus could not forget his sweet wife, but, yearning to enfold his dear one with phantom hands, the Thessalian returned in ghostly wise to his ancient home. There, whatsoe'er I be, as Cynthia's lover shall my shade be known; strong love o'erpasses even the shores of doom. There let the fair queens of old, whom the spoils of Troy gave to Argive husbands, come in a troop to greet me! Yet the beauty of none of these shall please me more than thine, and though the doom of old age delay thy coming long—may earth be kind and grant this boon!—yet shall the sight of thine ashes be dear to my weeping eyes: and like love long mayst thou that livest feel, when I am dust; then wheresoe'er death find me, it shall have lost its

SEXTI PROPERTI ELEGIARVM LIBER I

quam vereor, ne te contempto, Cynthia, busto
   abstrahat ei![1] nostro pulvere iniquus Amor,
cogat et invitam lacrimas siccare cadentes!
   flectitur assiduis certa puella minis.
quare, dum licet, inter nos laetemur amantes:
   non satis est ullo tempore longus amor.

XX

Hoc pro continuo te, Galle, monemus amore,
   (id tibi ne vacuo defluat ex animo)
saepe imprudenti fortuna occurrit amanti:
   crudelis Minyis dixerit Ascanius.
est tibi non infra speciem, non nomine dispar,
   Theiodamanteo proximus ardor Hylae:
hunc tu, sive leges Vmbrae sacra[2] flumina silvae,
   sive Aniena tuos tinxerit unda pedes,
sive Gigantea spatiabere litoris ora,
   sive ubicumque vago fluminis hospitio,   10
Nympharum semper cupidas defende rapinas
   (non minor Ausoniis est amor Adryasin[3]);
ne tibi sit duros[4] montes et frigida saxa,
   Galle, neque experto[5] semper adire lacus:
quae miser ignotis error perpessus in oris
   Herculis indomito fleverat Ascanio.

---

[1] ei *Aldina 1515* : e *NAF*.
[2] Vmbrae sacra *Hoeufft* : umbrosae *NAF*.
[3] Adryasin *Struvius* : adriacis *NAF*.
[4] sit duros *Lipsius* : sint duri *NAF*.
[5] experto *Livineius* : expertos *NAF*.

sting. Yet, Cynthia, I have a fear that thou mayst spurn my tomb, and some cruel passion part thee from my dust, and force thee, though loth, to dry thy falling tears. Continued threats may bend the will even of a loyal maid. Wherefore, while yet may be, let us love and be merry together. Eternity itself is all too brief for love.

XX

Take this my warning, Gallus, in return for thine unfailing love: let it not slip from thy thoughtless mind: "Fortune oft proves adverse to the heedless lover"; so might Ascanius tell thee, that wreaked his spite upon the Minyae.

[5] Thou hast a love most like to Hylas, child of Theodamas, one not less fair nor of humbler birth. Beware then, whether thou wanderest by the holy streams of Umbrian forests, or Anio's waters lave thy feet, or walk'st thou on the marge of the Giant's strand, or wheresoe'er a river's wandering waters welcome thee, beware and from thy love ward off the hands of nymphs that burn to steal (the Ausonian Dryads love as warmly as their sisters loved), lest it be thy fate ever to visit cruel mountain and icy crag and lakes, that thou hast tried to thy cost. Such woes the ill-starred wanderer Hercules suffered in a far land and bewailed by the shores of the relentless Ascanius. For they say that of old Argos

SEXTI PROPERTI ELEGIARVM LIBER I

namque ferunt olim Pagasae navalibus Argon
   egressum[1] longe Phasidos isse viam,
et iam praeteritis labentem Athamantidos undis
   Mysorum scopulis applicuisse ratem   20
hic manus heroum, placidis ut constitit oris,
   mollia composita litora fronde tegit.
at comes invicti iuvenis processerat ultra
   raram sepositi quaerere fontis aquam
hunc duo sectati fratres, Aquilonia proles,
   hunc super et Zetes, hunc super et Calais,
oscula suspensis instabant carpere palmis,
   oscula et alterna ferre supina fuga
ille sub extrema pendens secluditur ala
   et volucres ramo summovet insidias.   30
iam Pandioniae cessit[2] genus Orithyiae:
   a dolor! ibat Hylas, ibat Hamadryasin.
hic erat Arganthi Pege sub vertice montis
   grata domus Nymphis umida Thyniasin,
quam supra nullae pendebant debita curae
   roscida desertis poma sub arboribus,
et circum irriguo surgebant lilia prato
   candida purpureis mixta papaveribus.
quae modo decerpens tenero pueriliter ungui
   proposito florem praetulit officio,   40
et modo formosis incumbens nescius undis
   errorem blandis tardat imaginibus.
tandem haurire parat demissis flumina palmis
   innixus dextro plena trahens umero.

---

[1] egressum *Ellis*. egressam *NAF*.
[2] cessit ς: cesset *NAF*. cessat ς.

set sail from the dockyards of Pagasa and went forth on the long way to Phasis, and at last, the waves of Helle past, moored his bark on Mysia's rockbound coast. Here the band of heroes went forth upon the peaceful shore and carpeted the ground with a soft coverlet of leaves. But the comrade of the young unvanquished hero ranged afar to seek the scarce waters of some distant spring. Him the two brothers followed, Zetes and Calais, the North Wind's sons, and, bowing o'er him, both pressed on to embrace him with hovering hands and snatch a kiss and bear it from his upturned face, each as in turn they fled. But the boy, swept off his feet, hides clinging to one by his pinion's backmost edge, and with a branch wards off the other's wingèd wiles. At last the children of Orithyia, Pandion's daughter, retired discomfited, and Hylas, alas! went upon his way, went to be the wood-nymphs' prey.

[33] Here beneath the peak of Arganthus' mount lay the well of Pege, the watery haunt so dear to Bithynia's nymphs, o'er which from lonely trees there hung dewy apples that owed naught to the hand of man, and round about in a water-meadow sprang snowy lilies mingled with purple poppies. And there, in boyish delight, he gently plucked them with soft finger-tips, preferring the flowers to his chosen task; and now in artless wonder bent over the fair waters and prolonged his truancy with gazing at their mirrored charms. At length he made ready to stretch forth his hands to the waves and draw water therefrom, leaning on his right shoulder and raising a plenteous draught. But, smitten with passion at

SEXTI PROPERTI ELEGIARVM LIBER I

cuius ut accensae Dryades candore puellae
   miratae solitos destituere choros,
prolapsum leviter facili traxere liquore:
   tum sonitum rapto corpore fecit Hylas;
cui procul Alcides iterat responsa, sed illi
   nomen ab extremis fontibus aura refert.   50
his, o Galle, tuos monitus servabis amores,
   formosum Nymphis credere visus Hylan.

XXI

"Tv, qui consortem properas evadere casum,
   miles ab Etruscis saucius aggeribus,
quid nostro gemitu turgentia lumina torques?
   pars ego sum vestrae proxima militiae.
sic te servato, ut possint gaudere parentes,
   ne soror acta tuis sentiat e lacrimis:
Gallum per medios ereptum Caesaris enses
   effugere ignotas non potuisse manus;
et quaecumque[1] super dispersa invenerit ossa
   montibus Etruscis, nesciat[2] esse mea."   10

      [1] quaecunque *NAF:* quicunque ⱺ.
      [2] nesciat *Phillimore:* haec sciat *NAF.*

the sight of that snowy shoulder, the Hamadryads in wonder ceased their wonted dance. Easily from where he lay reclined they dragged him through the yielding flood. Then Hylas as they seized his body uttered a cry, whereto in answer Alcides shouted again, again, and yet again; but the breezes bore him back from the fountain's edge naught save the echo of the name.

[51] Warned by this tale, my Gallus, thou shalt keep thy love secure, thou that aforetime didst seem to entrust thy Hylas to the nymphs.

XXI

"Soldier, that hastenest to escape thy comrades' doom, flying wounded from the Etruscan ramparts,[1] and turnest thy swollen eyes at the sound of my moaning, I am one of thy nearest comrades in arms. So save thyself, that thy parents may rejoice over thy safety, nor thy sister learn my fate from the silent witness of thy tears; how Gallus, though he escaped through the midst of Caesar's swordsmen, yet could not escape the hand of some unknown spoiler; and whatever bones she may find scattered on the mountains of Tuscany, let her not know them to be mine."

[1] *I.e*, of Perusia. See Index, *s. v.* Perusinus.

SEXTI PROPERTI ELEGIARVM LIBER I

XXII

Qvalis et unde genus, qui sint mihi, Tulle, Penates,
  quaeris pro nostra semper amicitia.
si Perusina tibi patriae sunt nota sepulcra,
  Italiae duris funera temporibus,
cum Romana suos egit discordia civis;
  (sic, mihi praecipue, pulvis Etrusca, dolor,
tu proiecta mei perpessa es membra propinqui,
  tu nullo miseri contegis ossa solo)
proxima supposito contingens Vmbria campo
  me genuit terris fertilis uberibus.　　　　　　10

XXII

Tullus, thou askest ever in our friendship's name, what is my rank, whence my descent, and where my home. If thou knowest our country's graves at Perusia, the scene of death in the dark hours of Italy, when civil discord maddened the citizens of Rome (hence, dust of Tuscany, art thou my bitterest sorrow, for thou hast borne the limbs of my comrade that were cast out unburied, thou shroudest his ill-starred corpse with never a dole of earth), know then that where Umbria, rich in fertile lands, joins the wide plain that lies below, there was I born.

BOOK II

LIBER SECVNDVS

I

Qvaeritis, unde mihi totiens scribantur amores,
   unde meus veniat mollis in ore liber.
non haec Calliope, non haec mihi cantat Apollo,
   ingenium nobis ipsa puella facit.
sive illam Cois fulgentem incedere cogis,
   hoc totum e Coa veste volumen erit;
seu vidi ad frontem sparsos errare capillos,
   gaudet laudatis ire superba comis;
sive lyrae carmen digitis percussit eburnis,
   miramur, faciles ut premat arte manus;   10
seu cum poscentes somnum declinat ocellos,
   invenio causas mille poeta novas;
seu nuda erepto mecum luctatur amictu,
   tum vero longas condimus Iliadas;
seu quidquid fecit sive est quodcumque locuta,
   maxima de nihilo nascitur historia.
quod mihi si tantum, Maecenas, fata dedissent,
   ut possem heroas ducere in arma manus,
non ego Titanas canerem, non Ossan Olympo
   impositam, ut caeli Pelion esset iter,   20

THE SECOND BOOK

I

You ask me, from what source so oft I draw my songs of love and whence comes my book that sounds so soft upon the tongue. 'Tis not Calliope nor Apollo that singeth these things; 'tis my mistress' self that makes my wit. If thou wilt have her walk radiant in silks of Cos, of Coan raiment all this my book shall tell; or have I seen her tresses stray dishevelled o'er her brow, I praise her locks and she walks abroad in pride and gladness; or struck she forth music from the lyre with ivory fingers, I marvel with what easy skill she sweeps her hands along the strings; or when she droops those eyes that call for sleep I find a thousand new themes for song; or if, flinging away her robe, she enter naked with me in the lists, then, then I write whole Iliads long. Whate'er she does, whate'er she says, from a mere nothing springs a mighty tale.

[17] But if, Maecenas, the Fates had granted me the power to lead the hosts of heroes into war, I would not sing the Titans, nor Ossa on Olympus piled, that Pelion might be a path to heaven. I'd sing not

SEXTI PROPERTI ELEGIARVM LIBER II

nec veteres Thebas, nec Pergama nomen Homeri,
 Xerxis et imperio bina coisse vada,
regnave prima Remi aut animos Carthaginis altae,
 Cimbrorumque minas et benefacta Mari:
bellaque resque tui memorarem Caesaris, et tu
 Caesare sub magno cura secunda fores.
nam quotiens Mutinam aut civilia busta Philippos
 aut canerem Siculae classica bella fugae,
eversosque focos antiquae gentis Etruscae,
 et Ptolomaeei litora capta Phari,   30
aut canerem Aegyptum et Nilum, cum atratus[1] in urbem
 septem captivis debilis ibat aquis,
aut regum auratis circumdata colla catenis,
 Actiaque in Sacra currere rostra Via;
te mea Musa illis semper contexeret armis,
 et sumpta et posita pace fidele caput:
 . . . . .[2]
Theseus infernis, superis testatur Achilles,
 hic Ixioniden, ille Menoetiaden.
sed neque Phlegraeos Iovis Enceladique tumultus
 intonet angusto pectore Callimachus,   40
nec mea conveniunt duro praecordia versu
 Caesaris in Phrygios condere nomen avos.
navita de ventis, de tauris narrat arator,
 enumerat[3] miles vulnera, pastor oves;

[1] atratus *Baehrens*. attractus *N*. attractatus *F*. tractus *ς*.
[2] *A couplet seems to have been lost, since something is needed to introduce the mythological parallels for the friendship of Augustus and Maecenas.*
[3] enumerat *AF*. et numerat *N*.

THE ELEGIES OF PROPERTIUS BOOK II

Thebes nor Troy's citadel, that is Homer's glory, nor yet how at Xerxes' bidding sea met sundered sea, nor, again, would I chant the primeval realm of Remus or the fierce spirit of lofty Carthage, the Cimbrian's threats or the service wrought by Marius for the State. But I would tell of the wars and the deeds of thy master Caesar, and next after mighty Caesar my thoughts should turn on thee. For oft as I sang of Mutina or Philippi, where Romans lie by Romans slain, or of the sea-fight and the rout by the Sicilian shore, the ruined hearths of Etruria's ancient race, and the capture of the shore where Ptolemy's Pharos stands; oft as I sang of Egypt and the Nile, what time in mourning garb he went humbly to Rome with his seven captive streams, or of the necks of kings bound about with chains of gold, and the prows of Actium speeding along the Sacred Way; so oft would my Muse weave thy name into those deeds, true heart in peace or war.

. . . . .

Theseus to the shades below, Achilles to the gods above, proclaim a comrade's love, the one of Ixion's child, the other of the son of Menoetius.

39 But neither would Callimachus' scant breath avail to thunder forth the strife 'twixt Jove and Enceladus on Phlegra's plains, nor has my heart power in verse severe to trace the line of Caesar to his Phrygian grandsires. The sailor talks of winds, the ploughman of oxen, the soldier counts o'er his wounds, the shepherd his

SEXTI PROPERTI ELEGIARVM LIBER II

nos contra angusto versantes proelia lecto:
    qua pote quisque, in ea conterat arte diem.
laus in amore mori: laus altera, si datur uno
    posse frui: fruar o solus amore meo!
si memini, solet illa leves culpare puellas,
    et totam ex Helena non probat Iliada.   50
seu mihi sunt tangenda novercae pocula Phaedrae,
    pocula privigno non nocitura suo,
seu mihi Circaeo pereundum est gramine, sive
    Colchis Iolciacis[1] urat aena focis,
una meos quoniam praedata est femina sensus,
    ex hac ducentur funera nostra domo.
omnes humanos sanat medicina dolores:
    solus amor morbi non amat artificem.
tarda Philoctetae sanavit crura Machaon,
    Phoenicis Chiron lumina Phillyrides,   60
et deus exstinctum Cressis Epidaurius herbis
    restituit patriis Androgeona focis,
Mysus et Haemonia iuvenis qua cuspide vulnus
    senserat, hac ipsa cuspide sensit opem.
hoc si quis vitium poterit mihi demere, solus
    Tantaleae[2] poterit tradere poma manu;
dolia virgineis idem ille repleverit urnis,
    ne tenera assidua colla graventur aqua;
idem Caucasia solvet de rupe Promethei
    bracchia et a medio pectore pellet avem.   70

[1] Iolciacis *Scaliger* · Colchiacis *NAF*.
[2] Tantaleae *Beroaldus*: Tantalea *NF*.

sheep, while we for our part tell of lovers' wars upon a narrow couch! Let each man pass his days in that wherein his skill is greatest. To die for love is glory; and glory yet again to have power to joy in one love only; ah, may I, and I alone, joy in the love that's mine. If memory fails me not, she is wont to blame fickle-hearted maids, and on account of Helen frowns on the whole Iliad. Though I be doomed to drink of the cup that the stepdame Phaedra brewed, the cup whereof her stepson [1] was destined to take no hurt, or must die of Circe's herbs; or though for me the Colchian witch heat the caldron on the fires of Iolcus, yet since one girl hath stolen away my senses, from her house only shall go forth my funeral train.

[57] Medicine cures all the anguish of mankind; love alone loves no physician of its ill. Machaon healed Philoctetes' limping feet, Chiron the son of Phillyra opened the eyes of Phoenix, the Epidaurian god restored the dead Androgeon to his father's hearth by power of Cretan herbs, and the Mysian youth received succour from the same Haemonian spear that dealt the wound. If any can take this frailty from me, he and he alone will be able to bring the apple to the hands of Tantalus; he too shall fill the casks from the maidens' [2] pitchers, that their tender necks be not bowed for ever by the burden of water; he too shall loose Prometheus' arms from the Caucasian crag and drive the vulture from his inmost heart.

[1] Hippolytus. This is the only known allusion to an attempt on the part of Phaedra to poison him.
[2] The Danaids.

SEXTI PROPERTI ELEGIARVM LIBER II

quandocumque igitur vitam mea fata reposcent,
    et breve in exiguo marmore nomen ero,
Maecenas, nostrae spes invidiosa iuventae,
    et vitae et morti gloria iusta meae,
si te forte meo ducet via proxima busto,
    esseda caelatis siste Britanna iugis,
taliaque illacrimans mutae iace verba favillae:
    " Huic misero fatum dura puella fuit."

II

Liber eram et vacuo meditabar vivere lecto;
    at me composita pace fefellit Amor.
cur haec in terris facies humana moratur?
    Iuppiter, ignosco [1] pristina furta tua.
fulva coma est longaeque manus, et maxima toto
    corpore, et incedit vel Iove digna soror,
aut cum Dulichias Pallas spatiatur ad aras,
    Gorgonis anguiferae pectus operta comis;
qualis et Ischomache Lapithae genus heroine,
    Centauris medio grata rapina mero;   10
Mercurio et sacris [2] fertur Boebeidos undis
    virgineum Brimo [3] composuisse latus.
cedite iam, divae, quas pastor viderat olim
    Idaeis tunicas ponere verticibus!
hanc utinam faciem nolit mutare senectus,
    etsi Cumaeae saecula vatis aget!

    [1] ignosco *n*   ignoro *NF*.
    [2] et sacris *Butler* · sacris *cod Barberinus*: satis *NF*.
    [3] Brimo *Turnebus*. primo *NF*.

71 Therefore when at last the Fates demand my life, and I shall be no more than a brief name on a little stone of marble, then, Maecenas, thou hope and envy of our Roman youth, and, whether I live or die, mine own true glory, if perchance thy journeying lead thee near my tomb, stay awhile thy British chariot with carven yoke, and weeping pay this tribute to the silent dust: "An unrelenting maid wrought this poor mortal's death."

II

I was free and thought henceforth to lie alone of nights; but though the truce was made, Love played me false. Why abides such mortal beauty upon earth? Jupiter, I pardon thy gallantries of olden time. Yellow is her hair, and tapering her hands, tall and full her figure, and stately her walk, worthy the sister of Jove or like to Pallas, when she strides to Dulichian altars, her breast veiled by the Gorgons' snaky locks. Fair is she as Ischomache, heroic child of the Lapithae, the Centaurs' welcome spoil in the revel's midst, or as Brimo when by the sacred waters of Boebeis she laid her virgin body at Mercury's side. Yield now, ye goddesses, whom of old the shepherd saw lay aside your raiment on the heights of Ida! And oh! may old age never mar that face, though she reach the years of the Cumaean prophetess.

SEXTI PROPERTI ELEGIARVM LIBER II

III

Qvi nullum tibi dicebas iam posse nocere,
   haesisti, cecidit spiritus ille tuus!
vix unum potes, infelix, requiescere mensem,
   et turpis de te iam liber alter erit.
quaerebam, sicca si posset piscis harena
   nec solitus ponto vivere torvus aper;
aut ego si possem studiis vigilare severis:
   differtur, numquam tollitur ullus amor.
nec me tam facies, quamvis sit candida, cepit
   (lilia non domina sint magis alba mea;   10
ut Maeotica nix minio si certet Hibero,
   utque rosae puro lacte natant folia),
nec de more comae per levia colla fluentes,
   non oculi, geminae, sidera nostra, faces,
nec si qua Arabio lucet bombyce puella
   (non sum de nihilo blandus amator ego):
quantum quod posito formose saltat Iaccho,
   egit ut euhantes dux Ariadna choros,
et quantum, Aeolio cum temptat carmina plectro,
   par Aganippeae ludere docta lyrae;   20
et sua cum antiquae committit scripta Corinnae,
   carminaque Erinnes[1] non putat aequa suis.
non tibi nascenti primis, mea vita, diebus
   candidus[2] argutum sternuit omen Amor?
haec tibi contulerunt caelestia munera divi,
   haec tibi ne matrem forte dedisse putes.

---

[1] -que Erinnes *Volscus, Beroaldus*: quae lyrines μυ. quae quivis *NF*.   [2] candidus *Macrobius*: ardidus *NF*.

THE ELEGIES OF PROPERTIUS BOOK II

III

Thou, that didst boast that nought could harm thee more, art caught in the snare: thy proud spirit has fallen. Scarce, poor wretch, canst thou find rest for a single month, and now a second book of shame shall tell of thy doings   I was as one that seeks whether a fish may live on the dry sands, or a fierce wild boar in the midst of unfamiliar waves, when I tried if I could pass the night in sterner studies. Love is but put off, extinguished never.

9 'Twas not her face, bright though it be, that won me. Lilies would not surpass my mistress for whiteness; 'tis as though Maeotic snows were to strive with Spanish vermilion, or rose-leaves floated amid stainless milk. 'Twas not her hair flowing trimly o'er her smooth neck, 'twas not the twin torches of her eyes, my lodestars, nor a girl shining in Arabian silks: not for such trifles as these am I a gallant lover! 'Tis rather that at the revel's close she dances wondrously, even as Ariadne led the Maenad dance; 'tis rather that when she essays to sing to the Aeolian lyre she rivals the harp of Aganippe in her skill to play, and challenges with her verse the writings of ancient Corinna, and counts not Erinna's songs the equals of her own.

23 My life, did not bright Love sneeze a shrill omen at thine hour of birth, when day-first dawned for thee? These heavenly gifts the gods, the gods bestowed, for I would not have thee think that 'twas thy mother gave them. Such boons no human

SEXTI PROPERTI ELEGIARVM LIBER II

non non humani partus sunt talia dona:
   ista decem menses non peperere bona.
gloria Romanis una es tu nata puellis:
   Romana accumbes prima puella Iovi,   30
nec semper nobiscum humana cubilia vises;
   post Helenam haec terris forma secunda redit.
hac ego nunc mirer si flagret nostra iuventus?
   pulchrius hac fuerat, Troia, perire tibi.
olim mirabar, quod tanti ad Pergama belli
   Europae atque Asiae causa puella fuit:
nunc, Pari, tu sapiens et tu, Menelae, fuisti,
   tu quia poscebas, tu quia lentus eras.
digna quidem facies, pro qua vel obiret Achilles;
   vel Priamo belli causa probanda fuit.   40
si quis vult fama tabulas anteire vetustas,
   hic dominam exemplo ponat in arte meam:
sive illam Hesperiis, sive illam ostendet Eois,
   uret et Eoos, uret et Hesperios.
his saltem ut tenear iam finibus! aut mihi, si quis,
   acrius ut moriar, venerit alter amor!
ac veluti primo taurus detractat aratra,
   post venit assueto mollis ad arva iugo,
sic primo iuvenes trepidant in amore feroces,
   dehinc domiti post haec aequa et iniqua ferunt. 50
turpia perpessus vates est vincla Melampus,
   cognitus Iphicli surripuisse boves;
quem non lucra, magis Pero formosa coegit,
   mox Amythaonia nupta futura domo.

parentage can confer, those charms ne'er sprang from mortal womb. Thou and thou only wast born to be the glory of Roman maids; thou shalt be the first maid of Rome to lie with Jove, nor shalt thou forever in our midst visit mortal couches[1] Helen wore this beauty once, and now 'tis come to earth again with thee.

[33] For thee then that our youth should burn, why should I wonder now? Better, O Troy, to have perished for Cynthia's sake. Of old I wondered that a girl should have been the cause of so mighty a conflict before the citadel of Troy, where Europe and Asia met in war. Now, Paris, I hold that thou, and thou, Menelaus, wert wise, thou that thou didst demand, thou that thou wert slow to reply. Worthy in sooth was such a face, that for it even Achilles should face death; even Priam could not but approve such cause for strife. If any desire to surpass the fame of all ancient pictures, let him take my mistress as model for his art; if he show her to the peoples of the West or to the peoples of the East, he will set the East and set the West afire.

[45] These bounds at least let me never more outstep! Or if I do, let another passion smite me, if such there be, that shall burn me with keener agony. As at first the ox refuses the plough, yet at length becomes familiar to the yoke and goes quietly to the fields, so do proud youths fret in the first ecstasy of love, then, calmer grown, bear good and ill alike. Melampus the seer endured dishonouring fetters, convicted of having stolen the kine of Iphiclus: yet 'twas not gain, but rather the fair face of Pero compelled him, Pero soon to be a bride in the halls of Amythaon.

---

[1] Or perhaps "with me this mortal couch."

SEXTI PROPERTI ELEGIARVM LIBER II

IV

Mvlta prius dominae delicta queraris oportet,
  saepe roges aliquid, saepe repulsus eas,
et saepe immeritos corrumpas dentibus ungues,
  et crepitum dubio suscitet ira pede!
nequiquam perfusa meis unguenta capillis,
  ibat et expenso planta morata gradu.
non hic herba valet, non hic nocturna Cytaeis,
  non Perimedeae [1] gramina cocta manus;
quippe ubi nec causas nec apertos cernimus ictus,
  unde tamen veniant tot mala caeca via est;   10
non eget hic medicis, non lectis mollibus aeger,
  huic nullum caeli tempus et aura nocet;
ambulat—et subito mirantur funus amici!
  sic est incautum, quidquid habetur amor.
nam cui non ego sum fallaci praemia vati?
  quae mea non decies somnia versat anus?
hostis si quis erit nobis, amet ille puellas:
  gaudeat in puero, si quis amicus erit.
tranquillo tuta descendis flumine cumba:
  quid tibi tam parvi litoris unda nocet?   20
alter saepe uno mutat praecordia verbo,
  altera vix ipso sanguine mollis erit.

[1] Perimedeae *Beroaldus on the authority of "some MSS.":* per medeae *NF.*

THE ELEGIES OF PROPERTIUS BOOK II

IV

OFT first must thou bemoan the transgressions of thy mistress, oft must thou ask a boon, and oft depart denied. Oft must thou bite thy nails for wrath at thine unmerited woe, and in anger stamp the ground with hesitating foot.

5 In vain was my hair drenched with perfumes, in vain my feet went lingeringly with measured step. For such a case as mine avails no drug, no Colchian sorceress of the night, no, nor the herbs Perimede's hands distilled. For here we see no cause nor whence the blow is dealt; dark is the path whereby so many griefs come none the less. In such a case the sick man needs no physician, no soft pillows; him no inclement season, no wind of heaven racks: he walks abroad, and on a sudden his friends marvel to see him dead. Whate'er love be, 'tis a strange thing, that none may guard against. For what lying seer have I not rewarded? What hag has not three times three pondered my dreams?

17 Let my enemies love women, my friends have their delight in a boy. For then thou descendest the tranquil stream in unimperilled bark. How can the waves of such a tiny shore do thee hurt? His heart is oft softened by a single word; she will scarce be appeased even by thy blood.

SEXTI PROPERTI ELEGIARVM LIBER II

V

Hoc verum est, tota te ferri, Cynthia, Roma,
    et non ignota vivere nequitia?
haec merui sperare? dabis mihi, perfida, poenas;
    et nobis aliquo,[1] Cynthia, ventus erit.
inveniam tamen e multis fallacibus unam,
    quae fieri nostro carmine nota velit,
nec mihi tam duris insultet moribus et te
    vellicet: heu sero flebis amata diu.
nunc est ira recens, nunc est discedere tempus:
    si dolor afuerit, crede, redibit amor.   10
non ita Carpathiae variant Aquilonibus undae,
    nec dubio nubes vertitur atra Noto,
quam facile irati verbo mutantur amantes:
    dum licet, iniusto subtrahe colla iugo.
nec tu non aliquid, sed prima nocte, dolebis;
    omne in amore malum, si patiare, leve est
at tu per dominae Iunonis dulcia iura
    parce tuis animis, vita, nocere tibi.
non solum taurus ferit uncis cornibus hostem,
    verum etiam instanti laesa repugnat ovis.   20
nec tibi periuro scindam de corpore vestes,
    nec mea praeclusas fregerit ira fores,
nec tibi conexos iratus carpere crines,
    nec duris ausim laedere pollicibus:
rusticus haec aliquis tam turpia proelia quaerat,
    cuius non hederae circuiere caput.

[1] aliquo *Bosscha*: aquilo *NF*.

THE ELEGIES OF PROPERTIUS BOOK II

V

Is this true, Cynthia, that through all Rome thy name is a byword, and that thou livest in open wantonness? Did I deserve to look for this? Faithless one, I will punish thee, and the wind shall bear me, Cynthia, to some other haven. Though all womankind be deceitful, yet out of so many I shall find one that will be glad to be made famous by my song, that will not with heart hard as thine heap insult on my head, but will revile *thy* name. Alas! loved for so long, too late will fall thy tears!

[9] Now is mine anger fresh, now is the time to part from thee: when the smart is over, believe me, love will return. Not so swiftly do the Carpathian waves change their hue beneath the North Wind's blasts, not so swiftly veers the dark storm-cloud before the South-West's shifting gale, as one word will lightly change the wrath of lovers. While yet thou mayst, Propertius, withdraw thy neck from the unjust yoke. Somewhat wilt thou suffer, but only on the first night; so but thou wilt endure, all love's ills are light.

[17] But oh! by the sweet laws of our mistress Juno do thou, my life, spare by thy waywardness to harm thyself. Not only the bull strikes at its foe with curved horn; even the ewe when hurt resists the aggressor. I will not rend thy raiment from thy faithless limbs, nor shall my anger break down the doors thou barrest against me; I would not venture in my wrath to tear thy plaited tresses, nor bruise thee with cruel fist. Let some boor seek combats base as this, around whose head the ivy ne'er hath twined. I will but write words, that thy lifetime

SEXTI PROPERTI ELEGIARVM LIBER II

scribam igitur, quod non umquam tua deleat aetas,
"Cynthia, forma potens; Cynthia, verba levis."
crede mihi, quamvis contemnas murmura famae,
hic tibi pallori, Cynthia, versus erit. 30

VI

Non ita complebant Ephyreae Laidos aedes,
ad cuius iacuit Graecia tota fores;
turba Menandreae fuerat nec Thaidos olim
tanta, in qua populus lusit Erichthonius;
nec quae deletas potuit componere Thebas,
Phryne tam multis facta beata viris.
quin etiam falsos fingis tibi saepe propinquos,
oscula nec desunt qui tibi iure ferant.
me iuvenum pictae facies, me nomina laedunt,
me tener in cunis et sine voce puer; 10
me laedet, si multa tibi dabit oscula mater,
me soror et cum quae[1] dormit amica simul:
omnia me laedent: timidus sum (ignosce timori)
et miser in tunica suspicor esse virum.
his olim, ut fama est, vitiis ad proelia ventum est,
his Troiana vides funera principiis;
aspera Centauros eadem dementia iussit
frangere in adversum pocula Pirithoum.
cur exempla petam Graium? tu criminis auctor,
nutritus duro, Romule, lacte lupae: 20
tu rapere intactas docuisti impune Sabinas:
per te nunc Romae quidlibet audet Amor.

[1] quae *Dousa*. qua *NF*.

shall not see effaced: "Cynthia, mighty is thy beauty; Cynthia, light are thy words." Believe me, though thou spurn the whisper of scandal, this verse will drive the colour from thy cheek.

VI

Not so was the house of Ephyrean Lais thronged, at whose doors all Greece lay bowed; nor even did Menander's Thais, the darling of the folk of Athens, gather about her such a swarm of gallants; nor Phryne, who might have restored the ruined walls of Thebes, so many a lover had brought her riches.

⁷ Aye, and oft thou feign'st false kindred and lackest not those that have a right to kiss thee. Jealous am I of the very portraits, the very names of young men, even of the tender boy in the cradle that knows not how to speak. Jealous shall I be of thy mother if she gives thee many a kiss, of thy sister and of the friend that may chance to sleep with thee. All things will awake my fears; I am a coward (pardon my cowardice), and beneath the woman's dress I, poor fool, suspect the presence of a man.

¹⁵ 'Twas by reason of such jealousies that of old, as the story goes, the world went forth to battle; such was the beginning of the slaughter before Troy. The same madness bade the Centaurs break embossed goblets in conflict against Pirithous. Why should I seek examples from the tales of Greece? Thou, Romulus, nurtured by the milk of the cruel she-wolf, didst give warrant for the crime; thou taughtest thy Romans to ravish unpunished the Sabine maids; thou art the cause that now there is naught Love dare not do at Rome. Happy was the wife of Admetus, happy

SEXTI PROPERTI ELEGIARVM LIBER II

felix Admeti coniunx et lectus Vlixis,
 et quaecumque viri femina limen amat!
templa Pudicitiae quid opus statuisse puellis,
 si cuivis nuptae quidlibet esse licet?
quae manus obscenas depinxit prima tabellas
 et posuit casta turpia visa domo,
illa puellarum ingenuos corrupit ocellos
 nequitiaeque suae noluit esse rudes. 30
a gemat, in terris ista qui protulit arte
 iurgia sub tacita condita laetitia!
non istis olim variabant tecta figuris:
 tum paries nullo crimine pictus erat
sed non immerito velavit aranea fanum
 et mala desertos occupat herba deos.
quos igitur tibi custodes, quae limina ponam,
 quae numquam supra pes inimicus eat?
nam nihil invitae tristis custodia prodest:
 quam peccare pudet, Cynthia, tuta sat est. 40
nos uxor numquam, numquam seducet[1] amica:
 semper amica mihi, semper et uxor eris.

VII

Gavisa est certe sublatam Cynthia legem,
 qua quondam edicta flemus[2] uterque diu,
ni nos divideret: quamvis diducere amantes
 non queat invitos Iuppiter ipse duos.

---

[1] seducet *Rothstein.* me ducet *NF.*
[2] flemus *cod. Beroaldi:* stemus *NF.*

the partner of Ulysses' bed, and every woman that loves her husband's home.

²⁵ What profits it for maids to found temples in honour of Chastity, if every bride is permitted to be whate'er she will? The hand that first painted lewd pictures, and set up objects foul to view in chaste homes, first corrupted the unsullied eyes of maids and refused to allow them to be ignorant of its own wantonness. May he groan in torment who by his vile art first wakened strife 'twixt lovers, strife lurking secret under silent joy![1] Not with such figures did men of old adorn their houses; then their walls had no foul deeds painted on them. But deservedly have cobwebs gathered o'er the temples and rank herbage has overgrown the neglected gods.

³⁷ What guardians then, what limits shall I set thee, thresholds o'er which no enemy's foot shall ever pass? For no stern guardian can save her that will not be saved: she alone is surely guarded, my Cynthia, who is ashamed to sin. As for me, no wife nor mistress shall ever steal me from thee; for me thou shalt at once be mistress and wife

VII

IN very truth Cynthia rejoiced when that law was swept away, at the making of which we both wept for many an hour, for fear it should divide us: though against their will not Jove himself could part a pair

---

[1] The reason seems to be that the contemplation of such pictures, though it may give silent pleasure, yet contains in germ the severance of lovers through infidelity.

SEXTI PROPERTI ELEGIARVM LIBER II

"At magnus Caesar." sed magnus Caesar in
    armis:
devictae gentes nil in amore valent.
nam citius paterer caput hoc discedere collo
    quam possem nuptae perdere more faces,
aut ego transirem tua limina clausa maritus,
    respiciens udis prodita luminibus.   10
a mea tum quales caneret tibi tibia somnos,
    tibia, funesta tristior illa tuba!
unde mihi patriis natos praebere triumphis?[1]
    nullus de nostro sanguine miles erit.
quod si vera meae comitarem[2] castra puellae,
    non mihi sat magnus Castoris iret equus.
hinc etenim tantum meruit mea gloria nomen,
    gloria ad hibernos lata Borysthenidas.
tu mihi sola places: placeam tibi, Cynthia, solus:
    hic erit et patrio nomine[3] pluris amor.   20

VIII

Eripitvr nobis iam pridem cara puella:
    et tu me lacrimas fundere, amice, vetas?
nullae sunt inimicitiae nisi amoris acerbae:
    ipsum me iugula, lenior hostis ero.
possum ego in alterius positam spectare lacerto?
    nec mea dicetur, quae modo dicta mea est?

---

[1] *A new elegy in NF.*
[2] comitarem ς: comitarent *NF.*
[3] nomine *Postgate:* sanguine *NF.*

THE ELEGIES OF PROPERTIUS BOOK II

of lovers. "Nay," say you, "but Caesar is mighty." True, but his might is the might of armies : to have vanquished nations counts for nothing in the world of love. For sooner would I suffer my head to be severed from my body than I could quench the fire of our passion at the whim of a bride, or, a wedded husband, pass thy house forever barred to me, and glance back with streaming eyes at the threshold I had betrayed. Ah! then of what slumbers would the pipe of the wedding company sing to thee, that pipe more sadly sounding than the trump of funeral!

[13] How should I furnish children to swell our country's triumphs? From my blood shall no soldier ever spring. But if I were to follow my mistress' camp (the one true camp for me!), not mighty enough for me were Castor's war-horse. 'Twas in Love's warfare that my fame won such renown, fame that has travelled to the wintry Borysthenidae. Thou only pleasest me; let me in like manner, Cynthia, be thy only pleasure: love such as this will be worth more to me than the name of father.

VIII

The girl I loved so long is being torn from my arms, and dost thou, my friend, forbid me to weep? No enmities are bitter save those of love; slay me if thou wilt, and my hatred shall be milder far. Can I bear to behold her reclined on another's arm? Shall she no more be called "mine," that was "mine" so lately? All things change: and loves

SEXTI PROPERTI ELEGIARVM LIBER II

omnia vertuntur: certe vertuntur amores:
   vinceris aut vincis, haec in amore rota est.
magni saepe duces, magni cecidere tyranni,
   et Thebae steterant altaque Troia fuit.   10
munera quanta dedi vel qualia carmina feci!
   illa tamen numquam ferrea dixit "Amo."[1]

VIIIa

Ergo iam multos nimium temerarius annos,
   improba, qui tulerim teque tuamque domum?
ecquandone tibi liber sum visus? an usque
   in nostrum iacies verba superba caput?
sic igitur prima moriere aetate, Properti?
   sed morere; interitu gaudeat illa tuo!
exagitet nostros Manes, sectetur et umbras,
   insultetque rogis, calcet et ossa mea!   20
[quid? non Antigonae tumulo Boeotius Haemon
   corruit ipse suo saucius ense latus,
et sua cum miserae permiscuit ossa puellae,
   qua sine Thebanam noluit ire domum?[2]]
sed non effugies: mecum moriaris oportet;
   hoc eodem ferro stillet uterque cruor.

[1] *The MSS. mark no break at this point. But 1–12 can stand by themselves and clearly do not belong to what follows. I therefore mark a new elegy*

[2] *Lines 21–24 cannot belong to their present context; the simile is too irrelevant. Housman would place them after* XXVIII. 40, *perhaps rightly.*

not least; conqueror thou art or conquered; so turns the wheel of love. Oft have leaders and lords of might fallen; Thebes stood of old and lofty Troy once was. What gifts I gave her, what songs I made for her! Yet never did she soften her iron heart nor say, "I love thee."

VIIIA

So then, have I, that through so many years too rashly have endured thee and thy household, cruel girl, have I ever seemed to thee aught save thy slave? Or wilt thou never cease to hurl words of scorn at me?

[17] So then, Propertius, must thou die in thine earliest youth? Nay, die! let her rejoice to see thee perish! Let her harry my ghost, and vex my shade, let her trample on my pyre and spurn my bones! [Why? Did not Boeotian Haemon die by Antigone's tomb, his side rent by the sword, and mingle his bones with those of the hapless maid, without whom he would not return to his Theban home?] But thou shalt not escape; thou must die with me, on this same steel must drip the blood of both! Such death shall

SEXTI PROPERTI ELEGIARVM LIBER II

quamvis ista mihi mors est inhonesta futura :
   mors inhonesta quidem, tu moriere tamen.[1]

. . . . .

ille etiam abrepta desertus coniuge Achilles
   cessare in tectis pertulit arma sua.   30
viderat ille fugas, tractos in litore Achivos,
   fervere et Hectorea Dorica castra face ;
viderat informem multa Patroclon harena
   porrectum et sparsas caede iacere comas,
omnia formosam propter Briseida passus :
   tantus in erepto saevit amore dolor.
at postquam sera captiva est reddita poena,
   fortem illum Haemoniis Hectora traxit equis.
inferior multo cum sim vel matre [2] vel armis,
   mirum, si de me iure triumphat Amor?   40

IX

ISTE quod est, ego saepe fui : sed fors et in hora
   hoc ipso eiecto [3] carior alter erit.
Penelope poterat bis denos salva per annos
   vivere, tam multis femina digna procis ;
coniugium falsa poterat differre Minerva,
   nocturno solvens texta diurna dolo ;
visura et quamvis numquam speraret Vlixen,
   illum exspectando facta remansit anus.

---

[1] *Some lines seem to have been lost at this point, if, indeed, 29-40 can be regarded as belonging at all to what precedes.*
[2] matre, *a MS. of L. Valla :* marte *NF.*
[3] eiecto ϛ. electo *NF.*

be for me a death of shame; but, shameful though it be, thou still shalt die.

 .   .   .   .   .

²⁹ Even the great Achilles when left forlorn, his love snatched from his side, endured that his arms should lie idle in his tent. He saw the rout, the Achaeans dragged along the shore, he saw the Dorian camp glow with the torch of Hector, he saw Patroclus lie low defiled with clotted sand, his streaming hair dabbled with blood; and all this he endured for the sake of the lovely Briseis. Such is the force and fierceness of grief when love is stolen away. But when with tardy retribution his captive was restored to him, it was the same Achilles dragged brave Hector at the heels of his Haemonian steeds. What wonder then if Love rightfully triumphs over me, that have neither mother nor armour like to his?

IX

WHAT yonder fool now is, I often was. Yet one day, it may be, he too shall be cast forth and another dearer to thy heart.

³ Penelope was able to live true to her vows for twice ten years, a woman worthy to be wooed of so many suitors; she was able to put off her marriage by her false weaving, in crafty wise, unravelling by night the weft of the day, and though she ne'er hoped to look on Ulysses' face again, she remained faithful in his house, grown old in waiting his return. Briseis

SEXTI PROPERTI ELEGIARVM LIBER II

nec non exanimem amplectens Briseis Achillen
   candida vesana verberat ora manu;   10
et dominum lavit maerens captiva cruentum,
   propositum fulvis[1] in Simoenta vadis,
foedavitque comas, et tanti corpus Achilli
   maximaque in parva sustulit ossa manu;
cum tibi nec Peleus aderat nec caerula mater,
   Scyria nec viduo Deidamia toro.[2]
tunc igitur veris gaudebat Graecia natis,
   tunc etiam felix inter et arma pudor.
at tu non una potuisti nocte vacare,
   impia, non unum sola manere diem!   20
quin etiam multo duxistis pocula risu:
   forsitan et de me verba fuere mala.
hic etiam petitur, qui te prius ante reliquit:
   di faciant, isto capta fruare viro!
haec mihi vota tuam propter suscepta salutem,
   cum capite hoc Stygiae iam poterentur aquae,
et lectum flentes circum staremus amici?
   hic ubi tum, pro di, perfida, quisve fuit?
quid si longinquos retinerer miles ad Indos,
   aut mea si staret navis in Oceano?   30
sed vobis facile est verba et componere fraudes:
   hoc unum didicit femina semper opus.
non sic incerto mutantur flamine Syrtes,
   nec folia hiberno tam tremefacta Noto,
quam cito feminea non constat foedus in ira,
   sive ea causa gravis sive ea causa levis.

---

[1] fulvis ς: fluviis *NF*.   [2] toro *Itali*: viro *NF*.

too, one arm about her dead Achilles, beat her fair cheeks with frenzied hand, and, captive as she was, with weeping washed the bloodstained corpse of her lord and master, where she had laid him in the yellow shallows of Simois; she cast ashes on her hair, and her small hand sufficed to hold the body and mighty bones of the great Achilles. For in that day, Achilles, neither Peleus nor thy sea-born mother, nor Scyrian Deidamia, whom thou leftest widowed, were by thy side.

[17] Thus in those days Greece was glad of her true children; then even in the camp did modesty flourish. But thou, impious one, couldst not forego the joys of even one night, couldst not abide alone for even one day. Nay, more, ye twain laughed loud over the wine-cup, and perchance spake evil words of me. And this man whom thou seekest is even he that first left thee of old. God grant thee joy enslaved by such a man!

[25] Is this the end of the vows I made for thy safety, when the waves of Styx had all but whelmed thy head, and round about thy bed we, thy friends, stood and wept? Where then was this lover of thine, O God, or what cared he?

[29] What wouldst thou do were I a soldier, kept far hence in distant Ind, or if my bark were moored in the western ocean? But 'tis easy for you to contrive false tales and deceits. This art alone has woman ne'er failed to learn. Not so swiftly do the Syrtes change before the veering gale, nor the leaves tremble before the wintry South Wind, but swifter far is plighted faith forgot in a woman's anger, be the cause grave or light.

SEXTI PROPERTI ELEGIARVM LIBER II

nunc, quoniam ista tibi placuit sententia, cedam:
    tela, precor, pueri, promite acuta magis,
figite certantes atque hanc mihi solvite vitam!
    sanguis erit vobis maxima palma meus.   40
sidera sunt testes et matutina pruina
    et furtim misero ianua aperta mihi,
te nihil in vita nobis acceptius umquam:
    nunc quoque eris, quamvis sic inimica mihi.
nec domina ulla meo ponet vestigia lecto:
    solus ero, quoniam non licet esse tuum.
atque utinam, si forte pios eduximus annos,
    ille vir in medio fiat amore lapis![1]

   .   .   .   .   .

non ob regna magis diris cecidere sub armis
    Thebani media non sine matre duces: 50
quam, mihi si media liceat pugnare puella,
    mortem ego non fugiam morte subire tua.

X

Sed tempus lustrare aliis Helicona choreis,
    et campum Haemonio iam dare tempus equo.
iam libet et fortes memorare ad proelia turmas
    et Romana mei dicere castra ducis.
quod si deficiant vires, audacia certe
    laus erit: in magnis et voluisse sat est.

---

[1] *Some lines have clearly been lost at this point, and I therefore mark a gap with Lachmann. Housman would insert* VIII. *3, 4.*

⁣³⁷ But now, since thou hast chosen this for thy path, I will yield. Bring forth, ye loves, yet sharper arrows, and vying with one another pierce my heart and let the vital spirit free. Great glory shall my life-blood bring ye! The stars are witness and the morning frost, and the door that stealthily oped to let me in, that there ne'er was aught in life more dear to my heart than thou; and thus I'll love thee still, though thou art so unkind. No mistress ever shall come into my bed; alone will I live, since thine I may not be. And oh, if perchance my life hath been spent in true service of the gods, may thy mate in the mid-course of passion become a stone.

. . . . .

⁣⁴⁹ In no more deadly strife did the Theban chieftains fight and fall to win a throne, while in their midst their mother strove to part them; nor from such death would I shrink, not though Cynthia strove to part us, if only so thou also mightest die.

X

But now 'tis time with other measures to range the slopes of Helicon; 'tis time to launch the Haemonian steed o'er the open plain; now would I sing of hosts brave in battle and tell of my chieftain's Roman camp. But should strength fail me, yet my daring shall win me fame: in mighty enterprises enough even to have willed success. Let early youth sing

SEXTI PROPERTI ELEGIARVM LIBER II

aetas prima canat Veneres, extrema tumultus:
    bella canam, quando scripta puella mea est.
nunc volo subducto gravior procedere vultu,
    nunc aliam citharam me mea Musa docet   10
surge, anima; ex humili iam carmine sumite vires,
    Pierides: magni nunc erit oris opus.
iam negat Euphrates equitem post terga tueri
    Parthorum et Crassos se tenuisse dolet:
India quin,[1] Auguste, tuo dat colla triumpho,
    et domus intactae te tremit Arabiae;
et si qua extremis tellus se subtrahit oris,
    sentiat illa tuas postmodo capta manus.
haec ego castra sequar; vates tua castra canendo
    magnus ero: servent hunc mihi fata diem!   20
ut caput in magnis ubi non est tangere signis,
    ponitur hac imos ante corona pedes,
sic nos nunc, inopes laudis conscendere carmen,
    pauperibus sacris vilia tura damus.
nondum etiam Ascraeos norunt mea carmina fontes,
    sed modo Permessi flumine lavit Amor.

XI

Scribant de te alii vel sis ignota licebit:
    laudet, qui sterili semina ponit humo.
omnia, crede mihi, tecum uno munera lecto
    auferet extremi funeris atra dies;

---

[1] quin *Beroaldus* · quis *NF*.

the charms of love, life's later prime the storm of war: war will I sing, now that I have set forth all my mistress' charms. Now would I go my way with grave frown stamped on serious brow; my Muse now bids me strike another lyre. Awake, my soul! Ye Pierid maids, leave these humble strains and take a stronger tone; the work that waits you needs a mighty voice.

[13] Now does Euphrates deny that the Parthian aims his backward shaft, and grieves that ever he cut short the return of the Crassi. Nay, even India, Augustus, bows her neck to grace thy triumph, and the house of virgin Arabia trembles before thee; and if there be any land withdrawn upon earth's furthest rim, captured hereafter let it feel thy mighty hand.

[19] This be the camp I follow. Great will I be among singers by singing of thy wars. Let destiny keep that glorious day in store for me.

[21] As when we cannot reach the head of some tall statue, our garland is laid thus humbly before its feet, so now, too weak to climb to the heights of thy glory's song, with lowly rite we give thee the incense of the poor. Not yet have my songs come to know the founts of Ascra; Love has but dipped them in Permessus' stream.[1]

XI

LET others write of thee; or be thou all unknown. Let him praise thee that will sow his harvest in a barren soil: all thy endowments, believe me, the last dark hour of funeral shall consume with thee on

---

[1] *I.e.*, "I have not attempted epic, but only erotic verse" The key to the passage is found in Verg. *Ecl.* vi. 64, where Gallus' call to write epic is symbolised by his summons from Permessus to receive the pipe of Hesiod of Ascra.

SEXTI PROPERTI ELEGIARVM LIBER II

et tua transibit contemnens ossa viator,
　　nec dicet " Cinis hic docta puella fuit."

XII

Qvicvmqve ille fuit, puerum qui pinxit Amorem,
　　nonne putas miras hunc habuisse manus?
is primum vidit sine sensu vivere amantes,
　　et levibus curis magna perire bona.
idem non frustra ventosas addidit alas,
　　fecit et humano corde volare deum:
scilicet alterna quoniam iactamur in unda,
　　nostraque non ullis permanet aura locis.
et merito hamatis manus est armata sagittis,
　　et pharetra ex umero Gnosia utroque iacet:　　10
ante ferit quoniam, tuti quam cernimus hostem,
　　nec quisquam ex illo vulnere sanus abit.
in me tela manent, manet et puerilis imago:
　　sed certe pennas perdidit ille suas;
evolat ei nostro quoniam de pectore nusquam,
　　assiduusque meo sanguine bella gerit.
quid tibi iucundum est siccis habitare medullis?
　　si pudor est, alio traice duella tua![1]
intactos isto satius temptare veneno:
　　non ego, sed tenuis vapulat umbra mea.　　20
quam si perdideris, quis erit qui talia cantet,
　　(haec mea Musa levis gloria magna tua est),
qui caput et digitos et lumina nigra puellae,
　　et canat ut soleant molliter ire pedes?

[1] pudor *v*: puer *NF*.　duella *Lipsius*: puella *NF*.　tua ς.
tuo *NF*.

the selfsame bier, and the traveller shall spurn thine ashes as he passes by, nor ever say: "This dust was once a learnèd maid."

XII

Whoe'er he was first painted Love in likeness of a boy, think'st thou not his hands had wondrous skill? He first saw that there is no wisdom in the lives of lovers, and that mighty blessings are lost through petty cares. He too with good reason gave him windy wings, and made him flit about the hearts of men; for of a truth we are ever tossed upon a shifting sea, and our breeze abides never in the same quarter. Rightly too is Love's hand armed with barbed arrows, and the Cnossian quiver hangs from his shoulders twain; for he strikes e'er from our fancied safety we may see the foe, nor does any go scatheless from the wound he deals.

[13] In me his darts stick fast, for me he still wears the form of a boy; but of a truth he has lost his wings, for nowhither, alas! flies he forth from my bosom, and tireless he wages war within my blood.

[17] What delight hast thou to dwell in this withered heart of mine? If thou hast aught of shame, elsewhere transfer thy warfare. Better far to assail those that have never felt the power of thy venomed shaft. 'Tis not I, but my wasted shadow, thou smitest: yet, if thou destroy me utterly, where wilt thou find one to chant such strains as these? (Slight though my Muse be, yet 'tis thy great renown.) Where wilt thou find one to sing the face, the hands, the dark eyes of my beloved, and how soft her footsteps fall?

SEXTI PROPERTI ELEGIARVM LIBER II

XIII

Non tot Achaemeniis armatur Erythra[1] sagittis,
  spicula quot nostro pectore fixit Amor.
hic me tam graciles vetuit contemnere Musas,
  iussit et Ascraeum sic habitare nemus,
non ut Pieriae quercus mea verba sequantur,
  aut possim Ismaria ducere valle feras,
sed magis ut nostro stupefiat Cynthia versu:
  tunc ego sim Inachio notior arte Lino.
non ego sum formae tantum mirator honestae,
  nec si qua illustres femina iactat avos: 10
me iuvet in gremio doctae legisse puellae,
  auribus et puris scripta probasse mea.
haec ubi contigerint, populi confusa valeto
  fabula: nam domina iudice tutus ero.
quae si forte bonas ad pacem verterit aures,
  possum inimicitias tunc ego ferre Iovis.

XIIIa

Qvandocvmqve igitur nostros mors claudet ocellos
  accipe quae serves funeris acta mei.
nec mea tunc longa spatietur imagine pompa,
  nec tuba sit fati vana querela mei;   20
nec mihi tunc fulcro sternatur lectus eburno,
  nec sit in Attalico mors mea nixa toro.

[1] Erythra *Housman*. Etrusca *NF*.

XIII

Not with so many Persian shafts is Erythra armed as the darts that Love hath planted in my breast 'Twas he forbade me to despise the trivial Muse and commanded me to dwell in the grove of Ascra; not in such wise that the Pierian oaks should follow my words, or that I should lead the wild beasts after me down Ismarus' vale, but rather that Cynthia should marvel at my verse. Thus should I win more fame than Inachian Linus.

[9] I marvel not only at comeliness of form, nor if a woman boasts glorious ancestry. Be it rather my joy to have read my verse as I lay in the arms of a learnèd maid and to have pleased her pure ears with what I write. When such bliss hath fallen to my lot, farewell the confused talk of the people; I will rest secure in the judgment of my mistress. If only she chance to turn her thoughts toward peace and hear me kindly, though Jove be angry, I can bear his wrath.

XIIIa

Wherefore, Cynthia, when at last death shall seal my eyes, hear thou the order of my funeral. For me let no procession walk with long array of masks, let no trumpet make vain wailing for my end. Let no last bed on posts of ivory be strewn for me, let not my dead body lie on a couch of cloth-of-gold; no

SEXTI PROPERTI ELEGIARVM LIBER II

desit odoriferis ordo mihi lancibus, adsint
 plebei parvae funeris exsequiae.
sat mea sit magno,¹ si tres sint pompa libelli,
 quos ego Persephonae maxima dona feram.
tu vero nudum pectus lacerata sequeris,
 nec fueris nomen lassa vocare meum,
osculaque in gelidis pones suprema labellis,
 cum dabitur Syrio munere plenus onyx.   30
deinde, ubi suppositus cinerem me fecerit ardor,
 accipiat Manes parvula testa meos,
et sit in exiguo laurus super addita busto,
 quae tegat exstincti funeris umbra locum,
et duo sint versus: QVI NVNC IACET HORRIDA PVLVIS,
 VNIVS HIC QVONDAM SERVVS AMORIS ERAT.
nec minus haec nostri notescet fama sepulcri,
 quam fuerant Phthii busta cruenta viri.
tu quoque si quando venies ad fata, memento,
 hoc iter ad lapides cana veni memores.   40
interea cave sis nos aspernata sepultos:
 non nihil ad verum conscia terra sapit.
atque utinam primis animam me ponere cunis
 iussisset quaevis de Tribus una Soror!
nam quo tam dubiae servetur spiritus horae?
 Nestoris est visus post tria saecla cinis:
cui si tam longae ² minuisset fata senectae
 Gallicus ³ Iliacis miles in aggeribus,

---

¹ magno *Phillimore* magna *NF*.
² cui si tam longae *Livincius*· quis tam longaevae *NF*.
³ Gallicus *NF, probably corrupt*. bellicus *Behot*: Ilius *Lachmann*.

line of attendants with sweet-scented platters for me, only the humble obsequies that mark a poor man's death.

[25] Costly enough shall be my funeral train if three little books go with me to the grave, that I may bear them to Persephone as my most precious offering. And thou shalt follow, thy breast all bare and torn, nor shalt thou weary of calling upon my name, but shalt imprint the last kiss upon my clay-cold lips, when the casket of onyx with its gift of Syrian nard is bestowed upon me. Then when the fire beneath hath burned me to an ash, let a tiny earthen urn receive my ghost, and over my little tomb let a laurel be planted to o'ershade the spot, where the fire of death hath ceased to burn; and thereon be these two verses: HE THAT NOW LIES NAUGHT BUT UNLOVELY DUST, ONCE SERVED ONE LOVE AND ONE LOVE ONLY.

[37] So shall the fame of my sepulchre be blazoned abroad no less than the bloody tomb of the Phthian hero. And whene'er thou too shalt come to thy death, do thou come gray-haired by the old path to the stones that guard my memory. Meanwhile see thou despise me not in my tomb. Not all unconscious and witless of the truth are the ashes of man.

[43] And ah! would that any one of the three Sisters had ordained that I should die, while yet I lay in the cradle. For to what end is man's breath kept whole in him, breath that any moment may cease to be? Not till three generations of men had past away were Nestor's ashes seen: yet had some Phrygian warrior from the ramparts of Troy cut short the long-drawn doom of his old age, he ne'er had seen the body

SEXTI PROPERTI ELEGIARVM LIBER II

non ille Antilochi vidisset corpus humari,
   diceret aut "O mors, cur mihi sera venis?"   50
tu tamen amisso non numquam flebis amico:
   fas est praeteritos semper amare viros.
testis, qui niveum quondam percussit Adonem
   venantem Idalio vertice durus aper;
illis formosus[1] iacuisse paludibus, illuc
   diceris effusa tu, Venus, isse coma.
sed frustra mutos revocabis, Cynthia, Manes:
   nam mea qui poterunt ossa minuta loqui?

XIV

Non ita Dardanio gavisus Atrida triumpho est,
   cum caderent magnae Laomedontis opes;
nec sic errore exacto laetatus Vlixes,
   cum tetigit carae litora Dulichiae;
nec sic Electra, salvum cum aspexit Oresten,
   cuius falsa tenens fleverat ossa soror;
nec sic incolumem Minois Thesea vidit,
   Daedalium lino cum duce rexit iter;
quanta ego praeterita collegi gaudia nocte:
   immortalis ero, si altera talis erit.   10
at dum demissis supplex cervicibus ibam,
   dicebar sicco vilior esse lacu.
nec mihi iam fastus opponere quaerit iniquos,
   nec mihi ploranti lenta sedere potest.

---

[1] formosus *Postgate*: formosum *NF*.

of Antilochus laid in earth, nor cried aloud : "O death ! why tarriest thou so late e'er thou come to me?"

51 Yet thou, when thou hast lost thy friend, wilt sometimes weep for him; undying love is the due of the loved and lost. Witness the cruel boar that struck snow-white Adonis as he hunted on the Idalian peak. There in the marsh, 'tis said, he lay in his beauty; thither, 'tis said, thou wentest, Venus, thy tresses unbound. But in vain, Cynthia, shalt thou recall my voiceless shade to life; for what answer shall my crumbled bones have strength to make?

XIV

Not so did Atrides rejoice in his triumph over Troy, when the vast wealth of Laomedon fell in ruin; not so glad was Ulysses, when, his wanderings o'er, he reached the shore of his beloved Dulichia; not so happy Electra, when she saw Orestes safe and sound, o'er whose feigned ashes[1] she had wept, clasping them to her heart; not with such joy did the daughter of Minos behold Theseus come forth unscathed, when the guiding thread led him through the Daedalian maze. All their gladness was naught, compared with the joys that were mine last night. Come such another night, and I shall be immortal! (Yet when I went my way a suppliant with drooping head she spoke of me as more worthless than a pool run dry.) No more does she meet me with cruel disdain, no more can she sit unmoved at the voice of my complaint.

[1] A reference to the *Electra* of Sophocles, where Orestes returns home under a false name bearing an urn supposed to contain his ashes.

SEXTI PROPERTI ELEGIARVM LIBER II

atque utinam non tam sero mihi nota fuisset
  condicio! cineri nunc medicina datur.
ante pedes caecis lucebat semita nobis:
  scilicet insano nemo in amore videt.
hoc sensi prodesse magis: contemnite, amantes!
  sic hodie veniet, si qua negavit heri. 20
pulsabant alii frustra dominamque vocabant:
  mecum habuit positum lenta puella caput.
haec mihi devictis potior victoria Parthis,
  haec spolia, haec reges, haec mihi currus erunt.
magna ego dona tua figam, Cytherea, columna,
  taleque sub nostro nomine carmen erit:
HAS PONO ANTE TVAS TIBI, DIVA, PROPERTIVS AEDES
  EXVVIAS, TOTA NOCTE RECEPTVS AMANS.
nunc ad te, mea lux, veniet mea litore navis
  servata. an mediis sidat onusta vadis? 30
quod si forte aliqua nobis mutabere culpa,
  vestibulum iaceam mortuus ante tuum!

XV

O ME felicem! o nox mihi candida! et o tu
  lectule deliciis facte beate meis!
quam multa apposita narramus verba lucerna,
  quantaque sublato lumine rixa fuit!
nam modo nudatis mecum est luctata papillis,
  interdum tunica duxit operta moram.
illa meos somno lassos patefecit ocellos
  ore suo et dixit "Sicine, lente, iaces?"

¹⁵ And would that her terms of peace had not been made known to me so late! To dust and ashes now this healing is given. The way shone clear before my feet; but men love-maddened one and all are blind.

¹⁹ This I have found to be the sovereign cure: lovers, disdain your loves! So, if she have refused you yesterday, she will come to your arms to-day. Others in vain beat at my mistress' door and called her by name; but unmoved she laid her head upon my breast. Dearer to me this victory than the conquest of Parthia: be these my spoils, my captive kings, my triumphal car. Rich offerings, Cytherea, will I fix on the pillars of thy shrine, and such shall be the verse beneath my name: THESE SPOILS, O GODDESS, I PROPERTIUS HANG BEFORE THY SHRINE, FOR ONE WHOLE NIGHT LONG MY MISTRESS TOOK ME TO HER HEART. Now, Cynthia, shall my bark come safe home to thee—or is it doomed to sink with all its wares in shoal-water?[1] Nay, if thou change toward me through any fault of mine, may I lie dead before thy threshold!

XV

How happy is my lot! O night that was not dark for me! and thou beloved couch blessed by my delight! How many sweet words we interchanged while the lamp was by, and how we strove together when the light was gone! For now she struggled with me with breasts uncovered, now veiling herself in her tunic checked my advance. With a kiss she unsealed mine eyes weighed down with slumber and said: "Dost thou lie thus, thou sluggard?" How

---

[1] *I.e.*, in sight of shore.

SEXTI PROPERTI ELEGIARVM LIBER II

quam vario amplexu mutamus bracchia! quantum
 oscula sunt labris nostra morata tuis!
non iuvat in caeco Venerem corrumpere motu:
 si nescis, oculi sunt in amore duces.
ipse Paris nuda fertur periisse Lacaena,
 cum Menelaeo surgeret e thalamo;
nudus et Endymion Phoebi cepisse sororem
 dicitur et nudae concubuisse deae.
quod si pertendens animo vestita cubaris,[1]
 scissa veste meas experiere manus:
quin etiam, si me ulterius provexerit ira,
 ostendes matri bracchia laesa tuae.
necdum inclinatae prohibent te ludere mammae:
 viderit haec, si quam iam peperisse pudet.
dum nos fata sinunt, oculos satiemus amore:
 nox tibi longa venit, nec reditura dies.
atque utinam haerentes sic nos vincire catena
 velles, ut numquam solveret ulla dies!
exemplo vinctae tibi sint in amore columbae,
 masculus et totum femina coniugium.
errat, qui finem vesani quaerit amoris:
 verus amor nullum novit habere modum.
terra prius falso partu deludet arantes,
 et citius nigros Sol agitabit equos,
flumınaque ad caput incipient revocare liquores,
 aridus et sicco gurgite piscis erit,
quam possim nostros alio transferre dolores:
 huius ero vivus, mortuus huius ero.

[1] cubaris *Muretus*: cubares *O*.

oft we shifted our arms and varied our embrace; how long my kisses lingered on thy lips!

[11] There is no joy in spoiling love's delights by sightless motion: know, if thou knowest it not, that in love the eyes are guides. Paris himself is said to have been undone by love when he saw the Spartan naked, as she rose from the couch of Menelaus. Naked was Endymion when he impassioned Phoebus' sister, and naked they say he lay with the naked goddess.

[17] But if thou hardenest thine heart and wilt lie clothed, thou shalt have thy raiment rent and feel the violence of my hands. Nay more, if anger carry me further yet, thou shalt show thy mother how thine arms are bruised. Not yet do drooping breasts forbid thee to make merry; that be her care that hath borne a child and counts it shame. While the Fates grant it, let us glut our eyes with love: the long night hasteneth on for thee that knows no dawning. And oh! that thou wouldst bind us in this embrace with such a chain that never the day might come to break its power! Be doves thine example: they are yoked together in love, male and female made one by passion. He errs that seeks to set a term to the frenzy of love; true love hath no bound. Sooner will earth mock the ploughman by bearing fruit out of season, and the Sun-god drive the steeds of night, rivers begin to recall their waters to their fount, the deep dry up and leave its fish athirst, than I shall be able to transfer my love to another; hers will I be in life and hers in death.

SEXTI PROPERTI ELEGIARVM LIBER II

quod mihi si tecum tales concedere noctes
   illa velit, vitae longus et annus erit.
si dabit haec multas, fiam immortalis in illis:
   nocte una quivis vel deus esse potest.   40
qualem si cuncti cuperent decurrere vitam
   et pressi multo membra iacere mero,
non ferrum crudele neque esset bellica navis,
   nec nostra Actiacum verteret ossa mare,
nec totiens propriis circum oppugnata triumphis
   lassa foret crines solvere Roma suos.
haec certe merito poterunt laudare minores:
   laeserunt nullos pocula nostra deos.
tu modo, dum lucet, fructum ne desere vitae!
   omnia si dederis oscula, pauca dabis.   50
ac veluti folia arentes liquere corollas,
   quae passim calathis strata natare vides,
sic nobis, qui nunc magnum speramus amantes,
   forsitan includet crastina fata dies.

XVI

Praetor ab Illyricis venit modo, Cynthia, terris,
   maxima praeda tibi, maxima cura mihi.
non potuit saxo vitam posuisse Cerauno?
   a, Neptune, tibi qualia dona darem!
nunc sine me plena fiunt convivia mensa,
   nunc sine me tota ianua nocte patet.
quare, si sapis, oblatas ne desere messes
   et stolidum pleno vellere carpe pecus;

37
But if she be willing again to grant me such nights as last, one year will be long life for me. If she give me many, they will make me immortal; one such night might make any man a god!

41
Ah! if all men desired to pass their life as I, and lie with limbs weighed down by deep draughts of wine, nor cruel steel would there be nor ships of war, nor would our bones be tossed in the deep of Actium; nor would Rome, so oft beleaguered with triumphs o'er her own kin, be weary of tearing her hair for grief. This at least shall those that come after be able to praise in us: our wine-cups never outraged any god.

49
Cynthia, do thou only while the light is yet with thee forsake not the joy of life! Give me all thy kisses, yet shall they be all too few; and as leaves drop from withered wreaths and thou mayst see them bestrew the cups and float therein, so we that love and whose hopes are high perchance shall find to-morrow close our doom.

XVI

Of late, Cynthia, a praetor came from the land of Illyria, to thee the hugest plunder, to me the hugest care. Could he not have lost his life by the Ceraunian rocks? Ah, Neptune, what gifts would I have given thee!

5
Now feasts are spread on laden tables, and I am not there! Now all night long thy door stands open, but not for me! Wherefore, if thou art wise, neglect not the harvest offered thee and pluck thy stolid beast, while yet his fleece is whole! Then when his gifts are

SEXTI PROPERTI ELEGIARVM LIBER II

deinde, ubi consumpto restabit munere pauper,
   dic alias iterum naviget Illyrias! 10
Cynthia non sequitur fasces nec curat honores,
   semper amatorum ponderat una sinus.
at tu nunc nostro, Venus, o succurre dolori,
   rumpat ut assiduis membra libidinibus!
ergo muneribus quivis mercatur amorem?
   Iuppiter, indigna merce puella perit.
semper in Oceanum mittit me quaerere gemmas,
   et iubet ex ipsa tollere dona Tyro.
atque utinam Romae nemo esset dives, et ipse
   straminea posset dux habitare casa! 20
numquam venales essent ad munus amicae,
   atque una fieret cana puella domo.
numquam septenas noctes seiuncta cubares,[1]
   candida tam foedo bracchia fusa viro,
non quia peccarim (testor te), sed quia vulgo
   formosis levitas semper amica fuit.
barbarus exclusis[2] agitat vestigia lumbis—
   et subito felix nunc mea regna tenet!
aspice quid donis Eriphyla invenit amaris,
   arserit et quantis nupta Creusa malis. 30
nullane sedabit nostros iniuria fletus?
   an dolor hic vitiis nescit abesse tuis?[3]
tot iam abiere dies, cum me nec cura theatri
   nec tetigit Campi, nec mea mensa iuvat.
at pudeat certe, pudeat!—nisi forte, quod aiunt,
   turpis amor surdis auribus esse solet.

---

[1] numquam ... cubares *Itali*: non quia ... cubaris *NF*.
[2] excussis ς.   [3] tuis ς : suis *NF*.

THE ELEGIES OF PROPERTIUS BOOK II

spent and he left poor, bid him set sail again to fresh Illyrias.

¹¹ Cynthia follows not the rods of office, cares naught for honours; her lovers' purse she ever weighs as none other can. But do thou, Venus, aid me in my grief; let his insatiate lusts break all his strength.

¹⁵ So then shall any stranger purchase her love with gifts? Jove! 'tis an unworthy thing that such traffic should have power to corrupt the heart of woman. Ever she sends me to the marge of ocean to seek her gems, and bids me bring gifts from Tyre itself. Would that no men at Rome were wealthy and that our lord and master himself dwelt in a thatched[1] cottage. Never then would one's mistress sell herself for a gift, but girls would grow grey in the house of one only lover. Never wouldst thou lie far from me for seven nights long, thy white arms lapped about so foul a lover; nor dost thou thus because I have sinned—to that I call thee to testify—but because the fair are ever faithless.

²⁷ A barbarian shut out from bliss[2] stamps at thy door, and lo! of a sudden a blessing falls on him and now he rules where I once reigned supreme.

²⁹ See what bitter woe gifts brought to Eriphyla, and in what agony the bride Creusa burned! Will all the wrong thou dost me ne'er assuage my tears? or must this grief of mine attend thy sins for ever? So many days have past away since the theatre and the Campus lost all charms for me, and my table ceased to please. Yet truly shame, yea, shame should set me free! But, perchance, as men say, dishonourable

---

[1] An allusion to the so-called *casa Romuli*, preserved on the Palatine. Cp. IV. i. 9.   [2] If *excussis . . . lumbis* be read, translate "worn out by his lusts."

cerne ducem, modo qui fremitu complevit inani
 Actia damnatis aequora militibus:
hunc infamis amor versis dare terga carinis
 iussit et extremo quaerere in orbe fugam   40
Caesaris haec virtus et gloria Caesaris haec est:
 illa, qua vicit, condidit arma manu.
sed quascumque tibi vestes, quoscumque smaragdos,
 quosve dedit flavo lumine chrysolithos,
haec videam rapidas in vanum ferre procellas:
 quae tibi terra, velim, quae tibi fiat aqua.
non semper placidus periuros ridet amantes
 Iuppiter et surda neglegit aure preces.
vidistis toto sonitus percurrere caelo,
 fulminaque aetheria desiluisse domo: 50
non haec Pleiades faciunt neque aquosus Orion,
 nec sic de nihilo fulminis ira cadit;
periuras tunc ille solet punire puellas,
 deceptus quoniam flevit et ipse deus.
quare ne tibi sit tanti Sidonia vestis,
 ut timeas, quotiens nubilus Auster erit.

XVII

MENTIRI noctem, promissis ducere amantem,
 hoc erit infectas sanguine habere manus!
horum ego sum vates, quotiens desertus amaras
 explevi noctes, fractus utroque toro.

love is ever deaf. Behold the chief, who of late filled the waves of Actium with the fruitless groaning of the soldiers he dragged down to death! 'Twas infamous love bade him wheel his ships and turn his back to the foe and seek flight in the utmost bounds of earth. This is Caesar's claim to virtue, this Caesar's claim to glory; the hand that conquered sheathed the sword in peace.

43 But, oh that I may see all his gifts, the fine raiment, the emeralds and the yellow-gleaming chrysolite, borne by swift storms into empty space; may they become vile earth or water in thy hands! Not always does Jove calmly laugh at lovers' perjuries and turn a deaf ear to prayer. Thou hast perceived the thunderclap run through all the sky, and the levin bolt leap from its airy home. 'Tis neither the Pleiades nor dark Orion that brings these things to pass; 'tis not for nothing that the wrath of the lightning falls. 'Tis then that Jove is wont to punish faithless girls, since he also once wept for a woman's treachery. Wherefore count not thy Sidonian raiment worth the terror thou must feel whene'er the South Wind rolls up clouds of storm.

XVII

To make a false tryst for a night, to beguile a lover with promises, why, 'tis to have his blood upon thy hands. These sorrows do I sing, as oft as I pass lonely nights of bitterness, anguished to think of how thou liest, and how I.

SEXTI PROPERTI ELEGIARVM LIBER II

vel tu Tantalea moveare ad flumina sorte,
   ut liquor arenti fallat ab ore sitim;
vel tu Sisyphios licet admirere labores,
   difficile ut toto monte volutet onus;
durius in terris nihil est quod vivat amante,
   nec, modo si sapias, quod minus esse velis.   10
quem modo felicem invidia admirante ferebant,
   nunc decimo admittor vix ego quoque die.
nunc iacere e duro corpus iuvat, impia, saxo,
   sumere et in nostras trita venena manus;
nec licet in triviis sicca requiescere luna,
   aut per rimosas mittere verba fores.
quod quamvis ita sit, dominam mutare cavebo:
   tum flebit, cum in me senserit esse fidem.

XVIII[1]

Assidvae multis odium peperere querelae:
   frangitur in tacito femina saepe viro.
si quid vidisti, semper vidisse negato!
   aut si quid doluit forte, dolere nega!

XVIIIa

Qvid mea si canis aetas canesceret annis,
   et faceret scissas languida ruga genas?
at non Tithoni spernens Aurora senectam
   desertum Eoa passa iacere domo est:

---

[1] *I have given these verses, which, as Rossberg pointed out, are alien to their context, the rank of a separate elegy.*

⁵ Be thou smitten with compassion for the fate of Tantalus at the waterside, when thou seest how the water sinks from his parched mouth and mocks his thirst; or marvel at the toil of Sisyphus, how he rolls his stubborn burden up all the mountain slope; yet know that there is naught on earth more suffering than a lover, nor aught a wise man would less wish to be. I who was once accounted happy, I whom men envied and admired, I now have entry scarce every tenth day. Now gladly, impious maid, would I cast myself from some hard rock or take distilled poison into my hands. No more can I lie in the streets beneath the cold, clear moon nor cry my words through the chinks of thy door!

¹⁷ Yet though these things be so, I will have a care not to change my mistress; then will she weep, when she feels that I am true.

XVIII

Continued complainings beget disgust in many a heart; oft doth a silent lover bend a woman's will. If aught thou hast espied, deny thou sawest aught, or if aught perchance hath pained thee deny the pain!

XVIIIa

What if my youthful prime were white with the white hair of eld, and drooping wrinkles furrowed my cheeks?

⁷ Tithonus was old, yet Aurora despised him not, nor suffered him to lie lonely in the chambers of the

SEXTI PROPERTI ELEGIARVM LIBER II

illum saepe suis decedens fovit in undis
    quam prius adiunctos sedula lavit equos;   10
illum ad vicinos cum amplexa quiesceret Indos,
    maturos iterum est questa redire dies;
illa deos currum conscendens dixit iniquos,
    invitum et terris praestitit officium.
cui maiora senis Tithoni gaudia vivi,
    quam gravis amisso Memnone luctus erat.
cum sene non puduit talem dormire puellam
    et canae totiens oscula ferre comae.
at tu etiam iuvenem odisti me, perfida, cum sis
    ipsa anus haud longa curva futura die.   20
quin ego deminuo curam, quod saepe Cupido
    huic malus esse solet, cui bonus ante fuit.

XVIIIB[1]

Nvnc etiam infectos demens imitare Britannos,
    ludis et externo tincta nitore caput?
ut natura dedit, sic omnis recta figura est:
    turpis Romano Belgicus ore color.
illi sub terris fiant mala multa puellae,
    quae mentita suas vertit inepta comas!
deme: mihi certe poteris formosa videri;
    mi formosa satis, si modo saepe venis.   30
an si caeruleo quaedam sua tempora fuco
    tinxerit, idcirco caerula forma bona est?
cum tibi nec frater nec sit tibi filius ullus,
    frater ego et tibi sim filius unus ego.

[1] *Separated from the preceding by Kuinoel.*

East. Oft as she departed did she caress him amid the waves where she hath her home, or ever turning to her task she washed her yoked steeds, and when nigh Ind she laid her down to rest in his embrace she made moan that day returned too soon. As she climbed her car she cried, "High heaven is unkind," and offered unwilling service to the world. Deeper her joy, while old Tithonus lived, than heavy her grief when Memnon perished. So fair a maid as she had no shame to sleep beside an aged man, nor to heap kisses on his hoary locks.

19 But thou, faithless, hatest me for all my youth, though thyself at no far distant day shalt be a stooping crone. Still my care grows less when I remember that Cupid oft frowns on him to whom of old he was so kind.

XVIIIb

EVEN now, mad girl, dost ape the painted Briton and wanton with foreign dyes upon thy cheek? Beauty is ever best as nature made it; foul shows the Belgian rouge on Roman cheeks. May many an ill befall the maid in hell, that in her folly dyes her hair with lying hue. Away with these things! I at least shall find thee fair; fair enough art thou to me if only thou visit me often. If one stain her brows with azure dye, does that make azured beauty fair?

33 Thou hast no brother nor any son, wherefore let me and me alone be to thee at once both brother and son. Let thine own bed ever keep thee

SEXTI PROPERTI ELEGIARVM LIBER II

ipse tuus semper tibi sit custodia lectus,
　nec nimis ornata fronte sedere velis.
credam ego narranti, noli committere, famae:
　et terram rumor transilit et maria.

XIX

Etsi me invito discedis, Cynthia, Roma,
　laetor quod sine me devia rura colis.
nullus erit castis iuvenis corruptor in agris,
　qui te blanditiis non sinat esse probam;
nulla neque ante tuas orietur rixa fenestras,
　nec tibi clamatae somnus amarus erit.
sola eris et solos spectabis, Cynthia, montes
　et pecus et fines pauperis agricolae.
illic te nulli poterunt corrumpere ludi,
　fanaque peccatis plurima causa tuis. 10
illic assidue tauros spectabis arantes,
　et vitem docta ponere falce comas;
atque ibi rara feres inculto tura sacello,
　haedus ubi agrestes corruet ante focos;
protinus et nuda choreas imitabere sura;
　omnia ab externo sint modo tuta viro.
ipse ego venabor: iam nunc me sacra Dianae
　suscipere et Veneri ponere vota iuvat.
incipiam captare feras et reddere pinu
　cornua et audaces ipse monere canes; 20
non tamen ut vastos ausim temptare leones
　aut celer agrestes comminus ire sues.

safe from scandal, nor sit thou with face too much adorned. I shall believe tales that rumour tells of thee; therefore sin not; scandal o'erleaps the bounds of land and sea.

XIX

Though, Cynthia, 'tis against my will that thou departest from Rome, glad am I that 'tis in the country far from paths of man thou dwellest without me. In those chaste fields thou shalt find no seductive youth whose flatteries shall not permit thee to be honest, nor shall any brawl arise before thy windows, nor shall thy slumber be made bitter by cries upon thy name. Lone shalt thou dwell and on lone mountains gaze, on flocks and the lands of poor farmers. There will no games have power to corrupt thee, no temples, most frequent cause of all thy sins; there shalt thou behold the tireless oxen plough, and the vine lay aside her foliage at the sickle's skilful touch, and there shalt thou bear a scanty offering of incense to some rude shrine, where the kid shall fall before a rustic altar; then bare-legged shalt thou imitate the country dance, if only there be no danger from the espial of some town-bred man.

[17] I myself will hunt; now straightway 'tis my joy to perform sacrifice to Diana, my vows to Venus laid aside. I will begin to snare wild beasts, to nail trophies of horns to the pine-tree, and with mine own voice urge on the bold hounds: yet would I never dare to assail the lion fell, or with speedy foot go face the wild boar of the field. Daring

SEXTI PROPERTI ELEGIARVM LIBER II

haec igitur mihi sit lepores audacia molles
   excipere et stricto figere avem calamo,
qua formosa suo Clitumnus flumina luco
   integit, et niveos abluit unda boves.
tu quotiens aliquid conabere, vita, memento
   venturum paucis me tibi Luciferis.
sic me nec solae poterunt avertere silvae,
   nec vaga muscosis flumina fusa iugis,   30
quin ego in assidua mutem tua nomina lingua:
   absenti nemo non nocuisse velit.

XX

Qvid fles abducta gravius Briseide? quid fles
   anxia captiva tristius Andromacha?
quidve mea de fraude deos, insana, fatigas?
   quid quereris nostram sic cecidisse fidem?
non tam nocturna volucris funesta querela
   Attica Cecropiis obstrepit in foliis,
nec tantum Niobe bis sex ad busta superba[1]
   sollicito lacrimas defluit a Sipylo.
me licet aeratis astringant bracchia nodis,
   sint mea vel Danaes condita membra domo,   10
in te ego et aeratas rumpam, mea vita, catenas,
   ferratam Danaes transiliamque domum.
de te quodcumque ad surdas mihi dicitur aures:
   tu modo ne dubita de gravitate mea.
ossa tibi iuro per matris et ossa parentis
   (si fallo, cinis heu sit mihi uterque gravis!)

---

[1] superba *Beroaldus* · superbe *NF*.

enough for me to catch the timid hare, or pierce birds with arrows from the quiver, where Clitumnus shrouds his fair streams in his own belovèd grove, and with his waters laves the snow-white kine.

[27] Do thou, my love, oft as thou meditatest aught, remember that I shall be with thee in a few more dawns. So as thou rememberest this, neither the lonely woods nor the wandering streams upon the mossy hills can stay me from repeating thy name with tireless tongue; for one and all are ready to wrong an absent lover.

XX

Why weepst thou more bitterly than Briseis torn from Achilles' side? Why weepst with anxious eyes more sadly than captive Andromache? Or why, mad girl, weariest thou the ears of the gods with complaint of my perfidy? Why moanest thou that my loyalty to thee has sunk so low? Not so shrilly does the mourning bird of Attica make her moan embowered in Cecropian leafage, not so does proud Niobe by twice six tombs stream tears down sorrowing Sipylus.

[9] Though my arms were bound with gyves of bronze, though my limbs were immured in Danae's tower, yet for thy sake, my life, would I break bonds of brass and leap o'er the iron walls of Danae's tower. My ears are deaf to all men say of thee; only do thou likewise doubt not my steadfastness. By my mother's, by my father's bones I swear—if I lie, may either ghost take vengeance on me!—that I will abide true

SEXTI PROPERTI ELEGIARVM LIBER II

me tibi ad extremas mansurum, vita, tenebras:
   ambos una fides auferet, una dies.
quod si nec nomen nec me tua forma teneret,
   posset servitium mite tenere tuum.   20
septima iam plenae deducitur orbita lunae,
   cum de me et de te compita nulla tacent:
interea nobis non numquam[1] ianua mollis,
   non numquam[1] lecti copia facta tui.
nec mihi muneribus nox ulla est empta beatis:
   quidquid eram, hoc animi gratia magna tui.
cum te tam multi peterent, tu me una petisti:
   possum ego naturae non meminisse tuae?
tum me vel tragicae vexetis Erinyes, et me
   inferno damnes, Aeace, iudicio,   30
atque inter Tityi volucres mea poena vagetur,
   tumque ego Sisyphio saxa labore geram!
nec tu supplicibus me sis venerata tabellis:
   ultima talis erit quae mea prima fides.
hoc mihi perpetuo ius est, quod solus amator
   nec cito desisto nec temere incipio.

XXI

A qvantvm de me Panthi tibi pagina finxit,
   tantum illi Pantho ne sit amica Venus!
sed tibi iam videor Dodona verior augur.
   uxorem ille tuus pulcher amator habet!

---

[1] non numquam *F:* non unquam *N.*

to thee, my life, until darkness close my day; one selfsame love, one selfsame hour, shall sweep us both away.

¹⁹ But if neither the glory of thy name nor thy beauty kept me true, yet would the mildness of thy yoke do so. The seventh full moon has spun its course since every street corner hath been speaking of me and thee, and all this time not seldom hath thy door been kind, not seldom have I been admitted to thy bed. Yet not a night have I bought with sumptuous gifts; whate'er I have been in thine eyes, I owe to thy goodwill; great is my debt. Many sought thee, but thou hast sought me only; can I forget the kindness of thy nature? If I do, may ye, Furies of tragedy, plague me, and thou, Aeacus, pass on me the doom of the underworld. May my penalty be one of Tityus' ranging vultures, and may I carry rocks with labour worthy Sisyphus.

³³ But do thou beseech me no more with suppliant tablets: my loyalty shall be at the close what it was when it began. Herein forever am I justified: alone of lovers I neither rashly begin nor rashly end my love.

XXI

Ah, deep as the falsehoods Panthus has told thee of me be Venus' displeasure against Panthus. Yet, to-day thou deemst me a prophet truer than Dodona's shrine. That goodly lover of thine hath taken him

SEXTI PROPERTI ELEGIARVM LIBER II

tot noctes periere ? nihil pudet ? aspice, cantat
    liber : tu nimium credula, sola iaces.
et nunc inter eos tu sermo es, te ille superbus
    dicit se invito saepe fuisse domi.
dispeream, si quicquam aliud quam gloria de te
    quaeritur : has laudes ille maritus habet.   10
Colchida sic hospes quondam decepit Iason :
    eiecta est (tenuit[1] namque Creusa) domo.
sic a Dulichio iuvene est elusa Calypso :
    vidit amatorem pandere vela suum.
a nimium faciles aurem praebere puellae,
    discite desertae non temere esse bonae !
huic quoque, qui restet,[2] iam pridem quaeritur alter :
    experta in primo, stulta, cavere potes.
nos quocumque loco, nos omni tempore tecum
    sive aegra pariter sive valente sumus.   20

XXII

Scis here mi multas pariter placuisse puellas ;
    scis mihi, Demophoon, multa venire mala.
nulla meis frustra lustrantur compita plantis ;
    o nimis exitio nata theatra meo,
sive aliquis molli diducit candida gestu
    bracchia, seu varios incinit ore modos !
interea nostri quaerunt sibi vulnus ocelli,
    candida non tecto pectore si qua sedet,

---

[1] tenuit ϛ : tenuis *NFL*.
[2] restet *Phillimore*. restat *NFL*.

a wife! Have so many nights been spent in vain? Hast thou no shame? See, he is free and sings for joy; thou once too credulous now liest lonely; and now the twain speak amongst themselves of thee; he scornfully says that thou oft didst visit his house against his will. May I perish if he aims at aught else than to triumph for his conquest of thee: such is the praise that he the husband wins.

[11] So of old the stranger Jason deceived the maid of Colchis: she was cast forth from her home, for Creusa held her room. So was Calypso tricked by the Dulichian youth: she saw her lover spread his sails for flight. Ye maids, o'erprone to lend an ear to lovers, learn, left forlorn, not rashly to be kind.

[17] Yet for days thou hast been seeking another, who shall be faithful! Fool, the lesson thou hadst from the first should have taught thee caution! My heart, where'er I be, whate'er the hour, in sickness and in health, is with thee still.

XXII

Thou knowst that yesterday many a beauty pleased my impartial eyes; thou knowst, Demophoon, that thence springs many an ill for me. No street is there that my feet range in vain. Alas! the theatre was made too oft to be my doom, whether some beauty spreads out white arms with voluptuous motion, or pours from her lips a varied strain of song. And all the while mine eyes seek their own hurt, if some fair one sits with breast unveiled,

SEXTI PROPERTI ELEGIARVM LIBER II

sive vagi crines puris in frontibus errant,
    Indica quos medio vertice gemma tenet.   10
quae si forte aliquid vultu mihi dura negarat,
    frigida de tota fronte cadebat aqua.
quaeris, Demophoon, cur sim tam mollis in omnis?
    quod quaeris, "quare" non habet ullus amor.
cur aliquis sacris laniat sua bracchia cultris
    et Phrygis insanos caeditur ad numeros?
uni cuique dedit vitium natura creato:
    mi fortuna aliquid semper amare dedit.
me licet et Thamyrae cantoris fata sequantur,
    numquam ad formosas, invide, caecus ero.   20
sed tibi si exiles videor tenuatus in artus,
    falleris: haud umquam est culta labore Venus.
percontere licet: saepe est experta puella
    officium tota nocte valere meum.
Iuppiter Alcmenae geminas requieverat Arctos,
    et caelum noctu bis sine rege fuit;
nec tamen idcirco languens ad fulmina venit:
    nullus amor vires eripit ipse suas.
quid, cum e complexu Briseidos iret Achilles?
    num[1] fugere minus Thessala tela Phryges?   30
quid, ferus Andromachae lecto cum surgeret Hector?
    bella Mycenaeae non timuere rates?
ille vel hic, classes poterant vel perdere muros:
    hic ego Pelides, hic ferus Hector ego.
aspice uti caelo modo sol modo luna ministret:
    sic etiam nobis una puella parum est.

[1] num *FL*. non *N*.

or if her wandering locks stray o'er a snowy brow, clasped at the crown with an Indian gem. And if perchance by her look she said me nay in aught, cold streams of sweat streamed from all my brow.

[13] Dost thou ask, Demophoon, why my heart is so tender to one and all? Love knows not the meaning of thy question "Why?" Why do some gash their arms with sacred knives, and cut their limbs to the sound of the Phrygian pipe? To each at birth nature allotted a vice; to me fortune allotted the doom that I should ever be in love. Though the fate of Thamyras the singer come upon me, never, my grudging friend, will I be blind to beauty.

[21] But if to thee my limbs seem shrunk and thin, thou errest; it has ne'er been a hardship to me to serve Venus. 'Tis a lawful question; often a girl has found my passion could outlast the hours of night. Jove for Alcmena's sake made the stars of the Bear to slumber two nights long, and heaven twice was kingless through the dark; yet he was not therefore faint when he returned to the thunderbolt. Never doth love exhaust its own strength. What befell when Achilles came from Briseis' embrace? Did the Phrygians fly the less from the Thessalian's shafts? When fierce Hector rose from Andromache's bed, did not Mycenae's fleet tremble at the battle? Either hero could overthrow or ships or walls; I will be Achilles, or fierce Hector in the strife of love.

[35] See how 'tis now the moon and now the sun that serve the sky! Even so for me one love will not

SEXTI PROPERTI ELEGIARVM LIBER II

altera me cupidis teneat foveatque lacertis,
   altera si quando non sinit esse locum;
aut si forte irata meo sit facta ministro,
   ut sciat esse aliam, quae velit esse mea!   40
nam melius duo defendunt retinacula navim,
   tutius et geminos anxia mater alit.

XXIIa[1]

Avt si es dura, nega: sin es non dura, venito!
   quid iuvat at[2] nullo ponere verba loco?
hic unus dolor est ex omnibus acer amanti,
   speranti subito si qua venire negat.
quanta illum toto versant suspiria lecto,
   cum recipi, quem non noverit ille, necat![3]
et rursus puerum quaerendo audita fatigat,
   quem, quae[4] scire timet, quaerere fata iubet.   50

XXIII

Cvi fuit indocti fugienda haec[5] semita vulgi,
   ipsa petita lacu nunc mihi dulcis aqua est.
ingenuus quisquam alterius dat munera servo,
   ut promissa suae verba ferat dominae?
et quaerit totiens "Quaenam nunc porticus illam
   integit?" et "Campo quo movet illa pedes?"

---

[1] *Separated from the preceding by Renaissance scholars.*
[2] at *Baehrens:* et *NFL.*
[3] cum *v·* cur *NFL.* quem *ς:* quae *NFL* necat *Heinsius·* vetat *NFL.*   [4] quem quae *F.* quae quoque *L;* om. *N.*
[5] haec *ς·* et *NLF.*

suffice. If one receive me not, let another hold me and cherish me in passionate embrace; or if she be angered with my service of her, let her know that there is another who will gladly be mine. For a ship is safer when two cables hold it, and an anxious mother, if she rear twins, has less to dread.

XXIIA

Say "No!" if thou art unkind; or, if kind thou art, then come! But why take delight in waste of random words? This grief alone of all doth rack the lover's heart, if his mistress fails his hopes and comes not to the tryst. What sighs shake his frame as he tosses o'er all his couch, when the thought that now some unknown lover is admitted torments him even to death! Again and again he wearies his slave by asking, what he has heard already, and bidding him seek news of the fate he dreads to learn.

XXIII

I that once thought fit to shun this path trod by the vulgar herd, now find pleasure even in a draught from the common tank. Will any free-born man give money to another's slave to bring him the promised message of his mistress, and ask forever, "What shady colonnade now shields her from the sun?" or "Whither wend her footsteps on the Campus Martius?"

SEXTI PROPERTI ELEGIARVM LIBER II

deinde, ubi pertuleris, quos dicit fama labores
    Herculis, ut scribat "Muneris ecquid habes?"
cernere uti possis vultum custodis amari,
    captus et immunda saepe latere casa,   10
quam care semel in toto nox vertitur anno!
    a pereant, si quos ianua clausa iuvat!
contra, reiecto quae libera vadit amictu,
    custodum et nullo saepta timore, placet?
cui saepe immundo Sacra conteritur Via socco,
    nec sinit esse moram, si quis adire velit;
differet haec numquam, nec poscet garrula, quod te
    astrictus ploret saepe dedisse pater,
nec dicet "Timeo, propera iam surgere, quaeso:
    infelix, hodie vir mihi rure venit."   20
et quas Euphrates et quas mihi misit Orontes,
    me iuerint: nolim furta pudica tori;
libertas quoniam nulli iam restat amanti:
    si quis liber erit, nullus[1] amare volet.

XXIV

"Tv loqueris, cum sis[2] iam noto fabula libro
    et tua sit toto Cynthia lecta foro?"
cui non his verbis aspergat tempora sudor?
    aut pudor ingenuus, aut reticendus amor?
quod si tam facilis spiraret Cynthia nobis,
    non ego nequitiae dicerer esse caput,

---

[1] si quis . . . nullus *Foster;* nullus . . . si quis *NFL.*
[2] sis ς: sit *NFL.*

THE ELEGIES OF PROPERTIUS BOOK II

⁷ And then, when thou hast endured all the Herculean labours whereof fame tells, to receive a letter saying, "Hast thou any present for me?" or to win the privilege of facing a scowling guardian, or oft be hid a prisoner in some foul hovel, how costly is the night of joy that comes but once in the whole year! Perish the lovers that prefer the secrecy of closed doors!

¹³ On the other hand, she that walks at large, her cloak cast back from her head, and gladdens the eye, hedged in by no threatening guardian, she who treads the Sacred Way in loose shoes besmirched with mire, and makes no delay if any accost her, she will never put thee off, nor ask in chattering voice for that which thy niggard father will complain he has given so oft. She will not say: "I am afraid: haste thee, rise, I pray thee: unhappy man, 'tis to-day my husband returns from the country." Let the girls, that Euphrates and Orontes have sent for my delight, be all my joy: I hate those shamefaced thefts of love. Since no lover hath any freedom left him, no man that would be free will seek to love.

XXIV

" Dost thou talk thus, when thy book has become famous and made thee the talk of all the town, and thy Cynthia is read in all the forum?" Whose brow, that heard such words as these, would not be bathed in sweat, whether for honest modesty or for the shameful secret of his love? And yet if Cynthia smiled on me, as once she smiled, I should not now be called the crown of wantonness; my name would

SEXTI PROPERTI ELEGIARVM LIBER II

nec sic per totam infamis traducerer urbem,
   urerer et quamvis non bene,[1] verba darem.
quare ne tibi sit mirum me quaerere viles:
   parcius infamant: num tibi causa levis?   10
   .   .   .   .   .[2]

et modo pavonis caudae flabella superbae
   et manibus dura frigus habere pila,
et cupit iratum talos me poscere eburnos,
   quaeque nitent Sacra vilia dona Via.
a peream, si me ista movent dispendia, sed[3] me
   fallaci dominae iam pudet esse iocum!

XXIVa [4]

Hoc erat in primis quod me gaudere iubebas?
   tam te formosam non pudet esse levem?
una aut altera nox nondum est in amore peracta,
   et dicor lecto iam gravis esse tuo.   20
me modo laudabas et carmina nostra legebas:
   ille tuus pennas tam cito vertit amor?
contendat mecum ingenio, contendat et arte,
   in primis una discat amare domo:
si libitum tibi erit, Lernaeas pugnet ad hydras
   et tibi ab Hesperio mala dracone ferat,
taetra venena libens et naufragus ebibat undas,
   et numquam pro te deneget esse miser:

---
[1] urerer ς: ureret *NFL*. non bene *Housman*: nomine *NFL*
[2] *Some verses have clearly been lost here.*   [3] sed ς: si *NFL*
[4] *17–52 separated by Scaliger.*

not now be draggled in dishonour through all the town, and though my heart still burned with no seemly fire, still would I cheat the world.

⁹ Wherefore wonder not that now I seek common women; they are more sparing in slander. Seems that a trifling reason in your eyes? . . . [*And they are so expensive. Cynthia now asks me for some costly jewel;*] now demands a fan made from some proud peacock's tail, and would cool her hands by holding a hard ball of crystal; she angers me by bidding me demand ivory dice for her, and such worthless gifts as glitter in the Sacred Way. And yet, confound me if I grudge the expense! But now I am ashamed to be the laughing-stock of my faithless mistress!

XXIVa

CYNTHIA, was this the hope thou didst bid me cherish when our love began? Art not thou ashamed, being so fair, to be so fickle? Not yet have we spent one or two nights in love, and already thou tellest me I am irksome to thy couch. But now thou didst praise me and didst read my songs; does thy love so soon turn his wings to fly elsewhere?

²³ Let thy lover strive against me in wit and poetic skill, and first of all things let him learn to confine his love to one house only; if it be thy pleasure, let him fight with the Lernaean hydras, and fetch thee apples from the guardianship of the Hesperian dragon; let him drink gladly of foul poisons, or, shipwrecked, the sea wave, and never refuse to be wretched for thy sake (ah that thou wouldst prove

SEXTI PROPERTI ELEGIARVM LIBER II

(quos utinam in nobis, vita, experiare labores!)
   iam tibi de timidis iste protervus erit,   30
qui nunc se in tumidum iactando venit honorem:
   discidium vobis proximus annus erit.
at me non aetas mutabit tota Sibyllae,
   non labor Alcidae, non niger ille dies.
tu mea compones et dices " Ossa, Properti,
   haec tua sunt: eheu tu mihi certus eras,
certus eras eheu, quamvis nec sanguine avito
   nobilis et quamvis non ita[1] dives eras."
nil ego non patiar, numquam me iniuria mutat:
   ferre ego formosam nullum onus esse puto.   40
credo ego non paucos ista periisse figura,
   credo ego sed multos non habuisse fidem
parvo dilexit spatio Minoida Theseus,
   Phyllida Demophoon, hospes uterque malus.
iam tibi Iasonia nota est Medea carina
   et modo servato[2] sola relicta viro
dura est quae multis simulatum fingit amorem,
   et se plus uni si qua parare potest.
noli nobilibus, noli conferre beatis:
   vix venit, extremo qui legat ossa die   50
hi tibi nos erimus: sed tu potius precor ut me
   demissis plangas pectora nuda comis.

[1] non ita *Pontanus* · navita *NFL.*
[2] servato *N* om. *FL.*

me, my beloved, with such tasks as these !), and soon thou shalt find him a trembling coward that is now so forward, that by boasts of prowess has attained his proud place of honour in thy heart; next year shall see you parted. But a Sibyl's whole lifetime shall never alter my love, no, nor Alcides' toil, nor the dark hour of death. Thou shalt compose my ashes, and shalt say: " These are thy bones, Propertius; ah! but *thou* wast true to me! Ah! thou wast true, though sprung from no noble ancestry nor so rich as that other." I will suffer all things for thee; thy wrongs ne'er change my love; to endure one so fair is to me no burden.

[41] Many, I trow, have been smitten by thy fair form; but many, I trow, have broken troth with thee. It was but for a brief space that Theseus loved the daughter of Minos, that Demophoon adored Phyllis, a faithless pair of guests. Thou knowest well Medea borne on Jason's bark, and then left forlorn by the husband she but lately saved.

[47] Cruel is she that feigns false love for many, and has the heart to deck herself for many eyes. Compare me not with the noble and wealthy: scarce one of them shall come to gather up thine ashes at the end of all. I shall perform that duty for them; but rather I pray that thou mayest bewail me with bared bosom and thine hair unbound.

SEXTI PROPERTI ELEGIARVM LIBER II

XXV

Vnica nata meo pulcherrima cura dolori,
  excludit quoniam sors mea " saepe veni,"
ista meis fiet notissima forma libellis,
  Calve, tua venia, pace, Catulle, tua.
miles depositis annosus secubat armis,
  grandaevique negant ducere aratra boves,
putris et in vacua requiescit navis harena,
  et vetus in templo bellica parma vacat:
at me ab amore tuo deducet nulla senectus,
  sive ego Tithonus sive ego Nestor ero.   10
nonne fuit satius duro servire tyranno
  et gemere in tauro, saeve Perille, tuo?
Gorgonis et satius fuit obdurescere vultu,
  Caucasias etiam si pateremur aves
sed tamen obsistam. teritur robigine mucro
  ferreus et parvo saepe liquore silex:
at nullo dominae teritur sub limine amor, qui
  restat et immerita sustinet aure minas.
ultro contemptus rogat, et peccasse fatetur
  laesus, et invitis ipse redit pedibus.   20
tu quoque, qui pleno fastus assumis amore,
  credule, nulla diu femina pondus habet.
an quisquam in mediis persolvit vota procellis,
  cum saepe in portu fracta carina natet?
aut prius infecto deposcit praemia cursu,
  septima quam metam triverit ante rota?

THE ELEGIES OF PROPERTIUS BOOK II

XXV

O THOU beyond all women born to be, most fair, the burden of mine anguish, since mine ill fate debars me from the words "Come and come often!" my books shall make thy beauty known above all other; only do thou, Calvus, and thou, Catullus, grant me that this may be.

5 The soldier bowed with years sleeps no longer by the weapons he hath laid aside; oxen grown old refuse to draw the plough; the crumbling ship rests on the empty sands, and idle on the temple wall hangs the warrior's ancient shield. But never shall old age sunder me from love of thee, though I be old as Tithonus or as Nestor old. Were it not better to be a cruel tyrant's slave and groan within thy bull, savage Perillus? Better were it to turn to stone before the Gorgon's gaze or to endure the vultures of Caucasus. Yet will I persist. The blade of steel is eaten by rust, and drops of water oft wear down the flint. But the threshold of no mistress can wear down that love that abides firm and endures to listen to threats it has never deserved. Nay, the lover even answers disdain with supplications, and wrong with the confession that 'twas himself that sinned, and oft returns he with reluctant feet.

21 Thou too, credulous lover, that waxest proud because thy love is at the full, know that no woman has solid worth for long. Does any man perform his vows in mid-tempest, when many a ship swims shattered even in port? Or does any man demand the prize ere first for the seventh time the wheel hath

SEXTI PROPERTI ELEGIARVM LIBER II

mendaces ludunt flatus in amore secundi:
  si qua venit sero, magna ruina venit
tu tamen interea, quamvis te diligat illa,
  in tacito cohibe gaudia clausa sinu. 30
namque in amore suo semper sua maxima cuique
  nescio quo pacto verba nocere solent.
quamvis te persaepe vocet, semel ire memento:
  invidiam quod habet, non solet esse diu.
at si saecla forent antiquis grata puellis,
  essem ego quod nunc tu: tempore vincor ego.
non tamen ista meos mutabunt saecula mores:
  unus quisque sua noverit ire via.
at, vos qui officia in multos revocatis amores,
  quantum sic cruciat lumina vestra[1] dolor! 40
vidistis pleno teneram candore puellam,
  vidistis fusco, ducit[2] uterque color;
vidistis quandam Argivam prodente[3] figura,
  vidistis nostras, utraque forma rapit.
illaque plebeio vel sit sandycis amictu:
  haec atque illa mali vulneris una via est.
cum satis una tuis insomnia portet ocellis,
  una sit et cuivis femina multa mala.

XXVI

Vidi te in somnis fracta, mea vita, carina
  Ionio lassas ducere rore manus,

---

[1] vestra ς. nostra *NFL*.   [2] ducit *N*: dulcis *F* lucus *L*.
[3] Argivam *Baehrens*. argiva *NFL*. prodente *NFL*. prodire *N*.

grazed the goal? Deceitful is the play of the prospering gales of love; the passion that comes late in time brings with it mighty ruin. Yet do thou meanwhile, though she love thee, keep thy joys close within thy silent breast. For in love 'tis ever his own words that, how I know not, do the lover greatest hurt. Though oft she summon thee, have a care to go but once: that which is envied endures but for a brief space.

35 But should the times return that pleased the maids of old, I should be what thou now art; 'tis this vile age has conquered me. Yet these ill times shall never alter my heart: let each man have the wit to go his own way.

39 But ye that bid a man serve many loves, if thus ye live, what agony torments your eyes! Ye see a tender maid of whitest hue, or again another of darker brilliance: either hue attracts the eye. Ye see a girl whose form betrays the Greek, or, again, our Roman beauties; either beauty allures. Though she be clothed in plebeian garb or in robes of scarlet, 'tis by one and the same path that either cruel wound is dealt. Since one love can keep thine eyes from sleep long time enough, one woman were a host of ills for any man.

XXVI

IN my dreams I saw thee, light of my life, shipwrecked strike out with weary hands through the Ionian waves. I saw thee confess all thy falsehood

SEXTI PROPERTI ELEGIARVM LIBER II

et quaecumque in me fueras mentita fateri,
    nec iam umore graves tollere posse comas,
qualem purpureis agitatam fluctibus Hellen,
    aurea quam molli tergore vexit ovis.
quam timui, ne forte tuum mare nomen haberet,
    atque tua labens navita fleret aqua!
quae tum ego Neptuno, quae tum cum Castore fratri,
    quaeque tibi excepi, iam dea, Leucothoe!   10
at tu vix primas extollens gurgite palmas
    saepe meum nomen iam peritura vocas.
quod si forte tuos vidisset Glaucus ocellos,
    esses Ionii facta puella maris,
et tibi ob invidiam Nereides increpitarent,
    candida Nesaee, caerula Cymothoe.
sed tibi subsidio delphinum currere vidi,
    qui, puto, Arioniam vexerat ante lyram.
iamque ego conabar summo me mittere saxo,
    cum mihi discussit talia visa metus.   20

XXVIA[1]

Nvnc admirentur quod tam mihi pulchra puella
    serviat et tota dicar in urbe potens!
non, si Cambysae redeant et flumina Croesi,
    dicat "De nostro surge, poeta, toro."

[1] *Separated by Burmann.*

THE ELEGIES OF PROPERTIUS BOOK II

toward me and sink, unable to lift thine hair weighed down with brine, like Helle tossed upon the purple waves, whom once the sheep of gold bore on its soft back. How I feared, lest perchance that sea should take thy name, and the mariner might weep for thee as he sailed thy waves! What vows to Neptune did I then make, what vows to Castor and his brother and thee, Leucothoe, once mortal, now a goddess! But thou, scarce raising thy finger-tips over the surface of the deep, didst oft, as one that soon must perish, call upon my name.

[13] But if perchance Glaucus had espied thine eyes, thou hadst become a maid of the Ionian sea, and the Nereids would have chidden thee for envy, white Nesaee and azure Cymothoe. But I saw a dolphin hasten to thine aid, the same methinks that once bore Arion's lyre. I was even then striving to cast myself from the rocky height when terror dispelled the vision.

XXVIA

Now let men wonder that so fair a maid is my slave, and that all the city tells of my power! Though a Cambyses should return and the rivers of Croesus, never would she say, "Rise, poet, from my bed." For

SEXTI PROPERTI ELEGIARVM LIBER II

nam mea cum recitat, dicit se odisse beatos:
   carmina tam sancte nulla puella colit.
multum in amore fides, multum constantia prodest:
   qui dare multa potest, multa et amare potest.
seu mare per longum mea cogitet ire puella,
   hanc sequar, et fidos una aget aura duos;   30
unum litus erit sopitis unaque tecto
   arbor, et ex una saepe bibemus aqua;
et tabula una duos poterit componere amantis,
   prora cubile mihi seu mihi puppis erit.
omnia perpetiar: saevus licet urgeat Eurus;
   velaque in incertum frigidus Auster agat;
quicumque et venti miserum vexastis Vlixen,
   et Danaum Euboico litore mille rates;
et qui movistis duo litora, cum ratis Argo
   dux erat ignoto missa columba mari.   40
illa meis tantum non umquam desit ocellis,
   incendat navem Iuppiter ipse licet.
certe isdem nudi pariter iactabimur oris:
   me licet unda ferat, te modo terra tegat.
sed non Neptunus tanto crudelis amori,
   Neptunus fratri par in amore Iovi.
testis Amymone, latices dum ferret, in arvis [1]
   compressa, et Lernae pulsa tridente palus.
iam deus amplexu votum persolvit, at illi
   aurea divinas urna profudit aquas.   50
crudelem et Borean rapta Orithyia negavit:
   hic deus et terras et maria alta domat.

---

[1] dum *N*: cum *FL*. arvis *O*: Argis *ς*, *perhaps rightly*.

when she repeats my verse, she says that she hates wealthy suitors; no other maid does such reverent honour unto song. Fidelity in love is of much avail, of much avail is constancy; he that can make many a gift can have full many a love.

²⁹ Does my love think of sailing long leagues of sea, I will follow her. One breeze shall waft us on, a faithful pair, one shore shall give us rest when we sink in slumber, one tree overshadow us, and oft shall we drink from the selfsame spring. One plank shall yield a couch to lovers twain, whether my bed be strewn by prow or stern. I will endure all things, though the wild East Wind drive our bark and the South's chill blast sweep our sails, whither we know not; though all ye winds should blow that once tormented the hapless Ulysses and wrecked the thousand ships of Greece on Euboea's shore, and ye also that parted the two shores, when the dove was sent to Argus to guide his bark over an unknown sea If only she be never absent from my sight, let Jove himself fire our ship! For surely our naked corpses will be cast together upon the same shore; let the wave sweep me away, if only thou find burial in earth.

⁴⁵ But Neptune frowns not on love strong as ours; Neptune was Jove his brother's equal in the field of love. Witness Amymone, that in the meadows yielded to his embrace, that so she might find the fountain; witness Lerna's marsh smitten by the trident. Then did the god redeem his promise at the price of his embrace, and straightway for her an urn of gold poured forth a stream divine. Orithyia also denied that Boreas, the ravisher, was cruel; this god tames both earth and the deeps of ocean. Believe me, Scylla

SEXTI PROPERTI ELEGIARVM LIBER II

crede mihi, nobis mitescet Scylla, nec umquam
    alternante vacans[1] vasta Charybdis aqua;
ipsaque sidera erunt nullis obscura tenebris,
    purus et Orion, purus et Haedus erit.
quid mihi si ponenda tuo sit corpore vita?
    exitus hic nobis non inhonestus erit.

XXVII

At vos incertam, mortales, funeris horam
    quaeritis, et qua sit mors aditura via;
quaeritis et caelo, Phoenicum inventa, sereno,
    quae sit stella homini commoda quaeque mala!
seu pedibus Parthos sequimur seu classe Britannos,
    et maris et terrae caeca pericla viae.
rursus et obiectum fles tu caput esse tumultu[2]
    cum Mavors dubias miscet utrimque manus;
praeterea domibus flammam domibusque ruinas,
    neu subeant labris pocula nigra tuis.   10
solus amans novit, quando periturus et a qua
    morte, neque hic Boreae flabra neque arma timet.
iam licet et Stygia sedeat sub harundine remex,
    cernat et infernae tristia vela ratis:
si modo clamantis revocaverit aura puellae,
    concessum nulla lege redibit iter.

---

[1] vacans *Ayrmann*: vorans *NFL*.
[2] fles tu *Housman*: fletus *N*: flemus *FL*. caput *NF*: capiti *L*. tumultu *cod. Mus. Brit. 23766*: tumultum *NFL*.

will grow kind for us, and wild Charybdis also, that ceases never from her ebb and flow. Nor shall any darkness obscure the stars. Clear shall Orion be, and clear the Kid. Nay, what if I should breathe my last upon thy body! No dishonour will be mine in such an end as this.

XXVII

Yet do ye mortals inquire after the uncertain hour of death, and of the path by which your doom shall draw anigh, and in the unclouded heaven ye seek by the art the Phoenicians found of old what star is good, what star is ill for man. Whether on foot we follow the flying Parthian or with our fleet attack the Briton, blind are the perils both by land and sea. And again thou weepest that thy life is threatened by the storm of war, when Mars on this side and on that mingles the wavering ranks; thou dreadest also fire for thy house and ruin, and tremblest lest thou put cups of dark poison to thy lips. The lover only knows when and by what death he shall perish, and fears nor weapons nor blasts of the North Wind. Yea, even though he sit at the oar among the reeds of Styx and gaze on the dismal sails of the boat of hell, if the faint whisper of his mistress' voice cry out and call him back from the dead, he will return over that road that the eternal ordinance hath sealed.

SEXTI PROPERTI ELEGIARVM LIBER II

XXVIII

Ivppiter, affectae tandem miserere puellae:
　tam formosa tuum mortua crimen erit.
venit enim tempus, quo torridus aestuat aer,
　incipit et sicco fervere terra Cane
sed non tam ardoris culpa est neque crimina caeli,
　quam totiens sanctos non habuisse deos.
hoc perdit miseras, hoc perdidit ante puellas:
　quidquid iurarunt, ventus et unda rapit.
num[1] sibi collatam doluit Venus? illa peraeque
　prae se formosis invidiosa dea est.　　　　　　10
an contempta tibi Iunonis templa Pelasgae?
　Palladis aut oculos ausa negare bonos?
semper, formosae, non nostis parcere verbis.
　hoc tibi lingua nocens, hoc tibi forma dedit
sed tibi vexatae per multa pericula vitae
　extremo venit mollior hora die.
Io versa caput primos mugiverat annos:
　nunc dea, quae Nili flumina vacca bibit.
Ino etiam prima terris aetate vagata est:
　hanc miser implorat navita Leucothoen.　　　　20
Andromede monstris fuerat devota marinis:
　haec eadem Persei nobilis uxor erat.
Callisto Arcadios erraverat ursa per agros:
　haec nocturna suo sidere vela regit.
quod si forte tibi properarint fata quietem,
　illa sepulturae fata beata tuae,

[1] num *FL*. non *N*.

THE ELEGIES OF PROPERTIUS BOOK II

XXVIII

JUPITER, at length have pity on my mistress, stricken sore; the death of one so fair will be accounted to thee for a crime. For the season has come when the scorching air seethes with heat and earth begins to glow beneath the parching Dog-star. But 'tis not so much the fault of the heat, nor hath heaven so much the blame for her illness, as that so oft she hath spurned the sanctity of the gods. This is it that undoes hapless girls, aye, and hath undone many; wind and water sweep away their every oath.

[9] Was Venus vexed that thou wast compared with her? She is a jealous goddess to all alike, that vie with her in loveliness. Or didst thou spurn the temple of Pelasgian Juno, or deny that Pallas' eyes were fair? Ye beauties, never have ye learned to spare your words; Cynthia, thou owest this to thine offending tongue and to thy beauty. But anguished as thou hast been through many a deadly peril, at last hath come an hour of greater ease. So Io wore a strange guise and lowed all her earlier years; but now she is a goddess, that once drank Nilus' waters in likeness of a cow. Ino also wandered o'er the earth in her prime; but now she is called Leucothoe, and 'tis on her the hapless sailor calls for aid. Andromeda was doomed to the monsters of the deep, yet even she became the far-famed wife of Perseus. Callisto wandered as a bear over the fields of Arcadia; now with her own star's light she guides the sails of mariners through the dark.

[25] Yet if it chance that the Fates hasten down on thee the eternal rest, the Fates of funeral made

SEXTI PROPERTI ELEGIARVM LIBER II

narrabis Semelae, quo sit formosa periclo,
  credet et illa, suo docta puella malo;
et tibi Maeonias omnes heroidas inter
  primus erit nulla non tribuente locus.   30
nunc, utcumque potes, fato gere saucia morem:
  et deus et durus vertitur ipse dies.
hoc tibi vel poterit coniunx ignoscere Iuno:
  frangitur et Iuno, si qua puella perit.
[1] deficiunt magico torti sub carmine rhombi,
  et iacet exstincto laurus adusta foco;
et iam Luna negat totiens descendere caelo,
  nigraque funestum concinit omen avis.
una ratis fati nostros portabit amores
  caerula ad infernos velificata lacus.   40
sed[2] non unius quaeso, miserere duorum!
  vivam, si vivet: si cadet illa, cadam.
pro quibus optatis sacro me carmine damno:
  scribam ego " Per magnum est salva puella Iovem";
ante tuosque pedes illa ipsa operata sedebit,
  narrabitque sedens longa pericla sua.

XXVIIIa [3]

HAEC tua, Persephone, maneat clementia, nec tu,
  Persephonae coniunx, saevior esse velis.
sunt apud infernos tot milia formosarum:
  pulchra sit in superis, si licet, una locis!   50

[1] *A new elegy in Nμ, no break in FL.*
[2] sed *N :* si *FL.*
[3] *Separated by Lachmann.*

blest for thee, thou shalt tell Semele what dangers beauty brings; and she, taught by her own misfortune, will believe thee: and among all the Maeonian heroines thou by consent of all shalt have the foremost place. Now as best thou may, bear thyself reverently towards destiny on thy couch of pain; heaven and the cruel hour of death alike may change. Even Juno, the jealous wife, will forgive thee for thy beauty; even Juno is touched with pity for a maiden's death.

35 Now cease the wheels[1] whirled to the magic chant, the altar fire is dead and the laurel lies in ashes. Now the moon refuses to descend so oft from heaven, and the bird of night sings ominous of death. One murky boat of destiny shall bear our loves together, setting sail to the pools of Hell. But pity not one only, I pray thee, Jupiter; pity the twain of us. If she lives, I will live; if she dies, I too will die. Wherefore if my prayer be granted I bind myself with this solemn verse, to write: THE MIGHT OF JOVE HATH SAVED MY MISTRESS; and she herself after she hath sacrificed to thee will sit before thy feet, and seated there will tell of the long perils she has passed.

XXVIIIA

PERSEPHONE, may thy mercy endure, nor mayest thou, that hast Persephone for spouse, be over-cruel. There are so many thousand beauties among the dead; let one fair one, if so it may be, abide on earth. With

---

[1] The *rhombus* is probably an instrument known as a "bull-roarer," still used by savage tribes. It consists of a perforated piece of wood attached to a string: when whirled round it emits a loud booming sound.

SEXTI PROPERTI ELEGIARVM LIBER II

vobiscum est Iope, vobiscum candida Tyro,
   vobiscum Europe nec proba Pasiphae,
et quot Troia[1] tulit vetus et quot Achaia formas,
   et Phoebi et Priami diruta regna senis:
et quaecumque erat in numero Romana puella,
   occidit: has omnes ignis avarus habet.
nec forma aeternum aut cuiquam est fortuna perennis:
   longius aut propius mors sua quemque manet.
tu quoniam es, mea lux, magno dimissa periclo,
   munera Dianae debita redde choros,   60
redde etiam excubias divae nunc, ante iuvencae;
   votivas noctes et mihi solve decem.

XXIX

HESTERNA, mea lux, cum potus nocte vagarer,
   nec me servorum duceret ulla manus,
obvia nescio quot pueri mihi turba minuta
   venerat (hos vetuit me numerare timor);
quorum alii faculas, alii retinere sagittas,
   pars etiam visa est vincla parare mihi.
sed nudi fuerant. quorum lascivior unus,
   "Arripite hunc," inquit, "iam[2] bene nostis eum:
hic erat, hunc mulier nobis irata locavit."
   dixit, et in collo iam mihi nodus erat.   10
hic alter iubet in medium propellere, at alter,
   "Intereat, qui nos non putat esse deos!

---

[1] Troia *NFL, perhaps corrupt*: Phthia *Huschke*.
[2] iam *N*: nam *FL*.

you is Iope, with you snowy Tyro, with you Europe and impious Pasiphae, and all the beauties that Troy and Achaea bore of old, Troy the fallen realm of Phoebus and the old man Priam. And all the fair, that Rome may rank with these, have perished : all these the greedy pyre hath taken for its own. Neither beauty nor fortune abideth everlastingly for any; sooner or later death awaiteth all.

59 Since then, light of mine eyes, thou hast escaped from mighty peril, render Diana the dance thou owest for offering; and as is due, keep vigil in honour of her who, once a heifer, is now a goddess, and on my behalf pay her ten nights of worship.

XXIX

YESTERNIGHT, light of mine eyes, when I wandered heavy with wine and with never a servant's hand to lead me home, a crowd of tiny boys met me; how many I know not, for fear forbade me count them. Some carried little torches and others arrows, while some seemed even to make ready fetters for me. Yet naked were they all. Then one that was more wanton than the rest cried : " Seize him, for ye know him well of old. This is he that the angry woman delivered to us." He spake, and straightway a noose was about my head. Another then bade them thrust me into their midst, while a third cried : " Perish the man that deems us not divine! Whole hours hath she waited

SEXTI PROPERTI ELEGIARVM LIBER II

haec te non meritum totas exspectat in horas:
  at tu nescio quas quaeris, inepte, fores.
quae cum Sidoniae nocturna ligamina mitrae
  solverit atque oculos moverit illa graves,
afflabunt tibi non Arabum de gramine odores,
  sed quos ipse suis fecit Amor manibus.
parcite iam, fratres, iam certos spondet amores;
  et iam ad mandatam venimus ecce domum."   20
atque ita me in tectum duxerunt rursus amicae:[1]
  "I nunc et noctes disce manere domi."

XXIXa [2]

Mane erat, et volui, si sola quiesceret illa,
  visere: at in lecto Cynthia sola fuit.
obstipui: non illa mihi formosior umquam
  visa, neque ostrina cum fuit in tunica,
ibat et hinc castae narratum somnia Vestae,
  neu sibi neve mihi quae nocitura forent:
talis visa mihi somno dimissa recenti.
  heu quantum per se candida forma valet!   30
"Quid?[3] tu matutinus," ait "speculator amicae,
  me similem vestris moribus esse putas?
non ego tam facilis: sat erit mihi cognitus unus,
  vel tu vel si quis verior esse potest.
apparent non ulla toro vestigia presso,
  signa volutantis[4] nec iacuisse duos.

---

[1] in tectum duxerunt . . . amicae *G. Fischer* in lecto duxerunt . . . amictu *NFL*   [2] *Separated by Guyetus.*
[3] quid *ς* · quod *NFL*.   [4] volutantis *L*. voluntatis *NF*

thee, though little thou deservest it, while thou, fool, didst seek another's door. When she has loosened the strings of her nightcap of Sidonian purple and turns on thee her slumber-laden eyes, then will sweet odours breathe upon thee such as the herbs of Araby ne'er gave, but Love himself made with his own hands. Spare him now, brothers; now he pledges that his love shall be true: and lo! we have come to the house whither we were bidden." Thus did they lead me back to my mistress' house. "Go now," they cried, "and learn to stay at home of nights."

XXIXa

'Twas morn and I wished to see if alone she took her rest, and behold Cynthia was in her bed alone. I stood amazed; for never seemed she to mine eyes more fair, not even when, clad in purple tunic, she went to lay her dreams before chaste Vesta, for fear some ill might threaten herself and me. So seemed she to me, as she woke from her fresh slumber. Ah, how great is the power of beauty unadorned! "What!" quoth she, "thou that spiest thus early on thy mistress, deemst thou that my ways are like to thine? I am not so fickle: 'tis enough for me to know one lover such as thee, or one perchance of truer love than thine. There are no signs of impress on the couch, the marks of lovers taking their delight, no signs that two have lain therein. See! from my

SEXTI PROPERTI ELEGIARVM LIBER II

 aspice ut in toto nullus mihi corpore surgat
  spiritus admisso notus adulterio."
dixit, et opposita propellens savia dextra
  prosilit in laxa nixa pedem solea.   40
sic ego tam sancti custos retrudor[1] amoris:
  ex illo felix nox[2] mihi nulla fuit.

XXX

Nvnc tu, dure,[3] paras Phrygias nunc ire per undas 19
  et petere Hyrcani litora nauta[4] maris?   20
[spargere et[5] alterna communis caede Penates   21
  et ferre ad patrios praemia dira Lares?]   22
quo fugis a demens? nulla est fuga · tu licet usque 1
  ad Tanain fugias, usque sequetur Amor.
non si Pegaseo vecteris in aere dorso,
  nec tibi si Persei moverit ala pedes;
vel si te sectae rapiant talaribus aurae,
  nil tibi Mercurii proderit alta via.
instat semper Amor supra caput, instat amanti,
  et gravis ipse super libera colla sedet.
excubat ille acer custos et tollere numquam
  te patietur humo lumina capta semel.   10
et iam si pecces, deus exorabilis ille est,
  si modo praesentes viderit esse preces.

---

 [1] custos ς. custode *NL*. custodis *F*. retrudor *Postgate*.
reludor *N*. rector *FL*.   [2] nox ς: non *NFL*.
 [3] dure *cod. vet. Beroaldi* dura *FL*. non tamen immerito *N*.
 [4] nauta *Hertzberg*: nota *NFL*.
 [5] spargere et *N*: spargereque *FL*.

152

bosom springs no deep-drawn breath, that, as thou knowest, might tell thee that I had been untrue." She spake, and with her right hand resisted and thrust away my kisses, and leapt forth from the bed, loose slippers on her feet. So was I rebuffed by her that kept her love so pure; since then no happy night has e'er been mine.

XXX

HARD-HEARTED, dost thou now make ready to cross the Phrygian waves, and on shipboard seek the shores of the Hyrcanian sea? [to sprinkle our common household gods with mutual slaughter and bring dread prizes to the home of thy fathers?][1]

[1] Whither fliest thou, mad heart? There is no escape. Fly as far as Tanais; Love will hunt thee down. Thou shalt not escape, though thou be borne aloft on the back of Pegasus, nor though the pinions of Perseus wing thy feet. Or should the cloven breezes sweep thee along on feathered sandals, yet will the lofty path of Mercury avail thee naught. Love swoops ever above thy head; Love swoops down upon the lover, and sits a heavy burden on the neck that once was free. He is a watcher that slumbers not nor sleeps, nor ever will he suffer thee to raise thine eyes from off the ground when once he has enslaved them; and yet shouldst thou go astray, he is a god whom prayers may appease, if he but see that they are prompt to

[1] 19, 20 placed before 1, 2 by Housman; the same critic marks 21, 22 as alien to the context, and suggests that they should follow I. XXII. 8.

SEXTI PROPERTI ELEGIARVM LIBER II

ista senes licet accusent convivia duri :
   nos modo propositum, vita, teramus iter.
illorum antiquis onerantur legibus aures :
   hic locus est in quo, tibia docta, sones,
quae non iure vado Maeandri iacta natasti,
   turpia cum faceret Palladis ora tumor.   18
una contentum pudeat me vivere amica ?   23
   hoc si crimen erit, crimen Amoris erit.
mi nemo obiciat. libeat tibi, Cynthia, mecum
   rorida muscosis antra tenere iugis.
illic aspicies scopulis haerere Sorores
   et canere antiqui dulcia furta Iovis,
ut Semela est combustus, ut est deperditus Io,
   denique ut ad Troiae tecta volarit avis ;   30
(quod si nemo exstat qui vicerit Alitis arma,
   communis culpae cur reus unus agor ?)
nec tu Virginibus reverentia moveris ora :
   hic quoque non nescit quid sit amare chorus ;
si tamen Oeagri quaedam compressa figura
   Bistoniis olim rupibus accubuit.
hic ubi te[1] prima statuent in parte choreae,
   et medius docta cuspide Bacchus erit,
tum capiti sacros patiar pendere corymbos :
   nam sine te nostrum non valet ingenium.   40

[1] te ς. me O.

rise. Let stern old men denounce those revels of love; only let us, my life, pursue our chosen path. Their ears are burdened with the precepts of antiquity; but this is the place where thou, skilled pipe, shouldst sound, thou that of old didst float along Maeander's shallows, where unjustly thou wast cast when thou didst swell the cheeks of Pallas and mar the fairness of her face.[1]

[23] Shall I feel shame to live content in the service of one mistress? If this be a crime, to Love's door shall the crime be laid; let no one charge me therewith! And, Cynthia, be it thy joy to dwell with me in dewy grottoes on the mossy hills. There shalt thou see the Sisters clinging to the crags, while they chant the sweet loves of Jove in olden time, how he was consumed with fire for Semele, how madly he loved Io, and then how in likeness of a bird he flew to the abodes of Troy. (But if none hath e'er had strength to o'ercome the might of the winged one, why am I alone accused of the crime that all must share?) Nor shalt thou, Cynthia, grieve the demure faces of the Holy Maids; even their choir knows what it is to love, if it be true that for all their chastity a certain Muse lay upon the rocks of Bistonia locked in the arms of one that seemed Oeagrus. And there, when they shall place thee in the foremost rank of their dance, and Bacchus stands in the midst with his wand of skill, then will I suffer the holy ivy berries to hang about my head; for without thee my wit availeth naught.

[1] Minerva first made a pipe of bone and played upon it; but, catching sight of her reflection in the Maeander, she perceived that her cheeks puffed out to play disfigured her beauty, and cast the pipe into the stream.

SEXTI PROPERTI ELEGIARVM LIBER II

XXXI [1]

Qvaeris, cur veniam tibi tardior? aurea Phoebi
　　Porticus a magno Caesare aperta fuit;
tanta erat in speciem Poenis digesta columnis,
　　inter quas Danai femina turba senis. 4
tum medium claro surgebat marmore templum, 9
　　et patria Phoebo carius Ortygia: 10
et duo Solis erant [2] supra fastigia currus;
　　et valvae, Libyci nobile, dentis opus,
altera deiectos Parnasi vertice Gallos,
　　altera maerebat funera Tantalidos.
deinde inter matrem deus ipse interque sororem
　　Pythius in longa carmina veste sonat. 16
hic equidem Phoebo visus mihi pulchrior ipso 5
　　marmoreus tacita carmen hiare lyra: 6
atque aram circum steterant armenta Myronis, 7
　　quattuor artificis, vivida signa, boves.[3] 8

XXXII [4]

Qvi videt, is peccat: qui te non viderit ergo,
　　non cupiet: facti lumina crimen [5] habent.
nam quid Praenesti dubias, o Cynthia, sortes,
　　quid petis Aeaei moenia Telegoni?

---

[1] *A new elegy in μ, no break in NFL.*
[2] et duo ... erant *Hertzberg* · et quo ... erat *NFL.*
[3] *5–8 transposed to follow 16 by Dousa.*
[4] *No break in NFL, separated by Beroaldus.*
[5] lumina crimen ς : crimina lumen *NFL.*

THE ELEGIES OF PROPERTIUS BOOK II

XXXI

Thou askest why I am late in coming to thee. To-day was the golden colonnade of Phoebus opened by mighty Caesar; so vast it was to view, laid out with Punic columns,[1] between which stood the many daughters of the old man Danaus. Next in the midst of all the temple rose built of shining marble and dearer to Phoebus than his Ortygian home. And on the topmost roof were two chariots of the Sun, and the doors were of Libyan ivory wrought in wondrous wise. One told the fearful tale of the Gauls hurled down from off Parnassus' peak,[2] and one the death of the daughter of Tantalus. And last between his mother and his sister stood the Pythian god himself, clad in long raiment, his voice uplifted in song. Fairer he seemed to me than Phoebus' self, as he sang with silent lyre and parted lips of stone. And round about the altar stood Myron's kine, four counterfeit oxen, statues that seemed to live.

XXXII

Who sees thee sins: he then that hath not seen thee will not desire thee: 'tis the eyes must bear the blame. Else why at Praeneste seekst thou oracles of double import? Why seekst thou the walls of Aeaean Telegonus? Why does thy chariot

---

[1] *I.e.*, of Punic marble: yellow marble stained with red, now known as *giallo antico*.
[2] In 278 B.C. the Gauls attacked Delphi, but were driven off by storm and earthquake. *Cp.* III XIII 51-54.

SEXTI PROPERTI ELEGIARVM LIBER II

cur tua te [1] Herculeum deportant esseda Tibur?
  Appia cur totiens te via Lanuvium? [2]
hoc utinam spatiere loco, quodcumque vacabis,
  Cynthia! sed tibi me credere turba vetat,
cum videt accensis devotam currere taedis
  in nemus et Triviae lumina ferre deae.   10
scilicet umbrosis sordet Pompeia columnis
  Porticus, aulaeis nobilis Attalicis,
et platanis creber pariter surgentibus ordo,
  flumina sopito quaeque Marone cadunt,
et leviter nymphis tota crepitantibus urbe
  cum subito Triton ore recondit aquam.
falleris, ista tui furtum via monstrat amoris:
  non urbem, demens, lumina nostra fugis!
nil agis, insidias in me componis inanes,
  tendis iners docto retia nota mihi.   20
sed de me minus est: famae iactura pudicae
  tanta tibi miserae, quanta meretur,[3] erit.
nuper enim de te nostras maledixit[4] ad aures
  rumor, et in tota non bonus urbe fuit.
sed tu non debes inimicae credere linguae:
  semper formosis fabula poena fuit.
non tua deprenso damnata est fama veneno:
  testis eris puras, Phoebe, videre manus.
sin autem longo nox una aut altera lusu
  consumpta est, non me crimina parva movent.   30

[1] cur tua te *Baehrens* curva te *N*. cur vatem *FL*.
[2] Lanuvium *Jortin*. dicit anum *N* ducit anum *FL*
[3] meretur *N*: mereris *FL*.   [4] nostras *f*. nostra *NFL*.
maledixit *Schneidewin*. me ledit *FLN*

bear thee so oft to Herculean Tibur? Why so oft does the Appian Way lead thee to Lanuvium?

7 Ah that thou wouldst walk here in all thine hours of leisure! but the world forbids me trust thee, when it beholds thee hurry in frenzy with kindled torches to the Arician grove, and bear lights in honour of the goddess Trivia. Forsooth, thou carest naught for Pompey's colonnade, with its shady columns, bright-hung with gold-embroidered curtains; naught for the avenue thick-planted with plane-trees rising in trim rows; nor the waters that flow from Maro's slumbering form and run, their Naiads babbling through all the streets of Rome, till at the last, with sudden plunge, they vanish in the Triton's mouth.[1]

17 Thou deceiv'st thyself; thy wanderings reveal some secret passion; 'tis not the city, 'tis my eyes thou flyest. Thou strivest in vain; empty are the wiles thou spinnest against me; with little skill thou spreadst familiar snares for me, whom experience has taught. But for myself it matters little; the loss of thine honest name will be no less great than it deserves to be. For of late rumour spake ill of thee in mine ears, and a tale of evil ran through all the city.

25 And yet thou shouldst not trust these bitter words; scandal has ever been the doom of beauty. Thine honour has ne'er been blasted by the crime of poisoning; thou, Phoebus, wilt bear witness that her hands are unsullied. And if thou hast spent one night or two in long-drawn wantoning, such petty

---

[1] The simplest explanation of this passage is that the waters issued from a statue of Maro, and disappeared into the mouth of a Triton. It has also been suggested that the Triton was an automaton that blew a blast upon a horn as a signal that the water should be cut off.

SEXTI PROPERTI ELEGIARVM LIBER II

Tyndaris externo patriam mutavit amore,
    et sine decreto viva reducta domum est.
ipsa Venus fertur[1] corrupta libidine Martis,
    nec minus in caelo semper honesta fuit.
quamvis Ida Parim pastorem dicat amasse
    atque inter pecudes accubuisse deam,
hoc et Hamadryadum spectavit turba sororum
    Silenique senes[2] et pater ipse chori;
cum quibus Idaeo legisti poma sub antro,
    supposita excipiens, Nai, caduca[3] manu.   40
an quisquam in tanto stuprorum examine quaerit
    "Cur haec tam dives? quis dedit? unde dedit?"
o nimium nostro felicem tempore Romam,
    si contra mores una puella facit!
haec eadem ante illam impune et Lesbia fecit:
    quae sequitur, certe est invidiosa minus.
qui quaerit Tatios veteres durosque Sabinos,
    hic posuit nostra nuper in urbe pedem.
tu prius et fluctus poteris siccare marinos,
    altaque mortali deligere astra manu,   50
quam facere, ut nostrae nolint peccare puellae:
    hic mos Saturno regna tenente fuit,
et cum Deucalionis aquae fluxere per orbem;
    at[4] post antiquas Deucalionis aquas,
dic mihi, quis potuit lectum servare pudicum,
    quae dea cum solo vivere sola deo?

---

[1] fertur *N*: quamvis *FL*.
[2] senes *Beroaldus* · senis *NFL*.
[3] Nai, caduca *Scaliger* · naica dona *NFL*.
[4] at *Palmer* . et *NFL*.

crimes vex me not a whit. The daughter of Tyndareus left her fatherland for the love of a stranger, and yet was brought home alive without condemnation. Venus herself is said to have been seduced by the lust of Mars, yet none the less had she honour alway in heaven. Though Ida's mount tell how a goddess[1] loved the shepherd Paris, and lay with him among his flocks, yet all this the band of sister Hamadryads beheld, and the old Sileni and the father of their company himself; and with them thou, Naiad, didst gather in the glens of Ida wild apples falling to thy hand upstretched beneath the boughs.

41 After a host of sinners such as these does any ask: "Why is she so rich?" "Who gave? Whence came his gifts?" O Rome in these our days, thy happiness is full to overflowing, if one girl act not as her fellows do. All these things did Lesbia before Cynthia, wherefore Lesbia's follower is of a surety less hateful He that hopes still to find the ancient Tatii, and the strict Sabine, has but lately set foot in our city. Sooner shalt thou have power to dry the waters of the deep and pluck down the lofty stars with mortal hand, than bring it to pass that our maids should refuse to sin. Such was the fashion in the reign of Saturn, and when Deucalion's waves overflowed the world; but after Deucalion's flood in the days of old, tell me, who was ever able to keep his bed chaste, what goddess could ever bide alone with

---

[1] Oenone, who was according to some legends a water-nymph.

SEXTI PROPERTI ELEGIARVM LIBER II

uxorem quondam magni Minois, ut aiunt,
   corrupit torvi candida forma bovis;
nec minus aerato Danae circumdata muro
   non potuit magno casta negare Iovi.   60
quod si tu Graias es tuque[1] imitata Latinas,
   semper vive meo libera iudicio!

XXXIII

Tristia iam redeunt iterum sollemnia nobis:
   Cynthia iam noctes est operata decem.
atque utinam pereant, Nilo quae sacra tepente
   misit matronis Inachis Ausoniis!
quae dea tam cupidos totiens divisit amantes,
   quaecumque illa fuit, semper amara fuit.
tu certe Iovis occultis in amoribus, Io,
   sensisti multas quid sit inire vias,
cum te iussit habere puellam cornua Iuno
   et pecoris duro perdere verba sono.   10
a quotiens quernis laesisti frondibus ora,
   mandisti et stabulis arbuta[2] pasta tuis!
an, quoniam agrestem detraxit ab ore figuram
   Iuppiter, idcirco facta superba dea es?
an tibi non satis est fuscis Aegyptus alumnis?
   cur tibi tam longa Roma petita via?
quidve tibi prodest viduas dormire puellas?
   sed tibi, crede mihi, cornua rursus erunt,

---

[1] es tuque *Baehrens*: tuque es *NFL*.
[2] mandisti *Palmer*: mansisti *NFL*. et *Heinsius*: om. *NFL*.
arbuta *Palmer* abdita *NFL*.

one god only? The wife of great Minos, once, 'tis said, was seduced by the snowy form of a fierce bull, nor was Danae girt in her tower of bronze less unable to keep her chastity and deny mighty Jove. But if thou hast taken the women of Greece and of Rome for patterns, live ever in freedom; I blame thee not.

XXXIII

ONCE more those dismal rites have returned to plague us: now for ten nights hath Cynthia sacrificed. And a curse upon the rites which the daughter of Inachus hath sent from the warm Nile to the matrons of Italy! The goddess that so oft hath sundered such ardent lovers, whoe'er she may have been, was always a bitter goddess. Yet, Io, in truth thou didst learn in thy secret loves with Jove what it is to tread many paths of wandering, when Juno bade thee wear horns upon thy girlish brow and lose thy speech in the harsh bellowings of kine. Ah! how oft didst thou gall thy mouth with oak-leaves, and in thy stall didst chew once more the arbutus, on which thou hadst fed! Hast thou become so haughty a goddess since Jupiter took away from thee thy wild shape? Hast thou not worshippers enough among the swart Egyptians? Why didst thou come such a long journey to Rome? What profits it thee that maids should sleep alone? Nay, believe me, thy horns will sprout again, or we will

SEXTI PROPERTI ELEGIARVM LIBER II

aut nos e nostra te, saeva, fugabimus urbe:
   cum Tiberi Nilo gratia nulla fuit.   20
at tu, quae nostro nimium placata dolore es,
   noctibus his vacui ter faciamus iter.
non audis et verba sinis mea ludere, cum iam
   flectant Icarii sidera tarda boves.
lenta bibis: mediae nequeunt te frangere noctes?
   an nondum est talos mittere lassa manus?
a pereat, quicumque meracas repperit uvas
   corrupitque bonas nectare primus aquas!
Icare, Cecropiis merito iugulate colonis,
   pampineus nosti quam sit amarus odor!   30
tuque o Eurytion vino Centaure peristi,
   nec non Ismario tu, Polypheme, mero.
vino forma perit, vino corrumpitur aetas,
   vino saepe suum nescit amica virum.
me miserum, ut multo nihil est mutata Lyaeo!
   iam bibe: formosa es: nil tibi vina nocent,
cum tua praependent demissae in pocula sertae,[1]
   et mea deducta carmina voce legis.
largius effuso madeat tibi mensa Falerno,
   spumet et aurato mollius in calice.   40
nulla tamen lecto recipit se sola libenter:
   est quiddam, quod vos[2] quaerere cogat Amor.
semper in absentes felicior aestus amantes:
   elevat assiduos copia longa viros.

---

[1] demissae ... sertae *N, Charisius.* demissa ... serta *FL.*
[2] vos *N:* nos *FL.*

chase thee, cruel goddess, from our city! There ne'er was love lost 'twixt Tiber and Nile.

[21] But thou, Cynthia, since my woes have more than appeased thee, let us, whom these nights kept idle, thrice make love's journey together.

[23] Thou hearest me not and lettest my words become a mockery, though Icarus' oxen are wheeling their slow-moving stars to the setting; thou drinkst unmoved; has midnight no power to weary thee? or is thy hand never tired of casting the dice? A curse on him that first introduced the pure juice of the grape and first spoilt wholesome water by mixing wine therein!

[29] Icarus, justly wast thou slain by the farmers of Cecrops' land; thou hast found how rueful is the scent of the vine. Thou also, centaur Eurytion, didst perish through wine-bibbing, and thou, Polyphemus, wast undone by the Ismarian grape. Wine marreth beauty, wine spoils our prime; and thanks to wine a mistress oft knows not her lover.

[35] Woe is me: deep draughts have changed thee not a whit: drink on; thou art beautiful, the wine does thee no hurt, when garlands hang over thy brow and droop into thy cups, and thou readest my verses with utterance soft and low. Let the board be drowned still deeper in floods of Falernian and more lusciously foam the wine in thy cup of gold! Yet no woman ever betakes her willingly to a lonely bed; there is a somewhat that Love compels all to seek. Woman's heart is kinder always towards absent lovers; long possession takes from the worth of the persistent wooer.

SEXTI PROPERTI ELEGIARVM LIBER II

XXXIV [1]

Cvr quisquam faciem dominae iam credat [2] Amori?
　sic erepta mihi paene puella mea est.
expertus dico, nemo est in amore fidelis:
　formosam raro non sibi quisque petit.
polluit ille deus cognatos, solvit amicos,
　et bene concordes tristia ad arma vocat.
hospes in hospitium Menelao venit adulter:
　Colchis et ignotum nonne secuta virum est?
Lynceu, tune meam potuisti, perfide, curam
　tangere? nonne tuae tum cecidere manus?　　10
quid si non constans illa et tam certa fuisset?
　posses in tanto vivere flagitio?
tu mihi vel ferro pectus vel perde veneno:
　a domina tantum te modo tolle mea.
te socium vitae, te corporis esse licebit,
　te dominum admitto rebus, amice, meis:
lecto te solum, lecto te deprecor uno:
　rivalem possum non ego ferre Iovem.
ipse meas solus, quod nil est, aemulor umbras,
　stultus, quod nullo [3] saepe timore tremo.　　20
una tamen causa est, cur crimina tanta remitto,
　errabant multo quod tua verba mero.
sed numquam vitae fallet me ruga severae:
　omnes iam norunt quam sit amare bonum.

---

[1] *No break in NFL, separated by Beroaldus.*
[2] iam credat *N*: non credit *FL*.
[3] nullo *Heinsius*: stulto *NFL*.

166

XXXIV

WHY should any one henceforth entrust his mistress' beauty to the care of Love? Thus was my beloved nearly stolen from me. I speak from experience; no man is ever faithful in love, and rarely does any, beholding beauty, seek not to make it his own. Love pollutes kinship, parts friends, and summons them, that are well agreed, to bitter strife. The adulterer, that was made welcome by Menelaus, was a stranger; and did not the woman of Colchis follow a lover whom she knew not?

[9] Lynceus, hadst thou the heart to touch my beloved? Did not thy hands, faithless friend, fall powerless then? What if she had not been so constant and so true? Couldst thou have lived in such guilt? Take my life with poison or the sword, only take thyself away from my mistress. Thou mayest be the comrade of my life and part never from my side; my friend, I make thee lord of all my fortune; 'tis only as partner in my love that I would have thee never. I cannot endure a rival, though he were Jove himself. I am jealous of mine own shadow, a thing of naught, fool that I am to tremble with causeless fear. One plea alone can make me pardon such a crime: deep draughts of wine had caused thy tongue to stray. Yet never shall thy brow, wrinkled with stern morality, deceive me: the world is old enough for all to know how good a thing is love.

SEXTI PROPERTI ELEGIARVM LIBER II

Lynceus ipse meus seros insanit amores!
   solum te nostros laetor adire deos
quid tua Socraticis tibi nunc sapientia libris
   proderit aut rerum dicere posse vias?
aut quid Erechthei tibi prosunt carmina plectri?[1]
   nil iuvat in magno vester amore senex.   30
tu satius Meropem Musis[2] imitere Philetan
   et non inflati somnia Callimachi.
nam rursus licet Aetoli referas Acheloi
   fluxerit ut magno fractus[3] amore liquor,
atque etiam ut Phrygio fallax Maeandria campo
   errat et ipsa suas decipit unda vias,
qualis et Adrasti fuerit vocalis Arion,
   tristis ad Archemori funera victor equus:
Amphiarea tibi non prosint[4] fata quadrigae
   aut Capanei magno grata ruina Iovi.   40
desine et Aeschyleo componere verba coturno,
   desine, et ad molles membra resolve choros.
incipe iam angusto versus includere torno,
   inque tuos ignes, dure poeta, veni.
tu non Antimacho, non tutior ibis Homero:
   despicit et magnos recta puella deos.
sed non ante gravis taurus succumbit aratro,
   cornua quam validis haeserit in laqueis,

[1] erecthei μ. erechti N. erethei FL. plectri *Palmer*. lecta NFL.

[2] Meropem Musis *Bergk, Schneidewin*: memorem musis N: musis memorem FL.

[3] fractus ϛ. tactus NFL.

[4] Amphiarea tibi nil prosint *Postgate*. non amphiareae prosint tibi NFL

THE ELEGIES OF PROPERTIUS BOOK II

²⁵ Late though it be, at last Lynceus, my friend, is mad with love! Of this only am I glad, that at last thou worshippest the gods we lovers serve. What will avail thee now thy wisdom drawn from Socratic books, what the power to set forth the cause of things? What avails thee the songs of the Athenian lyre? Thine ancient bard availeth naught against o'ermastering love. Do thou rather imitate in thy song Coan Philetas, and the dreams of restrained Callimachus. Now, though thou shouldst tell once more how the stream of Aetolian Achelous flowed shattered by the might of love, and withal how the deceitful wave of Maeander wanders in the Phrygian plain and perplexes its own channels, and how, mourning at the funeral of Archemorus, Adrastus' victorious steed Arion spake aloud, naught will avail thee the fate of the chariot of Amphiaraus, nor the overthrow of Capaneus that made glad the heart of Jove. Cease to frame verse shod with the buskin of Aeschylus, and bend thy limbs in the soft choric dance. Begin now to turn thy verses on a narrower lathe, and sing of thine own flames, hard-hearted poet. Thou shalt not be safer in thy goings than Antimachus or Homer:[1] for a comely girl despises even the power of the gods.

⁴⁷ Yet the stubborn bull yields not to the yoke of the plough, e'er his horns have been caught in the

---

[1] Propertius alludes to Antimachus' love for Lyde, and to the legend recorded by Hermesianax that Homer fell in love with Penelope.

169

SEXTI PROPERTI ELEGIARVM LIBER II

nec tu tam¹ duros per te patiens amores:
    trux tamen a nobis ante domandus eris.   50
harum nulla solet rationem quaerere mundi,
    nec cur fraternis Luna laboret equis,
nec si post Stygias aliquid rest arbiter undas,²
    nec si consulto fulmina missa tonent.
aspice me, cui parva domi fortuna relicta est
    nullus et antiquo Marte triumphus avi,
ut regnem mixtas inter conviva puellas
    hoc ego, quo tibi nunc elevor, ingenio!
mi lubet hesternis posito³ languere corollis,
    quem tetigit iactu certus ad ossa deus;   60
Actia Vergilio custodis litora Phoebi,
    Caesaris et fortes dicere posse rates,
qui nunc Aeneae Troiani suscitat arma
    iactaque Lavinis moenia litoribus.
cedite Romani scriptores, cedite Grai!
    nescio quid maius nascitur Iliade.
tu canis umbrosi subter pineta Galaesi
    Thyrsin et attritis Daphnin harundinibus,
utque decem possint corrumpere mala puellas
    missus et impressis haedus ab uberibus.   70
felix, qui viles pomis mercaris amores!
    huic licet ingratae Tityrus ipse canat.
felix intactum Corydon qui temptat Alexin
    agricolae domini carpere delicias!

[1] tam *FL*: iam *N*.
[2] rest arbiter undas *Munro*: restabit *NFL*. erumpnas *FL*. om. *N*.
[3] mi lubet . . . posito *Housman*: me iuvet . . . positum *NFL*. hesternis *v*: externis *N*: aeternis *FL*.

stout noose. Nor wilt thou of thyself be able to endure the hardships of love; first thou must have thy fierce spirit tamed by me. Never will girl inquire concerning the system of the universe, nor ask why the labours of the moon depend on her brother's steeds, nor if in truth there is a judge beyond the waves of Styx, nor if the crashing thunderbolts be hurled by an aiming hand. Look on me, to whom but a scanty fortune hath been left at home, whose ancestors ne'er triumphed for battles long ago, see how I reign at the banquet in the midst of a crowd of girls, thanks to the wit for which thou now makest light of me!

59 Be it mine to lie languidly among the wreaths of yesterday, for the god hath stricken me with aim unerring even to the bone. Be it for Vergil to sing the shores of Actium o'er which Phoebus watches, and Caesar's gallant ships of war; Vergil that now wakes to life the arms of Trojan Aeneas and the walls he founded on the Lavinian shore. Yield ye, bards of Rome, yield ye, singers of Greece! Something greater than the Iliad now springs to birth! Vergil, thou singest beneath the pine-woods of shady Galaesus[1] of Thyrsis, and Daphnis[2] with the well-worn pipe of reed, and how ten apples or a kid[3] fresh from the udder of its dam may win the love of a girl. Happy thou that thus cheaply buyest thy love with apples; to such a love may even Tityrus[4] sing, unkind though she be. Happy, too, Corydon, who seeks to win Alexis,[5] the darling of the farmer, his master, Alexis

[1] The allusion is probably to *Georg.* IV. 125. The Galaesus is not mentioned in the *Eclogues*.
[2] *Ecl.* V. and VII.   [3] *Ecl.* III. 70.   [4] *Ecl.* I.   [5] *Ecl.* II.

SEXTI PROPERTI ELEGIARVM LIBER II

quamvis ille sua lassus requiescat avena,
   laudatur faciles inter Hamadryadas.
tu canis Ascraei veteris praecepta poetae,
   quo seges in campo, quo viret uva iugo.
tale facis carmen docta testudine quale
   Cynthius impositis temperat articulis.   80
non tamen haec ulli venient ingrata legenti,
   sive in amore rudis sive peritus erit.
nec minor hic animis, ut sit minor ore,[1] canorus
   anseris indocto carmine cessit olor.
haec quoque perfecto ludebat Iasone Varro,
   Varro Leucadiae maxima flamma suae;
haec quoque lascivi cantarunt scripta Catulli,
   Lesbia quis ipsa notior est Helena;
haec etiam docti confessa est pagina Calvi,
   cum caneret miserae funera Quintiliae.   90
et modo formosa qui[2] multa Lycoride Gallus
   mortuus inferna vulnera lavit aqua!
Cynthia quin etiam versu laudata Properti,
   hos inter si me ponere Fama volet.

---

[1] hic *Housman*: his *NFL*. animis *N*: animi *FL*. ut sit minor *Housman*: aut sim minor *NFL* (minor ore canorus om. *N*).

[2] qui ς: quam *NFL*

THE ELEGIES OF PROPERTIUS BOOK II

yet unwon; even though he weary and rest from his piping, yet is he praised by the wanton Hamadryads. Thou singest also the precepts of Ascra's poet old, telling in what plains the corn grows green, and on what hills the vine. Such music makest thou as the Cynthian god modulates with fingers pressed upon his well-skilled lyre. Yet these songs of thine will fail to please none that reads, whether he be skilled in love or all unlearned; and the melodious " swan," less lofty of accent, yet no less inspired when he sings the songs of love, sinks not to tuneless cackle like the " goose."[1]

[85] Such sportive themes also did Varro sing when his tale of Jason was all told;[2] Varro, Leucadia's mightiest flame. Such are the songs that wanton Catullus wrote, whose Lesbia is better known than Helen. Such passion also the pages of learned Calvus did confess, when he sang of the death of hapless Quintilia; and dead Gallus too, that of late laved in the streams of Hell the many wounds dealt him by fair Lycoris. Nay, Cynthia also has been glorified by Propertius—if Fame shall grant me a place mid such as they.

[1] A punning reference to the poetaster Anser (= goose), suggested by Vergil, *Ecl.* IX. 36
[2] *I.e.*, after the publication of his translation of the *Argonautica* of Apollonius Rhodius

BOOK III

LIBER TERTIVS

I

Callimachi Manes et Coi sacra Philetae,
 in vestrum, quaeso, me sinite ire nemus.
primus ego ingredior puro de fonte sacerdos
 Itala per Graios orgia ferre choros.
dicite, quo pariter carmen tenuastis in antro?
 quove pede ingressi? quamve bibistis aquam?
a valeat, Phoebum quicumque moratur in armis!
 exactus tenui pumice versus eat,—
quo me Fama levat terra sublimis, et a me
 nata coronatis Musa triumphat equis, 10
et mecum in curru parvi vectantur Amores,
 scriptorumque meas turba secuta rotas.
quid frustra missis in me certatis habenis?
 non datur ad Musas currere lata via.
multi, Roma, tuas laudes annalibus addent,
 qui finem imperii Bactra futura canent;
sed, quod pace legas, opus hoc de monte Sororum
 detulit intacta pagina nostra via.
mollia, Pegasides, date vestro serta poetae:
 non faciet capiti dura corona meo. 20

THE THIRD BOOK

I

SHADE of Callimachus and sacred rites of Philetas, suffer me, I pray, to enter your grove. I am the first with priestly service from an unsullied spring to carry Italian mysteries among the dances of Greece.[1] Tell me, in what grotto did ye weave your songs together? With what step did ye enter? What sacred fountain did ye drink?

[7] Away with the man who keeps Phoebus tarrying among the weapons of war! Let verse run smoothly, polished with fine pumice. 'Tis by such verse as this that Fame lifts me aloft from earth, and the Muse, my daughter, triumphs with garlanded steeds, and tiny Loves ride with me in my chariot, and a throng of writers follows my wheels. Why strive ye against me vainly with loosened rein? Narrow is the path that leadeth to the Muses. Many, O Rome, shall add fresh glories to thine annals, singing that Bactra shall be thine empire's bound; but this work of mine my pages have brought down from the Muses' mount by an untrodden way, that thou mayest read it in the midst of peace.

[19] Pegasid Muses, give soft garlands to your poet: no hard crown will suit my brow. But that whereof

---

[1] *I.e.*, to write on Italian subjects in Greek style.

SEXTI PROPERTI ELEGIARVM LIBER III

at mihi quod vivo detraxerit invida turba,
   post obitum duplici faenore reddet Honos;[1]
omnia post obitum fingit maiora vetustas:[2]
   maius ab exsequiis nomen in ora venit.
nam quis equo pulsas abiegno nosceret arces,
   fluminaque Haemonio comminus isse viro,
Idaeum Simoenta, Iovis cum prole Scamandro,[3]
   Hectora per campos ter maculasse rotas?
Deiphobumque Helenumque et Pulydamanta et in armis
   qualemcumque Parim vix sua nosset humus.   30
exiguo sermone fores nunc, Ilion, et tu
   Troia bis Oetaei numine capta dei.
nec non ille tui casus memorator Homerus
   posteritate suum crescere sensit opus.
meque inter seros laudabit Roma nepotes:
   illum post cineres auguror ipse diem.
ne mea contempto lapis indicet ossa sepulcro
   provisum est Lycio vota probante deo.

II

Carminis interea nostri redeamus in orbem;
   gaudeat in solito tacta puella sono.
Orphea delenisse[4] feras et concita dicunt
   flumina Threicia sustinuisse lyra;

---

[1] reddet *f*: reddit *NFL*. honos *ς*: onus *NFL*.
[2] omnia *FL*: famae *N*. vetustas *FL*: vetustae *N*.
[3] cum prole Scamandro *G. Wolff*: cunabula parvi *FL*: om. *N*.
[4] delenisse *Ayrmann*: detinuisse *NL*: detenuisse *F*.

the envious throng have robbed me in life, Glory after death shall repay with double interest. After death lapse of years makes all things seem greater; after the rites of burial a name rings greater on the lips of men. Else who would know aught of the citadel shattered by the horse of fir-wood, or how rivers strove in mortal conflict with Haemonia's hero? Who would know aught of Idaean Simois and Scamander sprung from Jove, or that the chariot-wheel thrice dragged Hector foully o'er the plain? Scarce would their own land know Deiphobus, Helenus, and Pulydamas, and Paris that sorry warrior. Little talk now would there be of thee, Ilion, and of thee, Troy, twice captured by the power of Oeta's god. Nay, even Homer, that told thy fall, hath seen his work grow in fame through lapse of after-years. Me too shall Rome praise in the voices of late-born generations; myself I foresee that day beyond the fatal pyre. No man shall spurn the grave where the headstone marks my bones! So ordaineth Lycia's god, for he hath approved my vows.

II

MEANWHILE let us return to our wonted round of song; let the heart of my mistress be moved with joy at the old familiar music. They say that Orpheus with his Thracian lyre tamed wild beasts and stayed

SEXTI PROPERTI ELEGIARVM LIBER III

saxa Cithaeronis Thebas agitata per artem
    sponte sua in muri[1] membra coisse ferunt;
quin etiam, Polypheme, fera Galatea sub Aetna
    ad tua rorantes carmina flexit equos.
miremur, nobis et Baccho et Apolline dextro,
    turba puellarum si mea verba colit?   10
quod non Taenariis domus est mihi fulta columnis,
    nec camera auratas inter eburna trabes,
nec mea Phaeacas aequant pomaria silvas,
    non operosa rigat Marcius antra liquor;
at Musae comites et carmina cara legenti,
    nec[2] defessa choris Calliopea meis.
fortunata, meo si qua est celebrata libello!
    carmina erunt formae tot monumenta tuae.
nam neque Pyramidum sumptus ad sidera ducti,
    nec Iovis Elei caelum imitata domus,   20
nec Mausolei dives fortuna sepulcri
    mortis ab extrema condicione vacant.
aut illis flamma aut imber subducit honores,
    annorum aut ictus pondere[3] victa ruent.
at non ingenio quaesitum nomen ab aevo
    excidet: ingenio stat sine morte decus.

---

[1] in muri ς: in numeri *NL*, immineri *F*.
[2] nec *Baehrens* et *FL*: omitted by *N*.
[3] ictus *L*: ictu *NF*. pondere *NL* pondera *F*.

rushing rivers, and that Cithaeron's rocks were driven to Thebes by the minstrel's art and of their own will gathered to frame a wall. Nay, Galatea too beneath wild Etna turned her steeds that dripped with brine to the sound of thy songs, Polyphemus.

9 What marvel, when Bacchus and Apollo smile on me, that a host of maidens should adore my words? My house is not stayed on Taenarian columns; I have no ivory chamber with gilded beams; no orchards have I to vie with Phaeacia's trees, nor hath art built me grottoes watered by the Marcian fount. But the Muses are my comrades, and my songs are dear to them that read, nor ever is Calliope aweary with my dancing.[1]

17 Happy she that book of mine hath praised! My songs shall be so many memorials of thy beauty. For neither the Pyramids built skyward at such cost, nor the house of Jove at Elis that matches heaven, nor the wealth of Mausolus' tomb are exempt from the end imposed by death. Their glory is stolen away by fire or rain, or the strokes of time whelm them to ruin crushed by their own weight. But the fame that my wit hath won shall never perish: for wit renown endureth deathless.

[1] Or perhaps "music"

SEXTI PROPERTI ELEGIARVM LIBER III

III

Visvs eram molli recubans Heliconis in umbra,
 Bellerophontei qua fluit umor equi,
reges, Alba, tuos et regum facta tuorum,
 tantum operis, nervis hiscere posse meis;
parvaque tam magnis admoram fontibus ora,
 unde pater sitiens Ennius ante bibit;
et cecinit Curios fratres et Horatia pila,
 regiaque Aemilia vecta tropaea rate,
victricesque moras Fabii pugnamque sinistram
 Cannensem et versos ad pia vota deos,   10
Hannibalemque Lares Romana sede fugantes,
 anseris et tutum voce fuisse Iovem:
cum me Castalia speculans ex arbore Phoebus
 sic ait aurata nixus ad antra lyra:
" Quid tibi cum tali, demens, est flumine? quis te
 carminis heroi tangere iussit opus?
non hinc ulla tibi speranda est fama, Properti:
 mollia sunt parvis prata terenda rotis;
ut tuus in scamno iactetur saepe libellus,
 quem legat exspectans sola puella virum.   20
cur tua praescripto sevecta est pagina gyro?
 non est ingeni cumba gravanda tui.
alter remus aquas alter tibi radat harenas,
 tutus eris: medio maxima turba mari est."
dixerat, et plectro sedem mihi monstrat eburno,
 qua nova muscoso semita facta solo est.

THE ELEGIES OF PROPERTIUS BOOK III

III

METHOUGHT I lay in the soft shades of Helicon, where flows the fountain of Bellerophon's steed, and deemed I had the power with sinews such as mine to sing of thy kings, O Alba, and the deeds of thy kings, a mighty task. Already I had set my puny lips to those mighty fountains, whence father Ennius once slaked his thirst and sang of the Curian brothers and the javelins of the Horatii and the royal trophies borne in Aemilius' bark, of the victorious delays of Fabius, the fatal fight of Cannae and the gods that turned to answer pious prayers, of the Lares frighting Hannibal from their Roman home, and of Jove saved by the cackling goose.

[13] But of a sudden Phoebus espied me from his Castalian grove and spake thus, leaning on his golden lyre nigh to a cavern: "Madman, what hast thou to do with such a stream? Who bade thee essay the task of heroic song? Not hence, Propertius, mayest thou hope for fame! Soft are the meads o'er which thy little wheels must roll, that oft thy book may be read by some lonely girl, that waits her absent lover, and oft be cast upon the stool at her feet.[1] Why has thy page swerved from the ring prescribed for it? The shallop of thy wit can bear no heavy cargo! Let one oar skim the water, the other the sand; so shalt thou be safe: mighty is the turmoil in mid-sea." He spake, and with his ivory quill showed me a dwelling, where a new path had been made along the mossy floor.

---

[1] Two interpretations of this obscure couplet are possible: (a) the book is cast down on the arrival of the lover; (b) the reader is restless and keeps throwing the book down.

SEXTI PROPERTI ELEGIARVM LIBER III

hic erat affixis viridis spelunca lapillis,
    pendebantque cavis tympana pumicibus,
orgia¹ Musarum et Sileni patris imago
    fictilis et calami, Pan Tegeaee, tui;   30
et Veneris dominae volucres, mea turba, columbae
    tingunt Gorgoneo punica rostra lacu;
diversaeque novem sortitae rura Puellae
    exercent teneras in sua dona manus:
haec hederas legit in thyrsos, haec carmina nervis
    aptat, at illa manu texit utraque rosam.
e quarum numero me contigit una dearum
    (ut reor a facie, Calliopea fuit):
" Contentus niveis semper vectabere cycnis,
    nec te fortis equi ducet ad arma sonus.   40
nil tibi sit rauco praeconia classica cornu
    flare, nec Aonium tinguere Marte nemus;
aut quibus in campis Mariano proelia signo
    stent et Teutonicas Roma refringat opes,
barbarus aut Suevo perfusus sanguine Rhenus
    saucia maerenti corpora vectet aqua.
quippe coronatos alienum ad limen amantes
    nocturnaeque canes ebria signa fugae,
ut per te clausas sciat excantare puellas,
    qui volet austeros arte ferire viros."   50
talia Calliope, lymphisque a fonte petitis
    ora Philetaea nostra rigavit aqua.

        ¹ orgia *Heinsius*: ergo *NFL.*

THE ELEGIES OF PROPERTIUS BOOK III

27 Here was a green cave, its walls lined with pebbles, and timbrels hung from its hollowed stones; there hung also the mystic instruments of the Muses and the clay image of father Silenus, and thy reeds, O Pan of Tegea; and doves, birds of my lady Venus, the birds I love, dipped their red bills in the Gorgon's fount, while here and there the Maidens nine, to each of whom the lot hath given her several realm, busied their soft hands about their diverse gifts. One gathered ivy for the thyrsus-wand, another tuned her song to the music of the lyre, a third with either hand wove wreaths of roses.

37 Then one of the number of these goddesses laid her hand upon me—'twas Calliope,[1] as I deem by her face: "Thou shalt alway be content to be drawn by snowy swans, nor shall the tramp of the war-horse lead thee to battle. Care not thou with hoarse trumpet-blast to blare forth martial advertisement nor to stain Aonia's grove with war. Care not thou in what fields the battle is arrayed beneath Marius' standard, and Rome beats back the Teuton's power, nor where the wild Rhine, steeped with the Swabian's blood, bears mangled bodies down its sorrowing waves

47 "For thou shalt sing of garlanded lovers watching before another's threshold, and the tokens of drunken flight through the dark, that he who would cheat stern husbands by his cunning may through thee have power to charm forth his imprisoned love." So spake Calliope, and, drawing water from the fount, sprinkled my lips with the draught Philetas loved.

[1] It is probable that Propertius regards the name Calliope as meaning in Greek "fair-faced" instead of "sweet-voiced."

SEXTI PROPERTI ELEGIARVM LIBER III

IV

Arma deus Caesar dites meditatur ad Indos,
  et freta gemmiferi findere classe maris.
magna, viri, merces: parat ultima terra triumphos,
  Thybris, et Euphrates sub tua iura fluet;[1]
sera, sed Ausoniis veniet provincia virgis;
  assuescent Latio Partha tropaea Iovi.
ite agite, expertae bello date lintea prorae,
  et solitum armigeri ducite munus equi!
omina fausta cano. Crassos clademque piate!
  ite et Romanae consulite historiae! 10
Mars pater, et sacrae fatalia lumina Vestae,
  ante meos obitus sit precor illa dies,
qua videam spoliis oneratos Caesaris axes,
  ad vulgi plausus saepe resistere equos,
inque sinu carae nixus spectare puellae
  incipiam et titulis oppida capta legam,
tela fugacis equi et bracati militis arcus,
  et subter captos arma sedere duces!
ipsa tuam serva prolem, Venus: hoc sit in aevum,
  cernis ab Aenea quod superesse caput. 20
praeda sit haec illis, quorum meruere labores:
  mi sat erit Sacra[2] plaudere posse Via.

[1] Thybris ... fluet *Housman*: Tigris ... fluent *NFL*.
[2] mi *ς·* me *NFL.* sacra *N · om. L*: media *F.*

THE ELEGIES OF PROPERTIUS BOOK III

IV

Caesar our god plans war [1] against rich Ind and would cleave with his fleet the waters of the pearl-bearing sea. Great is the prize, men of Rome: furthest earth prepares triumphs for thee, Tiber, and Euphrates shall flow beneath thy sway. Late shall that province come beneath Ausonia's rods, yet it shall surely come; Parthia's trophies shall become familiar with Latin Jupiter. Go now, ye prows well skilled in war, unfurl your sails; ye war-horses, ply the task ye know so well! I sing you prospering omens. Avenge Crassus and his slaughter! Go forth and make fair the pages of Rome's story!

[11] O father Mars and ye fires of fate, that burn for holy Vesta, I implore you, may that day come ere I die, on which I shall see Caesar's chariots laden with spoils and his steeds halting at sound of the people's cheers; then as I lie reclined on the bosom of my beloved I will read the names of captured cities, and will turn mine eyes to gaze at the shafts that were hurled by flying horsemen, at the bows of trousered warriors and the chiefs that sit beneath their captured arms.

[19] Venus, keep safe thine offspring; may that life, that before thine eyes still preserves Aeneas' line, live through all ages! Be the spoil theirs whose toil has won it! Enough for me to be able to cheer them on the Sacred Way.

---

[1] An allusion to the expedition to Parthia, which actually took place in 20 B.C.

SEXTI PROPERTI ELEGIARVM LIBER III

V

Pacis Amor deus est, pacem veneramur amantes:
    sat[1] mihi cum domina proelia dura mea.
nec tantum[2] inviso pectus mihi carpitur auro,
    nec bibit e gemma divite nostra sitis,
nec mihi mille iugis Campania pinguis aratur,
    nec, miser, aera paro clade, Corinthe, tua.
o prima infelix fingenti terra Prometheo!
    ille parum caute pectoris egit opus.
corpora disponens mentem non vidit in arte:
    recta animi primum debuit esse via.   10
nunc maris in tantum vento iactamur, et hostem
    quaerimus, atque armis nectimus arma nova.
haud ullas portabis opes Acherontis ad undas:
    nudus ad infernas, stulte, vehere rates.
victor cum victis pariter miscebitur umbris:
    consule cum Mario, capte Iugurtha, sedes.
Lydus Dulichio non distat Croesus ab Iro:
    optima mors, carpta quae venit acta[3] die.
me iuvat in prima coluisse Helicona iuventa
    Musarumque choris implicuisse manus: 20
me iuvet et multo mentem vincire Lyaeo,
    et caput in verna semper habere rosa.

[1] sat *Livineius* stant *NFL.*
[2] tantum *Lachmann.* tamen *NFL.*
[3] carpta *Baehrens.* parca *NFL.* acta *NL.* apta *F.*

THE ELEGIES OF PROPERTIUS BOOK III

V

Love is a god of peace: we lovers worship peace: enough for me the hard warfare I wage with my mistress. My soul is not so racked with lust for hateful gold, nor drinks my thirst from cups of precious stone, nor is fat Campania ploughed for me by a thousand yokes, nor do I get me bronzes [1] from thy ruin, hapless Corinth.

[7] Ah! primeval earth so unkind to Prometheus' fashioning hand! With too little care he moulded the human heart. He ordered men's bodies, but forgot the mind as he plied his art; straight before all else should have been the path of the soul. Now o'er such wide seas are we tempest-tossed; we seek out a foe, and pile fresh war on war. Yet no wealth shalt thou carry to the waves of Acheron: naked, thou fool, thou shalt be borne to the ship of Hell. There victor and vanquished shades are mingled in equality of death: captive Jugurtha, thou sittest beside the consul Marius; Lydian Croesus is as Dulichian Irus! That death is best that comes apace when we have had our joy of life.

[19] My delight is it to have worshipped Helicon in my earliest youth and to have entwined my hands in the Muses' dance. Be it my delight also to bind my soul with deep Lyaean draughts and ever to have wreaths of spring roses about my brow. And when the

---

[1] An allusion to Corinthian bronze, said to have been formed by the accidental fusing of gold, silver, and bronze at the burning of Corinth by Mummius, 146 B.C.

SEXTI PROPERTI ELEGIARVM LIBER III

atque ubi iam Venerem gravis interceperit aetas,
   sparserit et nigras[1] alba senecta comas,
tum mihi naturae libeat perdiscere mores,
   quis deus hanc mundi temperet arte domum,
qua venit exoriens, qua deficit, unde coactis
   cornibus in plenum menstrua luna redit,
unde salo superant venti, quid flamine captet
   Eurus, et in nubes unde perennis aqua;   30
sit ventura dies mundi quae subruat arces,
   purpureus pluvias cur bibit arcus aquas,
aut cur Perrhaebi tremuere cacumina Pindi,
   solis et atratis luxerit orbis equis,
cur serus versare boves et plaustra Bootes,[2]
   Pleiadum spisso cur coit igne chorus,
curve suos finis altum non exeat aequor,
   plenus et in partis quattuor annus eat;
sub terris sint iura deum et tormenta Gigantum,
   Tisiphones atro si furit angue caput,   40
aut Alcmaeoniae furiae aut ieiunia Phinei,
   num rota, num scopuli, num sitis inter aquas,
num tribus infernum custodit faucibus antrum
   Cerberus, et Tityo iugera pauca novem,
an ficta in miseras descendit fabula gentis,
   et timor haud ultra quam rogus esse potest.
exitus hic vitae superest mihi: vos, quibus arma
   grata magis, Crassi signa referte domum.

[1] sparserit et *N*: sparsit et *FL*. nigras ϛ: integras *NFL*.
[2] plaustra Bootes ϛ: flamma palustra *FL*: flamma boon *N*.

burdening years have set a stay to love, and whitening age hath flecked my black locks, then be it my pleasure to learn the ways of nature, to learn what god rules by his wisdom this quarter of the world, how comes the rising moon, how wanes, and how each month its horns are orbed to the full; whence sweep the winds in triumph over the sea, what seeks the East Wind with his blast, and whence the clouds draw their unfailing water; whether a day shall come to o'erthrow the citadels of the world; why the bright bow drinks up the rain-water, why the peaks of Perrhaebian Pindus have trembled, why mourned the sun's disk with dark-robed steeds, why Boötes is late to turn his oxen and wain, why the band of Pleiads shine with close-set fires, why the deep outsteps not its bounds, and why the full year hath four seasons in its round; whether there be gods that rule underground and giants that suffer torment, and Tisiphone's brow be wild with black snakes; whether Alcmaeon be plagued with Furies and Phineus with fasting, whether there be the wheel, the rolling rock, the thirst in the water's midst; whether Cerberus guards with triple throat the cave of Hell, and nine acres are all too few for Tityos; or if the tale that hath come down to wretched mortals be an empty dream and there is naught to dread beyond the pyre. Such is the close of life that waits for me: do ye to whom arms are dearest bring home the standards of Crassus!

SEXTI PROPERTI ELEGIARVM LIBER III

VI

Dic mihi de nostra, quae sentis, vera puella:
  sic tibi sint dominae, Lygdame, dempta iuga.
num [1] me laetitia tumefactum fallis inani,
  haec referens, quae me credere velle putas?
omnis enim debet sine vano nuntius esse,
  maioremque timens servus habere fidem.
nunc mihi, si qua tenes, ab origine dicere prima
  incipe: suspensis auribus ista bibam.
sic, ut eam [2] incomptis vidisti flere capillis,
  illius ex oculis multa cadebat aqua?   10
nec speculum strato vidisti, Lygdame, lecto?
  ornabat niveas nullane gemma manus?
ac maestam teneris vestem pendere lacertis,
  scriniaque ad lecti clausa iacere pedes?
tristis erat domus, et tristes sua pensa ministrae
  carpebant, medio nebat et ipsa loco,
umidaque impressa siccabat lumina lana,
  rettulit et querulo iurgia nostra sono?
" Haec te teste mihi promissa est, Lygdame, merces?
  est poenae servo rumpere teste fidem.   20
ille potest nullo miseram me linquere facto,
  et qualem nolo [3] dicere habere domo!
gaudet me vacuo solam tabescere lecto.
  si placet, insultet, Lygdame, morte mea.

[1] num ς: non *N*: dum *FL*.
[2] sic, ut eam *Butler*· sicut eam *FL*: si cã *N*.
[3] et qualem nolo *Palmer*. et qualem nullo *N*: aequalem nulla *FL*.

THE ELEGIES OF PROPERTIUS BOOK III

VI

TELL me truly what thou thinkest of my love: so, Lygdamus, be the yoke of thy mistress taken from thy neck. Dost thou cheat me and make me swell with baseless joy, telling me such news as thou thinkst I would fain believe? Every messenger should be blameless of lying, and a slave should be all the truer by reason of his fear. Now set forth thy tale to me from the first beginning, if thou rememberest aught; I will listen with eager ears.

9 Did her tears rain even so when thou beheldest her weep with hair dishevelled? Didst thou see no mirror, Lygdamus, on her couch? Did no jewelled ring adorn her snowy hands? Didst thou see a sad-hued robe hang from her soft arms, and did her toilet caskets lie closed at the bed's foot? Was the house sad, and sad her handmaids as they plied their tasks, and was she knitting in their midst? Did she press the wool to her eyes to dry their moisture, and repeat my chidings with plaintive tone? "Is this the reward he promised me in thy hearing, Lygdamus? Perjury may be punished, though the witness be but a slave. Can he leave me thus to weep with never an act of love, and keep in his house one such as I would not name? He rejoices that I pine forlorn in my empty bed. If it please him, Lygdamus, let him mock me even in death! 'Twas by no winning ways, but by

SEXTI PROPERTI ELEGIARVM LIBER III

non me moribus illa, sed herbis improba vicit:
   staminea rhombi ducitur ille rota.
illum turgentis ranae portenta rubetae
   et lecta exuctis[1] anguibus ossa trahunt,
et strigis inventae per busta iacentia plumae,
   cinctaque funesto lanea vitta viro.   30
si non vana canunt mea somnia, Lygdame, testor,
   poena erit ante meos sera sed ampla pedes;
putris et in vacuo texetur aranea lecto:
   noctibus illorum dormiet ipsa Venus."
quae tibi si veris animis est questa puella,
   hac eadem rursus, Lygdame, curre via,
et mea cum multis lacrimis mandata reporta
   iram, non fraudes esse in amore meo,
me quoque consimili impositum torquerier igni:
   iurabo bis sex integer esse dies.   40
quod mihi si e tanto[2] felix concordia bello
   exstiterit, per me, Lygdame, liber eris.

VII

Ergo sollicitae tu causa, pecunia, vitae!
   per te immaturum mortis adimus iter;
tu vitiis hominum crudelia pabula praebes;
   semina curarum de capite orta tuo.
tu Paetum ad Pharios tendentem lintea portus
   obruis insano terque quaterque mari.

---

[1] exuctis *Burmann*   exectis *NL*. exactis *F*.
[2] e tanto *Lachmann*. tanto *NFL*.

magic herbs, that she, the wretch, hath conquered me: he is led captive by the magic wheel[1] whirled on its string. He is drawn to her by the monstrous charms of the swelling bramble-toad and by the bones she has gathered from dried serpents, by the owl-feathers found on low-lying tombs, and the woollen fillet bound about the doomed man.[2] I call thee to witness, Lygdamus; if my dreams lie not, he shall yield me vengeance, late, yet ample, as he grovels at my feet. The spider shall weave her mouldering threads about his empty couch, and Venus herself shall slumber on the night of their embrace."

35 If my love spake these words with truth in her soul, run back, Lygdamus, by the way thou camest. Bear back this message from me with many tears, that my passion may have stooped to anger, but never to guile, that I am tormented by like flame to hers: I will swear that for twice six days I have known no woman. Then if blest peace shall spring from such fierce war, as far as I may serve thee, Lygdamus, thou art free!

VII

Thou, therefore, money, art the cause that life is full of care! 'tis for thee we go down to death ere our time; 'tis thou that givest men's vices cruel nourishment, thou art the fount whence spring the seeds of woe: 'twas thou that thrice and four times didst whelm with raging seas Paetus that set his sails toward Pharos' haven.

[1] See note, p. 147.
[2] *I.e.*, the waxen image of the object of the spells.

SEXTI PROPERTI ELEGIARVM LIBER III

nam dum te sequitur, primo miser excidit aevo
    et nova longinquis piscibus esca natat;
et mater non iusta piae dare debita terrae
    nec pote cognatos inter humare rogos;   10
sed tua nunc volucres astant super ossa marinae,
    nunc tibi pro tumulo Carpathium omne mare est.
infelix Aquilo, raptae timor Orithyiae,
    quae spolia ex illo tanta fuere tibi?
aut quidnam fracta gaudes, Neptune, carina?
    portabat sanctos alveus ille viros.
Paete, quid aetatem numeras? quid cara natanti
    mater in ore tibi est? non habet unda deos
nam tibi nocturnis ad saxa ligata procellis
    omnia detrito vincula fune cadunt.   20
reddite corpus humo, posita est in gurgite vita;   25
    Paetum sponte tua, vilis arena, tegas;
et quotiens Paeti transibit nauta sepulcrum,
    dicat "Et audaci tu timor esse potes."
ite, rates curvate,[1] et leti texite causas:
    ista per humanas mors venit acta manus.   30
terra parum fuerat fatis, adiecimus undas:
    fortunae miseras auximus arte vias.
ancora te teneat, quem non tenuere penates?
    quid meritum dicas, cui sua terra parum est?
ventorum est, quodcumque paras: haud ulla carina
    consenuit, fallit portus et ipse fidem.
natura insidians pontum substravit avaris:
    ut tibi succedat, vix semel esse potest.

[1] curvate *Lendrum*: curvae *NFL*.

THE ELEGIES OF PROPERTIUS BOOK III

⁷ Poor wretch, while he followed thee he was snatched away from life's first bloom, and floats strange food for fishes far away. His mother might not give burial due to the dust of him that loved her, nor lay him in earth amid the ashes of his kin. But the birds of the sea stand now above thy bones, and thou hast for sepulchre the whole Carpathian main. Ah! cruel North Wind, ravished Orithyia's dread, what great harvest of spoil couldst thou win from him? Or why, Neptune, delightest thou in shipwreck? Righteous men were they that voyaged in that hull. Paetus, why count'st thou o'er thy years? Why, as thou swimmest, is thy dear mother's name upon thy lips? The wave hath no gods to hear thee. Thy cables were made fast to the rocks, but the storms of the night shore through their strands and swept them all away.

²⁵ Give back his body to earth, his life lies lost in the deep; sands without worth, drift at your will and cover Paetus And oft as the mariner passes Paetus' tomb let him say: "Thou canst bring terror even to the brave!" Go to now, build curving keels, weave engines of death: 'tis from man's hands come deaths like this. Earth was too small for death, we have added the waves: by our craft have we enlarged the cruel paths of fortune. Should the anchor hold thee, whom thy home could not hold? What shouldst thou say he merits, that finds his native land too small? Whate'er thou buildest is sport of the winds; no keel hath e'er grown old; even the haven keeps not faith. Nature with guile hath made the sea a path for greed: scarce once may success

SEXTI PROPERTI ELEGIARVM LIBER III

sunt Agamemnonias testantia litora curas, 21
   quae notat Argynni poena Mimantis aquas.[1] 22
hoc iuvene amisso classem non solvit Atrides, 23
   pro qua mactata est Iphigenia mora.[2] 24
saxa triumphales fregere Capharea puppes, 39
   naufraga cum vasto Graecia tracta salo est. 40
paulatim socium iacturam flevit Vlixes,
   in mare cui solum[3] non valuere doli.
quod si contentus patrio bove verteret agros,
   verbaque duxisset pondus habere mea,
viveret ante suos dulcis conviva Penates,
   pauper, at in terra nil, nisi fleret opes.[4]
non tulit haec Paetus, stridorem audire procellae
   et duro teneras laedere fune manus;
sed Chio thalamo aut Oricia terebintho
   et fultum pluma versicolore caput. 50
huic fluctus vivo radicitus abstulit ungues,
   et miser invisam traxit hiatus aquam;
hunc parvo ferri vidit nox improba ligno:
   Paetus ut occideret, tot coiere mala.
flens tamen extremis dedit haec mandata querelis,
   cum moribunda niger clauderet ora liquor:
" Di maris Aegaei quos sunt penes aequora,
     venti,
   et quaecumque meum degravat unda caput,

---

[1] Argynni *v.* agynni *N*: argioni *FL*. Mimantis aquas *Ellis*: minantis aquae *NFL*.
[2] *21–24 transposed by Scaliger after 38.*
[3] solum *ς*: soli *NFL*.
[4] nisi *ς*: ubi *NFL*. fleret opes *Baehrens*: flere potest *NFL*.

THE ELEGIES OF PROPERTIUS BOOK III

be thine. There are shores that bear witness to Agamemnon's woe, where the doom of Argynnus brands the waves of Mimas; for the loss of this boy Atrides would not launch his ships and for this tarrying was Iphigenia slain. The rocks of Caphareus brake a triumphant fleet, when shipwrecked Greece was engulfed by the wild brine. Ulysses wept the loss of his comrades one by one; against the sea alone his wiles had no power.

43 But if Paetus had been content to plough his fields with his father's kine, and had counted my words of weight, still would he live to feast in merriment before his household gods; poor though he were, yet on dry land would he have naught to beweep, save only lack of wealth. Paetus could not endure to hear the shrieking gale, nor to wound his delicate hands with the hard cordage; his rather to lie in a chamber of Chian marble or on a couch of Orician terebinth, his head propped on down of rainbow hues. Yet from him while still he lived did the wave rend his nails, and right loth, poor wretch, his gasping throat gulped down the waters: yet him did the wild night see borne on a slender plank: so many ills conspired for the death of Paetus Natheless with his last lamentations he gave this charge and wept, when the dark wave was closing his dying lips: " Ye gods of the Aegean that have power over the waters, ye winds and every wave that weighs down my head, whither snatch ye

SEXTI PROPERTI ELEGIARVM LIBER III

quo rapitis miseros primae lanuginis annos?
    attulimus nocuas[1] in freta vestra manus?   60
a miser alcyonum scopulis affligar acutis!
    in me caeruleo fuscina sumpta deo est.
at saltem Italiae regionibus evehat aestus:
    hoc de me sat erit si modo matris erit."
subtrahit haec fantem torta vertigine fluctus;
    ultima quae Paeto voxque diesque fuit.
o centum aequoreae Nereo genitore puellae,
    et tu materno tracta dolore Thetis;
vos decuit lasso supponere bracchia mento:
    non poterat vestras ille gravare manus: 70
at tu, saeve Aquilo, numquam mea vela videbis:
    aute fores dominae condar oportet iners.

VIII

Dvlcis ad hesternas fuerat mihi rixa lucernas,
    vocis et insanae tot maledicta tuae.
cum[2] furibunda mero mensam propellis et in me
    proicis insana cymbia plena manu.
tu vero nostros audax invade capillos
    et mea formosis unguibus ora nota,
tu minitare oculos subiecta exurere flamma,
    fac mea rescisso pectora nuda sinu!
nimirum veri dantur mihi signa caloris:
    nam sine amore gravi femina nulla dolet.   10

---

[1] nocuas *Housman*: longas *NFL*.
[2] cum *Beroaldus*: cur *NFL*.

the hapless years of my first bloom? Was there guilt on the hands that I brought to your seas? Ah! woe is me! The sharp rocks where the seamew nests shall batter me! The god of the blue deep hath smitten me with his trident. Yet at least may the tide cast me up on Italian shores: little though there be left of me, 'twill suffice if but it reach my mother." Even as he spake these words the wave with twisting eddy dragged him down; thus passed from Paetus speech and life together.

67 Ye hundred daughters of Nereus, maids of the sea, and thou Thetis, whom a mother's love once drew from out the deep, ye should have placed your arms beneath his weary chin: he was no heavy burden for your hands But thou, fierce wind of the North, never shalt thou see my sails; mine rather before my mistress' doors to lay me down, adventuring naught.

VIII

Right glad am I of our brawl by the lamplight yester-eve and all the railings of thy frenzied tongue, when mad with wine thou didst thrust away the table and cast goblets of wine at me with angry hand. Nay, be bold! Assail my hair and scar my face with thy fair talons! Threaten to hold fire beneath mine eyes and burn them from their sockets! Tear my raiment and leave my bosom bare!

9 In all this forsooth thou givest me tokens of thy passion's truth: never is woman vexed, save if her

SEXTI PROPERTI ELEGIARVM LIBER III

quae mulier rabida[1] iactat convicia lingua,
   haec[2] Veneris magnae volvitur ante pedes,
custodum gregibus circa se stipat euntem,
   seu sequitur medias, Maenas ut icta, vias,
seu timidam crebro dementia somnia terrent,
   seu miseram in tabula picta puella movet:
his ego tormentis animi sum verus haruspex,
   has didici certo saepe in amore notas.
non est certa fides, quam non in iurgia vertas:[3]
   hostibus eveniat lenta puella meis.   20
in morso aequales videant mea vulnera collo:
   me doceat livor mecum habuisse meam.
aut in amore dolere volo aut audire dolentem,
   sive tuas lacrimas sive videre meas,[4]
tecta superciliis si quando verba remittis,
   aut tua cum digitis scripta silenda notas.
odi ego quae numquam pungunt suspiria somnos:
   semper in irata pallidus esse velim.
dulcior ignis erat Paridi, cum Graia[5] per arma
   Tyndaridi poterat gaudia ferre suae: 30
dum vincunt Danai, dum restat barbarus Hector,
   ille Helenae in gremio maxima bella gerit
aut tecum aut pro te mihi cum rivalibus arma
   semper erunt: in te pax mihi nulla placet.

---

[1] rabida *Scaliger*   gravida *NFL*.
[2] haec *Livincius*· et *NFL*.
[3] iniurgia *N* iniuria *FL*. vertas *Vahlen*: versat *NL* vertat *F*.
[4] tuas ... meas *Sandstrom*: meas ... tuas *NFL*.
[5] Graia *Fruter*: grata *NFL*.

love be strong. She, that hurls taunts with raving tongue, lies grovelling at the feet of mighty Venus; she throngs herself close with flocks of guardians,[1] or rushes down the street like some frenzied Maenad; or wild dreams fright her timid soul continually, or the painted portrait of some girl fills her with woe. From all these torments of soul I draw sure auguries: these have I learned to be the signs of constant passion. No love is constant that cannot be provoked to quarrel: be girls that naught may move the fate of them that hate me.

21 Let my comrades see the wounds where her teeth have torn my neck; let dark bruises show that my love hath been with me. I would have sorrow myself in love, or else hear thine; I would see thy tears or else mine own, that fall if ever thou sendest secret messages with nodding brow, or with thy fingers writest words thou wouldst not speak aloud. I hate those sighs that never break through sleep: 'tis for an angry mistress I would ever be pale with longing. Sweeter to Paris was his passion's fire, when he must cleave his way through the hosts of Greece ere he could bring joy to his love, the daughter of Tyndareus. While the Danaans conquered, while savage Hector barred their path, he waged a mightier war in Helen's arms. Either with thee or for thee with my rival will I wage truceless war: where thou art, peace hath for me no pleasure.[2]

[1] *I.e.*, to excite her lover's jealousy and lure him back.
[2] Lit., where thou art concerned.

SEXTI PROPERTI ELEGIARVM LIBER III

VIIIa[1]

Gavde, quod nulla est aeque formosa: doleres,
  si qua foret: nunc sis iure superba licet.
at tibi, qui nostro nexisti[2] retia lecto,
  sit socer aeternum nec sine matre domus!
cui nunc si qua data est furandae copia noctis,
  offensa illa mihi, non tibi amica, dedit.   40

IX

Maecenas, eques Etrusco de sanguine regum,
  intra fortunam qui cupis esse tuam,
quid me scribendi tam vastum mittis in aequor?
  non sunt apta meae grandia vela rati.
turpe est, quod nequeas, capiti committere pondus
  et pressum inflexo mox dare terga genu.
omnia non pariter rerum sunt omnibus apta,
  palma[3] nec ex aequo ducitur ulla iugo.
gloria Lysippo est animosa effingere signa;
  exactis Calamis se mihi iactat equis;   10
in Veneris tabula summam sibi poscit Apelles;
  Parrhasius parva vindicat arte locum;
argumenta magis sunt Mentoris addita formae;
  at Myos exiguum flectit acanthus iter;

---

[1] *No break in NFL, separated by Butler.*
[2] nexisti *Priscianus and Diomedes*: tendisti *NFL*.
[3] palma ϛ: flamma *NFL*.

THE ELEGIES OF PROPERTIUS BOOK III

VIIIa

REJOICE that none is fair as thou! Thou wouldst grieve if there were any. But now thou hast just cause for pride.

37 But for thee, that didst spread a snare for our love, may thy wife's father live for ever and thy house ne'er have peace from her mother! If ever thou wast granted the boon of one stolen night, 'twas anger against me, not love for thee, that made her grant it.

IX

MAECENAS, knight sprung from the blood of Tuscan kings, that wouldst fain abide within thy fortune's scope, why dost thou launch me on so wide a sea of song? Such spreading canvas suits not a bark like mine.

5 It brings but shame to take upon thine head a burden that thou canst not bear, and soon to bow the knee and turn in flight. All things are not meet alike for all men; from different heights the palm of fame is won.[1] 'Tis Lysippus' glory to mould statues with all the fire of life; Calamis, methinks, boasts the perfection of his carven steeds; Apelles claims his highest glory from his painting of Venus; Parrhasius asserts his place by his miniature art; groups rather are the themes of Mentor's mould; in the works of Mys the acanthus winds on its brief way; the Jove

---

[1] The line is very obscure. The alternative is to take *iugo* =chariot-yoke and interpret "no prize is won by him whose car runs level with another's." Professor J. S. Reid conjectures *e Coo . . . illa*—"such glory is not to be won from the Coan [Philetean] Parnassus."

SEXTI PROPERTI ELEGIARVM LIBER III

Phidiacus signo se Iuppiter ornat eburno;
   Praxitelen Triopos venditat [1] urbe lapis.
est quibus Eleae concurrit palma quadrigae,
   est quibus in celeres gloria nata pedes;
hic satus ad pacem, hic castrensibus utilis armis:
   naturae sequitur semina quisque suae.   20
at tua, Maecenas, vitae praecepta recepi,
   cogor et exemplis te superare tuis.
cum tibi Romano dominas in honore secures
   et liceat medio ponere iura foro;
vel tibi Medorum pugnaces ire per hastas,[2]
   atque onerare tuam fixa per arma domum;
et tibi ad effectum vires det Caesar, et omni
   tempore tam faciles insinuentur opes;
parcis et in tenues humilem te colligis umbras:
   velorum plenos subtrahis ipse sinus   30
crede mihi, magnos aequabunt ista Camillos
   iudicia, et venies tu quoque in ora virum,
Caesaris et famae vestigia iuncta tenebis:
   Maecenatis erunt vera tropaea fides.
non ego velifera tumidum mare findo carina:[3]
   tota sub exiguo flumine nostra mora est.
non flebo in cineres arcem sedisse paternos
   Cadmi nec septem proelia clade pari;
nec referam Scaeas et Pergama Apollinis arces,
   et Danaum decimo vere redisse rates,   40

[1] Triopos *Richmond*: propria *NFL*.   venditat *Burmann*·
vindicat *NFL*.
[2] hastas *Markland*· hostes *NFL*.
[3] 35 om. *N*.

THE ELEGIES OF PROPERTIUS BOOK III

of Phidias arrays himself in a statue of ivory; the marble in Triops' city gives Praxiteles glory. Some race their victorious chariots[1] at Elis; for the swift feet of some was glory born; one was begotten for peace, another is meet for the weapons of war; each man follows the seeds of his own nature.

21 But I, Maecenas, have taken to heart thy rule of life, and am driven to vanquish thee with thine own example. Though as a magistrate of Rome thou mightest plant thine imperious axes where thou wouldst and deal justice in the Forum's midst; though thou mightest pass through the fierce Medians' spears and load thy house with trophies of arms; though Caesar gives thee strength for success, and at all seasons ready wealth pours into thy purse, yet holdest thou back and dost withdraw in lowly wise to modest shades, and of thine own choice furlest the swelling canvas of thy sails. Believe me, thy resolve shall rival the great deeds of Camillus, and thou also shalt be a name upon the lips of men, and thy footsteps shall accompany the fame of Caesar; thy loyalty, Maecenas, shall be thy true trophy of triumph. I cleave not the swelling sea with sail-borne keel: I do but loiter in the shelter of a little stream. I will not tell in tearful strain how Cadmus' citadel sank into ashes beneath the Father's fire,[2] nor of the seven fights, each closed with like disaster; I will not tell of the Scaean gate and Pergama, Apollo's citadel, nor how the Danaan ships returned in the tenth spring, when the wooden horse, wrought

---

[1] *palma quadrigae = quadriga quae palmam petit.*

[2] If *paternos* be correct (and there is no satisfactory correction), the phrase must mean "ashes resulting from the fatherhood" of Jupiter—*i.e.*, caused by the destruction of Semele and the palace of Cadmus at the birth of Bacchus, when Jupiter appeared in all his fiery glory to Semele.

SEXTI PROPERTI ELEGIARVM LIBER III

moenia cum Graio Neptunia pressit aratro
   victor Palladiae ligneus artis equus.
inter Callimachi sat erit placuisse libellos
   et cecinisse modis, Dore[1] poeta, tuis.
haec urant pueros, haec urant scripta puellas,
   meque deum clament et mihi sacra ferant!
te duce vel Iovis arma canam caeloque minantem
   Coeum et Phlegraeis Eurymedonta[2] iugis;
eductosque pares silvestri ex ubere reges,   51
   ordiar et caeso moenia firma Remo,   50
celsaque Romanis decerpta palatia tauris[3]   49
   crescet et ingenium sub tua iussa meum!
prosequar et currus utroque ab litore ovantes,
   Parthorum astutae tela remissa fugae,
castraque Pelusi Romano subruta ferro,
   Antonique graves in sua fata manus.
mollis tu coeptae fautor cape lora iuventae,
   dexteraque immissis da mihi signa rotis.
hoc mihi, Maecenas, laudis concedis, et a te est
   quod ferar in partes ipse fuisse tuas.   60

---

[1] Dore *Scriverius*. dure *NFL*.
[2] Eurymedonta *Huschke*: oromedonta *NFL*.
[3] *49 and 51 transposed by Peiper.*

by the cunning of Pallas, won the day and made the walls, that Neptune built, to be razed by the Greek plough. Enough for me to have found acceptance among the books of Callimachus and to have sung, O Dorian poet, in strains like thine. Let my writings kindle boys and girls to love! Let them acclaim me as a god and bring me sacrifice!

⁴⁷ Be thou my leader, then will I sing of the arms of Jove, of Coeus threatening heaven and Eurymedon on Phlegra's hills: then will I set forth to tell of the kings that were reared together at the wild beast's teat, of the walls that were established by the slaying of Remus, and of the lofty Palatine grazed by the steers of Rome; and my wit shall grow to the height of thy commands. I will hymn thy chariots that triumph from the East and from the West, the shafts now idle of the Parthian's crafty flight, the camp of Pelusium o'erthrown by the sword of Rome, and Antony whose own hands wrought his doom.

⁵⁷ Do thou but grant thy kindly favour, take the reins that guide my youthful course and give me favouring applause when my wheels speed forth in the race. This is the glory thou grantest me, Maecenas, and to thee 'tis due that men shall say that I, even I, have followed thine example.

X

Mirabar, quidnam misissent mane Camenae,
　　ante meum stantes sole rubente torum.
natalis nostrae signum misere puellae
　　et manibus faustos ter crepuere sonos.
transeat hic sine nube dies, stent aere venti,
　　ponat et in sicco molliter unda minax.
aspiciam nullos hodierna luce dolentes,
　　et Niobae lacrimas supprimat ipse lapis,
alcyonum positis requiescant ora querelis,
　　increpet absumptum nec sua mater Ityn.　　　　10
tuque, o cara mihi, felicibus edita pennis,
　　surge et poscentes iusta precare deos.
ac primum pura somnum tibi discute lympha,
　　et nitidas presso pollice finge comas:
dein qua primum oculos cepisti veste Properti
　　indue, nec vacuum flore relinque caput;
et pete, qua polles, ut sit tibi forma perennis,
　　inque meum semper stent tua regna caput.
inde coronatas ubi ture piaveris aras,
　　luxerit et tota flamma secunda domo,　　　　20
sit mensae ratio, noxque inter pocula currat,
　　et crocino nares murreus ungat onyx.
tibia nocturnis succumbat rauca choreis,
　　et sint nequitiae libera verba tuae,
dulciaque ingratos adimant convivia somnos,
　　publica vicinae perstrepat aura viae:

THE ELEGIES OF PROPERTIUS BOOK III

X

I WONDERED what omen the Muses had sent me as they stood before my couch in the red sunlight of dawn. They sent me a token that 'twas the birthday of my mistress, and thrice with propitious sound they clapped their hands. May this day pass to its close without a cloud, may the winds be motionless in heaven, and may the threatening wave sink to calm on the dry shore. To-day may I see none that mourn, and may even the rock that is Niobe withhold its tears. May the sea-birds' mouths have rest, hushed from their wailing, and the mother of Itys cease to moan his death.

11 And do thou, beloved, born under happy auguries, rise and pray to the gods that demand their due offering. First with pure water wash sleep from off thee, and with thy finger's impress tire thy shining hair. Next don that robe wherein thou first didst snare the eyes of Propertius, and let thy brows not lack a crown of flowers. And pray that the beauty that is thy might may endure alway, and that thou mayest be the queen of my heart for ever. Then when thou hast appeased the wreathèd altars with incense and their fire hath flashed its blessing through all the house, give thy thoughts to feasting. Let night speed mid the wine-cup, and let the casket of yellow onyx make glad our nostrils with oil of saffron; let the hoarse pipe blow for the midnight dance till it give o'er for weariness, and let thy wanton words come fast and free. Let the merry banquet keep unwelcome slumbers far, and let the air of the neighbouring street ring loud that all may hear. Let us

SEXTI PROPERTI ELEGIARVM LIBER III

sit sors et nobis talorum interprete iactu,
   quem gravibus pennis verberet ille puer.
cum fuerit multis exacta trientibus hora,
   noctis et instituet sacra ministra Venus,   30
annua solvamus thalamo sollemnia nostro,
   natalisque tui sic peragamus iter.

XI

Qvid mirare, meam si versat femina vitam
   et trahit addictum sub sua iura virum,
criminaque ignavi capitis mihi turpia fingis,
   quod nequeam fracto rumpere vincla iugo?
venturam melius praesagit navita mortem,[1]
   vulneribus didicit miles habere metum.
ista ego praeterita iactavi verba iuventa:
   tu nunc exemplo disce timere meo.
Colchis flagrantes adamantina sub iuga tauros
   egit et armigera proelia sevit humo,   10
custodisque feros clausit serpentis hiatus,
   iret ut Aesonias aurea lana domos.
ausa ferox ab equo quondam oppugnare sagittis
   Maeotis Danaum Penthesilea rates;
aurea cui postquam nudavit cassida frontem,
   vicit victorem candida forma virum.
Omphale in tantum formae processit honorem,
   Lydia Gygaeo tincta puella lacu,

---

[1] venturam *NFL, perhaps corrupt*. ventorum *S. G. Owen.*
mortem *NFL:* motum *S. G. Owen.*

cast lots, let the fall of the dice reveal to us those whom the boy god lashes with heavy pinions. And then when the hours have been sped by many a goblet and Venus appoints those mysteries that wait on night, let us with all solemnity perform the anniversary's rite in our chamber, and thus complete the path of thy natal day.

XI

WHY marvellest thou that a woman sways my life and drags my manhood captive beneath her rule? Why falsely dost thou hurl at me the foul taunt of cowardice, because I cannot snap my chains and break my yoke? 'Tis the mariner best foretells his coming doom, 'tis wounds that teach the soldier fear. I once spake boasts like thine in my past youth: now let my example teach thee to be afraid.

[9] The witch of Colchis drove the fiery bulls beneath the adamantine yoke and sowed battles in the warrior-bearing earth, and closed the fierce, gaping jaws of the guardian snake, that the fleece of gold might go to Aeson's halls. Maeotian Penthesilea once dared on horseback to assail the Danaan ships with her arrows, even she whose bright beauty conquered the conquering hero, when the helm of gold laid bare her brow. Omphale, the maid of Lydia, bathed in the Gygean lake, rose to such renown of beauty that

SEXTI PROPERTI ELEGIARVM LIBER III

ut, qui pacato statuisset in orbe columnas,
   tam dura traheret mollia pensa manu. 20
Persarum statuit Babylona Semiramis urbem,
   ut solidum cocto tolleret aggere opus,
et duo in adversum mitti [1] per moenia currus
   nec possent tacto stringere ab axe latus;
duxit et Euphratem medium, quam condidit, arcis,[2]
   iussit et imperio subdere [3] Bactra caput.
nam quid ego heroas, quid raptem in crimine divos?
   Iuppiter infamat seque suamque domum.
quid, modo quae nostris opprobria vexerit armis
   et famulos inter femina trita suos, 30
coniugis obsceni pretium Romana poposcit
   moenia et addictos in sua regna Patres?
noxia Alexandria, dolis aptissima tellus,
   et totiens nostro Memphi cruenta malo,
tris ubi Pompeio detraxit harena triumphos!
   tollet nulla dies hanc tibi, Roma, notam.
issent Phlegraeo melius tibi funera campo,
   vel tua si socero colla daturus eras.
scilicet incesti meretrix regina Canopi,
   una Philippeo sanguine adusta nota, 40
ausa Iovi nostro latrantem opponere Anubim,
   et Tiberim Nili cogere ferre minas,
Romanamque tubam crepitanti pellere sistro,
   baridos et contis rostra Liburna sequi,

[1] mitti *Tyrrell* · missi *NFL*.
[2] quam *FL*. qua *N*. arcis *Bachrens* arces *NFL*.
[3] subdere *Burmann*. surgere *NFL*.

he, who had set up his pillars in the world he had tamed to peace, with horny hands plucked soft tasks of wool. Semiramis stablished Babylon, the Persian's city, in such wise that it rose a solid mass with wall of brick, and two chariots might be sent to meet each other nor graze their sides with touching axles; and through the midst of the citadel which she founded she led Euphrates, and bade Bactra bow its head to her sway.

27 Why should I tell of heroes, why taunt the gods with sin? Jove brings shame on himself and on his house. Why should I tell of her that of late heaped insults on our arms, that woman who found lovers even among her slaves, and claimed the walls of Rome and the Senate enslaved to her tyranny as a fee from her foul paramour? Guilty Alexandria, land most skilled in guile, and Memphis so often bloodstained with our woe, where the sand robbed Pompey of his three triumphs! No day shall ever free thee of this stain, O Rome! Better for thee, Pompey, had thy funeral gone forth on the Phlegrean plain,[1] or hadst thou been doomed to bow thy neck to thy wife's father! Forsooth the harlot queen of unchaste Canopus, the one disgrace branded on Rome by the race of Philip, dared to match barking Anubis against our Roman Jove, to force Tiber to endure the threats of Nile, to drive out the Roman trumpet with rattling sistrum[2] and with poled barge to pursue the Liburnian galley, to stretch her foul curtains[3] on the

[1] Pompey fell ill at Naples in 50 B.C. Propertius says he would have been happier had he died then. The Phlegrean plains are near Naples. See Index.
[2] The *sistrum* was a rattle used in the worship of Isis.
[3] *I e.*, mosquito-nets.

SEXTI PROPERTI ELEGIARVM LIBER III

foedaque Tarpeio conopia tendere saxo,
  iura dare et statuas inter et arma Mari. 46
septem urbs alta iugis, toto quae praesidet orbi, 57
  femineas¹ timuit territa Marte minas.² 58
quid nunc Tarquinii fractas iuvat esse secures, 47
  nomine quem simili vita superba notat,
si mulier patienda fuit? cape, Roma, triumphum
  et longum Augusto salva precare diem! 50
fugisti tamen in timidi vaga³ flumina Nili:
  accepere tuae Romula vincla manus.
bracchia spectavi sacris admorsa colubris,
  et trahere occultum membra soporis iter.
" Non hoc, Roma, fui⁴ tanto tibi cive verenda!"
  dixit et assiduo lingua sepulta mero. 56
Curtius expletis statuit monumenta lacunis, 61
  at Decius misso proelia rupit equo,
Cochtis abscissos testatur semita pontes,
  est⁵ cui cognomen corvus habere dedit:
haec di condiderant, haec di quoque moenia servant:
  vix timeat salvo Caesare Roma Iovem.
nunc ubi Scipiadae classes, ubi signa Camilli,
  aut modo Pompeia Bospore capta manu, 68
Hannibalis spolia et victi monumenta Syphacis, 59
  et Pyrrhi ad nostros gloria fracta pedes?⁶ 60

---

¹ femineo *Postgate*: femineas *NFL*.
² 57, 58 *transposed by Butler after 46. 58 om. N.*
³ vaga ς: vada *NFL*.   ⁴ fui ς: fuit *NFL*.
⁵ est *Puccius* et *NFL*.
⁶ 59, 60 *transposed by Passerat after 68.*

Tarpeian rock, and to give judgment amid the arms and statues of Marius. The city high-throned on the seven hills, the queen of all the world, was terrified by a woman's might and feared her threats! What boots it now to have broken the axes of Tarquin, whose proud life brands him with the name of "proud," if we must needs endure a woman's tyranny? Rome, take thy triumph and, saved from doom, implore long life for Augustus. Yet didst thou fly, O queen, to the wandering streams of timorous Nile! Thy hands received the chains of Rome. I saw her arms bitten by the sacred asps, I saw her limbs drink in slumber as it worked its secret way. "Thou needst not have feared me, Rome, with such a citizen to guard thee!" so spake even the tongue that deep draughts of wine had enslaved.

[61] Curtius closed the gulf and made himself an everlasting memorial: Decius brake the battle-line with charging steed; the path of Cocles still tells of the cutting of the bridge: and one there is who won his name from a raven. The gods founded these walls, and the gods protect them; while Caesar lives scarce should Rome fear the wrath of Jove! Now where are Scipio's fleets, where the standards of Camillus, or thou, O Bosporus, so lately captured by the might of Pompey? Where are the spoils of Hannibal and the trophies of conquered Syphax, and Pyrrhus' glory

SEXTI PROPERTI ELEGIARVM LIBER III

Leucadius versas acies memorabit Apollo: 69
    tantum operis belli sustulit una dies. 70
at tu, sive petes portus seu, navita, linques,
    Caesaris in toto sis memor Ionio.

XII

Postvme, plorantem potuisti linquere Gallam,
    miles et Augusti fortia signa sequi?
tantine ulla fuit spoliati gloria Parthi,
    ne faceres [1] Galla multa rogante tua?
si fas est, omnes pariter pereatis avari,
    et quisquis fido praetulit arma toro!
tu tamen iniecta [2] tectus, vesane, lacerna
    potabis galea fessus Araxis aquam.
illa quidem interea fama tabescet inani,
    haec tua ne virtus fiat amara tibi, 10
neve tua Medae laetentur caede sagittae,
    ferreus aurato neu cataphractus equo,
neve aliquid de te flendum referatur in urna:
    sic redeunt,[3] illis qui cecidere locis.
ter quater in casta felix, o Postume, Galla!
    moribus his alia coniuge dignus eras!
quid faciet nullo munita puella timore,
    cum sit luxuriae Roma magistra suae?[4]
sed securus eas: Gallam non munera vincent,
    duritiaeque tuae non erit illa memor. 20

[1] faceres *N*. facias *FL*.   [2] iniecta *Itali*: intecta *NFL*.
[3] sic redeunt ς: si credunt *N*. si credent *FL*.
[4] suae ς; tuae *NFL*.

broken beneath our feet? Leucadian Apollo shall tell how the hosts were turned to flight: one day of war swept away so vast an armament! But do thou, O mariner, whether thou seekest or leavest the haven, remember Caesar o'er all the Ionian main.

XII

Postumus, hadst thou the heart to leave Galla weeping and to follow the gallant standards of Augustus to the wars? Was any glory from Parthia's spoils worth aught to thee, when thy Galla oft prayed thee not to go? If it be lawful, may all ye that are greedy for gold perish alike, and with you the man that loves arms more than a faithful bride!

[7] Yet thou, madman, with thy cloak cast about thee for covering shalt drink the water of Araxes from thy helmet when thou art weary; and she meanwhile will pine at each idle rumour, for fear lest thy valour cost thee dear, or lest the Median arrows rejoice in thy death or the mailed soldier on his gilded steed; or lest some scanty relics of thee be brought home in an urn for her to weep; thus they return that perish in those lands

[15] Thrice and four times blest, O Postumus, art thou in Galla's chastity! With a heart like thine thou wast worthy of a different spouse! What will a woman do with no fear for safeguard, when there is Rome to teach its luxury? But go without fear; no gifts shall conquer Galla and she will not remember

nam quocumque die salvum te fata remittent,
　　pendebit collo Galla pudica tuo
Postumus alter erit miranda coniuge Vlixes:
　　non illi longae tot nocuere morae,
castra decem annorum, et Ciconum mons Ismara, Calpe,
　　exustaeque tuae mox, Polypheme, genae,
et Circae fraudes, lotosque herbaeque tenaces,
　　Scyllaque et alternas scissa Charybdis aquas,
Lampeties Ithacis veribus mugisse iuvencos
　　(paverat hos Phoebo filia Lampetie),　　　　　　30
et thalamum Aeaeae flentis fugisse puellae,
　　totque hiemis noctes totque natasse dies,
nigrantesque domos animarum intrasse silentum,
　　Sirenum surdo remige adisse lacus,
et veteres arcus leto renovasse procorum,
　　errorisque sui sic statuisse modum.
nec frustra, quia casta domi persederat uxor.
　　vincit Penelopes Aelia[1] Galla fidem.

XIII

QVAERITIS, unde avidis nox sit pretiosa puellis,
　　et Venerem exhaustae damna querantur opes.
certa quidem tantis causa et manifesta ruinis:
　　luxuriae nimium libera facta via est.
Inda cavis aurum mittit formica metallis,
　　et venit e Rubro concha Erycina salo,

[1] Aelia *Passerat*: laelia *NFL*.

thy cruelty. For whensoe'er fate sends thee home in safety, chaste Galla shall hang about thy neck. Postumus shall be another Ulysses with a wife to wake men's wonder: no hurt did Ulysses suffer from his long tarrying, no hurt from the ten years' leaguer, from Ismara the Ciconians' mount, from Calpe, and thereafter the burning of thine eye, O Polyphemus; no hurt from the guile of Circe, the lotos with its binding spell, nor from Scylla and Charybdis, cloven with alternate ebb and flow, nor when Lampetie's oxen bellowed on the Ithacan spits (Lampetie, Phoebus' daughter, had pastured them for her sire), nor when he fled from the couch of Acaea's weeping queen, or swam the deep so many nights and days, entered the dark halls of the silent ghosts, and with his rowers drew nigh the Siren's pools, revived his ancient bow with the suitors' slaughter, and thus set a term to his wanderings. And not in vain, for his wife had remained true to him at home. Aelia Galla shall surpass Penelope's fidelity.

XIII

YE ask, wherefore the greed of women makes their love so costly, and wherefore our empty coffers cry out that Venus has been their bane. Clear and undoubted is the cause of such vast ruin; the path of luxury has grown overfree. The Indian ant[1] sends gold from the caves of the mine, the nautilus

[1] Both Pliny and Herodotus assert that somewhere in India gold-dust was brought from underground by ants in winter, and in summer stolen by the Indians, the ants having retired to their nests owing to the heat.

SEXTI PROPERTI ELEGIARVM LIBER III

et Tyros ostrinos praebet Cadmea colores,
    cinnamon et multi pastor odoris Arabs:
haec etiam clausas expugnant arma pudicas,
    quaeque gerunt[1] fastus, Icarioti, tuos.   10
matrona incedit census induta nepotum
    et spolia opprobrii nostra per ora trahit.
nulla est poscendi, nulla est reverentia dandi,
    aut si qua est, pretio tollitur ipsa mora.
felix Eois lex funeris una maritis,
    quos Aurora suis rubra colorat equis!
namque ubi mortifero iacta est fax ultima lecto,
    uxorum fusis stat pia turba comis,
et certamen habent leti, quae viva sequatur
    coniugium: pudor est non licuisse mori.   20
ardent victrices et flammae pectora praebent,
    imponuntque suis ora perusta viris.
hoc genus infidum nuptarum, hic nulla puella
    nec fida Euadne nec pia Penelope.
felix agrestum quondam pacata iuventus,
    divitiae quorum messis et arbor erant!
illis munus erant decussa[2] Cydonia ramo,
    et dare puniceis plena canistra rubis,
nunc violas tondere manu, nunc mixta referre
    lilia virgineos lucida per calathos,   30
et portare suis vestitas frondibus uvas
    aut variam plumae versicoloris[3] avem.
his tum blanditiis furtiva per antra puellae
    oscula silvicolis empta dedere viris.

[1] gerunt *Scioppius:* terunt *NFL.*
[2] decussa *FL:* discussa *N.*
[3] versicoloris ς. viricoloris *NFL:* vitricoloris *Ellis.*

shell comes from the Red Sea; Cadmean Tyre sends hues of purple, and the Arab shepherd rich-scented cinnamon. These weapons storm the hearts even of close-guarded virgins and such as are cold as thou, O daughter of Icarius. Matrons go forth arrayed in spendthrifts' fortunes and flaunt the spoils of infamy before our eyes. No shame is there in asking or in giving; or if any there be, even reluctance is banished at a price.

15 Blest is that peerless law for the burial of Eastern husbands, whom the crimson dawn colours with her steeds! For when the last torch is set to the dead man's bier his wives stand round, a pious company with streaming hair, and struggle for death one with another, who living shall follow her dead lord; 'tis shame to be debarred from death. The victors burn and offer their breasts to the flame and lay charred faces on their husband's body. But here the race of brides is faithless; here doth no woman show Evadne's faith or Penelope's loyalty.

25 Happy the young that dwelt in peace of old, whose wealth was in harvest and orchard. Their offerings were Cydonian apples shaken from the bough; they gave baskets filled with purple brambles, now with their hands plucked violets, now brought home shining lilies mingled together in the maidens' paniers, and carried grapes clad in their own leaves or some dappled bird of rainbow plumage. Bought by such wooing as this were the kisses that girls gave their silvan lovers in secret caves. A roe-

SEXTI PROPERTI ELEGIARVM LIBER III

hinnulei[1] pellis totos operibat amantis,
  altaque nativo creverat herba toro,
pinus et incumbens laetas[2] circumdabat umbras;
  nec fuerat nudas poena videre deas;
corniger atque dei vacuam pastoris in aulam
  dux aries saturas ipse reduxit oves;   40
dique deaeque omnes, quibus est tutela per agros,
  praebebant nostris[3] verba benigna focis:
" Et leporem, quicumque venis, venaberis, hospes,
  et si forte meo tramite quaeris avem:
et me Pana tibi comitem de rupe vocato,
  sive petes calamo praemia, sive cane."
at nunc desertis cessant sacraria lucis:
  aurum omnes victa iam pietate colunt.
auro pulsa fides, auro venalia iura,
  aurum lex sequitur, mox sine lege pudor.   50
torrida sacrilegum testantur limina[4] Brennum,
  dum petit intonsi Pythia regna dei:
at mox[5] laurigero concussus vertice diras
  Gallica Parnasus sparsit in arma nives.
te[6] scelus accepto Thracis Polymestoris auro
  nutrit in hospitio non, Polydore, pio.[7]
tu quoque ut auratos gereres, Eriphyla, lacertos,
  dilapsis nusquam est Amphiaraus equis.

[1] hinnulei *Scaliger*: atque hinuli *N*: atque humili *FL*.
[2] letas *F*: lentas *NL*.   [3] nostris *Butler*: vestris *NFL*.
[4] limina *N*: lumina *FL*.   [5] mox *FL*: mons *N*.
[6] te *Itali*: et *NFL*   [7] pio *N*: tuo *FL*.

deer's skin was enough to cover two lovers, and the grass grew tall to make them nature's couch. The pine bowed o'er them and cast its rich shade about them; nor was it a sin to see goddesses naked: the horned ram of his own accord led back his ewes sated with grazing to the empty fold of the shepherd god. All gods and goddesses that guard the countryside spake kindly words to the hearths of men. "Stranger, whoe'er thou art that comest, thou shalt hunt the hare in my paths or the bird, if bird thou seekest: and whether thou pursuest thy prize with lime-rod or with hound, call me Pan from the crag to be thy comrade."

⁴⁷ But now the shrines lie neglected in deserted groves: piety is vanquished and all men worship gold. Gold has banished faith, gold has made judgment to be bought and sold, gold rules the law, and, law once gone, rules chastity as well.

⁵¹ Portals of burning fire [1] bear witness to the sacrilege of Brennus, when he assailed the Pythian realms of the god unshorn: and soon Parnassus shook its laurel-bearing peak and scattered its snows over the arms of Gaul. Thee, Polydorus, did guilty Polymestor, bought by the gold of Thrace, nurture with treacherous hospitality. That thou too, Eriphyla, mightest deck thy shoulders with gold, the steeds of Amphiaraus are sunken and earth knows him no more.

[1] See p. 157, note 2. The Gauls were discomfited by thunder and lightning, a snowstorm and a fall of rocks from Parnassus according to Pausanias.

SEXTI PROPERTI ELEGIARVM LIBER III

proloquar:—atque utinam patriae sim verus
 haruspex!—
frangitur ipsa suis Roma superba bonis.   60
certa loquor, sed nulla fides; neque enim Ilia
 quondam
verax Pergameis Maenas habenda malis:
sola Parim Phrygiae fatum componere, sola
 fallacem patriae serpere dixit equum.
ille furor patriae fuit utilis, ille parenti:
 experta est veros irrita lingua deos.

XIV

MVLTA tuae, Sparte, miramur iura palaestrae,
 sed mage virginei tot bona gymnasii,
quod non infames exercet corpore ludos[1]
 inter luctantes nuda puella viros,
cum pila veloces fallit per bracchia iactus,
 increpat et versi clavis adunca trochi,
pulverulentaque ad extremas stat femina metas,
 et patitur duro vulnera pancratio:
nunc ligat ad caestum gaudentia bracchia loris,
 missile nunc disci pondus in orbe rotat,   10
et modo Taygeti, crines aspersa pruina,   15
 sectatur patrios per iuga longa canes,[2]   16
gyrum pulsat equis, niveum latus ense revincit,   11
 virgineumque cavo protegit aere caput,

[1] ludos *Auratus*: laudes *NFL*.
[2] 15, 16 transposed after 10 by Housman.

226

THE ELEGIES OF PROPERTIUS BOOK III

[59] I will speak out; and may my country find me a true seer! Rome is being shattered by her own prosperity. I speak sure truth, but none believe me; for neither was the frenzied maid of Ilium ever to be deemed a true seer amid the woes of Troy: she only cried that Paris was building Phrygia's doom, she only that, freighted with treachery, the horse stole on her home. Her madness carried profit for her country and for her sire. The tongue that none believed proved that the gods were true.

XIV

At many of the laws of thy wrestling-grounds do I marvel, O Sparta, but most at the plenteous blessings of the schools where thy women train, inasmuch as a girl may without blame disport her body naked among wrestling men, when the swift-thrown ball cheats the player's grasp and the hooked rod clanks against the rolling hoop, and dust-besprinkled the woman stands at the race's furthest goal and endures wounds in the cruel boxing-match.[1] Now she binds the glove to her hands that rejoice in its thongs, now whirls in a circle the discus' flying weight; now with hoar-frost sprinkling her hair she follows her father's hounds o'er the long ridges of Taygetus, now tramples the ring with her steeds, girds the sword to her snowy flank and shields her virgin head with hollow

[1] The *pancratium* has no English equivalent: it was a rough-and-tumble fight combining boxing and wrestling.

SEXTI PROPERTI ELEGIARVM LIBER III

qualis Amazonidum nudatis bellica mammis
   Thermodontiacis turba lavatur aquis;   14
qualis et Eurotae Pollux et Castor harenis,[1]   17
   hic victor pugnis, ille futurus equis,
inter quos Helene nudis capere arma papillis
   fertur nec fratres erubuisse deos.   20
lex igitur Spartana vetat secedere amantes,
   et licet in triviis ad latus esse suae,
nec timor aut ulla est clausae tutela puellae,
   nec gravis austeri poena cavenda viri.
nullo praemisso de rebus tute loquaris
   ipse tuis: longae nulla repulsa morae.
nec Tyriae vestes errantia lumina fallunt,
   est neque odoratae cura molesta comae.[2]
at nostra ingenti vadit circumdata turba,
   nec digitum angusta est inseruisse via;   30
nec quae sint facies nec quae sint verba rogandi
   invenias: caecum versat amator iter.
quod si iura fores pugnasque imitata Laconum,
   carior hoc esses tu mihi, Roma, bono.

XV

Sic ego non ullos iam norim in amore tumultus,
   nec veniat sine te nox vigilanda mihi!
ut mihi praetexti pudor est velatus amictus[3]
   et data libertas noscere amoris iter,

---

[1] harenis *Volscus*: habenis *N*: athenis *FL*.
[2] odoratae *FL*: adoratae *N*. comae *Canter*. domi *NFL*.
[3] praetexti *N*: praetexta *FL*. amictus *L*. amicus *NF*.

bronze, like the warrior throng of Amazons who bathe bare-bosomed in Thermodon's stream, or as Pollux and Castor on Eurotas' sands, the one destined to conquer with his fists, the other with his steeds: amid these twain, men say, Helen bared her breasts and carried arms, nor called a blush to her brother's cheek.

[21] Thus Sparta's law forbids lovers to hold aloof and grants to each to walk by his mistress' side in the open streets; there none fear for her honour nor keep her under watch and ward: there none need dread the bitter vengeance of some stern husband. Thou needst no herald; thyself thou mayst speak of thine own business; no long delay shall affront thee. No raiment of Tyrian purple beguiles the wandering eyes of lovers, nor shall thy mistress vex thee with long tiring of her scented hair.

[29] But here my love goes girt by a vast crowd, leaving no narrow passage whereby so much as a finger may reach her. Nor canst thou discover what mien to wear nor with what words to proffer thy request: shrouded in darkness is the path o'er which the lover ponders. But if thou, O Rome, wouldst but follow the laws and wrestling of the Spartans, then wouldst thou be the dearer to me for this blessing.

XV

So may I know no further storms in my love, nor may ever the night come whereon I must lie wakeful without thee! When the modesty of my boyhood's garb[1] was hidden away, and freedom was given me

[1] Before the age of puberty boys wore a striped toga (*praetexta*). On reaching puberty they assumed the *toga virilis*, which was all of white.

SEXTI PROPERTI ELEGIARVM LIBER III

illa rudes animos per noctes conscia primas
    imbuit, heu nullis capta Lycinna datis!
tertius (haud multo minus est) cum ducitur annus,
    vix memini nobis verba coisse decem.
cuncta tuus sepelivit amor, nec femina post te
    ulla dedit collo dulcia vincla meo.   10

   .   .   .   .   .

[1] testis erit Dirce tam vero crimine saeva,
    Nycteos Antiopen accubuisse Lyco.
a quotiens pulchros ussit regina capillos,
    molliaque immites [2] fixit in ora manus!
a quotiens famulam pensis oneravit iniquis,
    et caput in dura ponere iussit humo!
saepe illam immundis passa est habitare tenebris,
    vilem ieiunae saepe negavit aquam.
Iuppiter, Antiopae nusquam succurris habenti
    tot mala? corrumpit dura catena manus.   20
si deus es, tibi turpe tuam servire puellam:
    invocet Antiope quem nisi vincta [3] Iovem?
sola tamen, quaecumque aderant in corpore vires,
    regales manicas rupit utraque manu.
inde Cithaeronis timido pede currit in arces
    nox erat, et sparso triste cubile gelu.
saepe vago [4] Asopi sonitu permota fluentis
    credebat dominae pone venire pedes.

---

[1] *At this point NFL mark a new elegy. Some verses have clearly fallen out*
[2] immites ς: immittens *NFL*.
[3] vincta ς: victa *NFL*.   [4] vago *F*: vaga *NL*.

to know the paths of love, 'twas she, Lycinna, won, ah me! by no gifts of mine, that initiated my innocent soul on those first nights wherein she shared my love. 'Tis now the third year since then, but little less, and I can scarce remember that ten words have passed between us. All things thy love has buried, nor since thee has any woman cast sweet chains about my neck.

[*Spare Lycinna, lest vengeance fall on thee!*] Dirce shall be my witness, Dirce maddened with anger by the tale none might gainsay, that Antiope, daughter of Nycteus, had lain with Lycus. Ah! how often did the queen burn her fair tresses and clutch her tender face with relentless hands! How often she loaded her handmaid with unjust tasks and bade her lay her head upon the hard ground! Often she suffered her to dwell in foul darkness, oft she refused even worthless water to allay her thirst. Jove, wilt thou never aid Antiope so deep in woe? The hard chains gall her hands. If thou art a god, 'tis shame that she whom thou didst love should be a slave; on whom should Antiope call from her chains save on Jove? Yet unaided, summoning all her body's strength, with either hand she brake the tyrant chains. Then with trembling feet she ran to the heights of Cithaeron. 'Twas night, and her couch was bitter with scattered frost. Oft scared by the wandering sound of the rushing Asopus, she deemed that the feet of her mistress were pursuing.

SEXTI PROPERTI ELEGIARVM LIBER III

et durum Zethum et lacrimis Amphiona mollem
   experta est stabulis[1] mater abacta suis.   30
ac veluti, magnos cum ponunt aequora motus,
   Eurus ubi adverso desinit ire Noto,[2]
litore sic tacito sonitus rarescit harenae,
   sic cadit inflexo lapsa puella genu.
sera, tamen pietas: natis est cognitus error.
   digne Iovis natos qui tueare senex,
tu reddis pueris matrem; puerique trahendam
   vinxerunt Dircen sub trucis ora bovis.
Antiope, cognosce Iovem: tibi gloria Dirce
   ducitur in multis mortem habitura locis.   40
prata[3] cruentantur Zethi, victorque canebat
   paeana Amphion rupe, Aracynthe, tua.
at tu non meritam parcas vexare Lycinnam:
   nescit vestra ruens ira referre pedem.
fabula nulla tuas de nobis concitet aures:
   te solam et lignis funeris ustus amem.

XVI

Nox media, et dominae mihi venit epistula nostrae:
   Tibure me missa iussit adesse mora,
candida qua geminas ostendunt culmina turres,
   et cadit in patulos nympha Aniena lacus.
quid faciam? obductis committam mene tenebris,
   ut timeam audaces in mea membra manus?

---

[1] stabulis ς. tabulis *NFL*.
[2] ubi adverso ... Noto *Lachmann*: sub adverso ... notho *N* in adversos ... notos *FL*.   [3] prata ς: parta *NFL*.

Her tears found Zethus unmoved and Amphion pitiful, when she, their mother, was driven from the steading that was of right her own. And as when the waves give over their huge heavings, what time the East Wind ceases to strive with the wind of the South-West, and so the shore is stilled and the sound of the wave-swept sand grows less and less, so gradually sank she down on her bended knee. At length, though late, they showed their love; her sons knew their error. Worthy wert thou, old man, to tend the sons of Jove; thou didst restore the mother to her boys, and they bound Dirce beneath the head of a fierce bull to be dragged to death. Antiope, recognise the power of Jove! Dirce, now thy proud boast, is drawn along to find death in many a spot. The fields of Zethus are red with blood, and Amphion sang the paean of victory on thy rocks, O Aracynthus.

[43] But do thou spare to torment guiltless Lycinna: anger of jealous woman knows no turning back. And may no tale concerning us ever alarm thine ears; may I love thee only even when the funeral pile hath consumed me.

XVI

'Twas midnight when a letter came to me from my mistress bidding me come without delay to Tibur, where the white hills heave up their towers to right and left and Anio's waters plunge into spreading pools. What should I do? Trust myself to the dark that shrouded all and tremble lest my limbs should be gripped by ruffian hands? Yet if I should

SEXTI PROPERTI ELEGIARVM LIBER III

at si distulero haec nostro mandata timore,
  nocturno fletus saevior hoste mihi.
peccaram semel, et totum sum pulsus[1] in annum:
  in me mansuetas non habet illa manus. 10
nec tamen est quisquam, sacros qui laedat amantes:
  Scironis media sic licet[2] ire via.
quisquis amator erit, Scythicis licet ambulet[3] oris,
  nemo adeo[4] ut noceat barbarus esse volet.
luna ministrat iter, demonstrant astra salebras,
  ipse Amor accensas praecutit[5] ante faces,
saeva canum rabies morsus avertit hiantis:
  huic generi quovis tempore tuta via est.
sanguine tam parvo quis enim spargatur amantis
  improbus, et cuius sit[6] comes ipsa Venus? 20
quod si certa meos sequerentur funera casus,
  tali[7] mors pretio vel sit emenda mihi.
afferet huc unguenta mihi sertisque sepulcrum
  ornabit custos ad mea busta sedens.
di faciant, mea ne terra locet ossa frequenti,
  qua facit assiduo tramite vulgus iter!
post mortem tumuli sic infamantur amantum.
  me tegat arborea devia terra coma,
aut humer ignotae cumulis vallatus harenae:
  non iuvat in media nomen habere via. 30

[1] pulsus *FL*. portus *N*.
[2] sic licet *ς*: scilicet *N*. si licet *FL*.
[3] Scythiae *inscriptio Pompeiana, C.I.L. 4, 1950.* ambulet *inscr. Pomp.*. ambulat *NFL*.
[4] adeo *inscr. Pomp.*. deo *NFL* feriat *inscr Pomp.*
[5] praecutit *Guyetus* percutit *NFL*.
[6] et cuius sit *Palmer:* exclusis fit *NFL*.
[7] tali *ς* · talis *NFL*.

put off obedience out of fear, her tears would be more terrible than any midnight foe. Once had I sinned, and was rejected for a whole year long. Against me her hands are merciless.

11 Yet there is none would hurt a lover: lovers are sacred: lovers might travel Sciron's road unscathed. A lover, though he walk on Scythia's shores, will find none so savage as to have heart to harm him. The moon lights his path; the stars show forth the rough places, and Love himself waves the flaming torch before him; the fierce watchdog turns aside his gaping fangs. For such as him the road is safe at any hour Who is so cruel as to embrue his hands in a lover's worthless blood, above all when Venus herself bears him company?

21 But did I know that if I perished I should surely receive due rites of burial, death would be worth the purchase at such price. She will bring unguents to my pyre and adorn my tomb with wreaths, she will sit beside my grave and keep watch there. God grant she place not my bones in some crowded spot, where the rabble journeys on the busy highway. Thus after death are lovers' tombs dishonoured. Let me be shadowed by leafy trees in some field far from the roadside; else let me be buried walled in by heaps of nameless sand. I would not that my name should be recorded amid the bustle of the street.

SEXTI PROPERTI ELEGIARVM LIBER III

XVII

Nvnc, o Bacche, tuis humiles advolvimur aris:
    da mihi pacato vela secunda, pater.
tu potes insanae Veneris compescere fastus,
    curarumque tuo fit medicina mero.
per te iunguntur, per te solvuntur amantes:
    tu vitium ex animo dilue, Bacche, meo.
te quoque enim non esse rudem testatur in astris
    lyncibus ad caelum vecta Ariadna tuis
hoc mihi, quod veteres custodit in ossibus ignes,
    funera sanabunt aut tua vina malum   10
semper enim vacuos nox sobria torquet amantes,
    spesque timorque animos[1] versat utroque modo.
quod si, Bacche, tuis per fervida tempora donis
    accersitus erit somnus in ossa mea,
ipse seram vitis pangamque ex ordine collis,
    quos carpant nullae me vigilante ferae.
dum modo purpureo cumulem[2] mihi dolia musto,
    et nova pressantis inquinet uva pedes,
quod superest vitae per te et tua cornua vivam,
    virtutisque tuae, Bacche, poeta ferar.   20
dicam ego maternos Aetnaeo fulmine partus,
    Indica Nysaeis arma fugata choris,
vesanumque nova nequiquam in vite Lycurgum,
    Pentheos in triplices funera grata greges,

---

[1] animos *Beroaldus* animo *NFL*.
[2] cumulem *Postgate:* numen *N*. numerem *L:* nũẽ *F*.

THE ELEGIES OF PROPERTIUS BOOK III

XVII

Now, O Bacchus, I cast me down before thine altars in lowly supplication; O father, give me peace and prosper my sails. Though Venus be frenzied, thou canst quell her scorn, and woes find healing from thy wine. By thee are lovers yoked, by thee set free; do thou, O Bacchus, wash this weakness from my soul. Thou also art not unversed in love; to that Ariadne rapt heavenward in thy lynx-drawn car bears witness among the stars. This curse that for many a year hath kept a fire ablaze within my bones only death or thy wine shall heal. For a sober night is always torment to lonely lovers, and hope and fear rack their spirits this way and that.

13 But if, O Bacchus, by thy gifts making my brain to burn thou shalt bring sleep to rest my bones, then will I sow vines and plant my hills with rows, and will watch that no beasts of the wild make havoc thereon. If only I may crown my vats with purple must and the new grape may dye my feet that tread the wine-press, then through all my life to come thou and thine horns shall give me life and men shall call me the poet of thy virtue, O Bacchus.

21 I will sing how the thunderbolt of Etna's forge blasted thy mother[1] and brought thee to the birth, how the warriors of Ind were driven in flight by Nysa's dancers, how Lycurgus maddened in vain over the new-found vine, how Pentheus' death brought joy

[1] See Semela, Index

SEXTI PROPERTI ELEGIARVM LIBER III

curvaque Tyrrhenos delphinum corpora nautas
   in vada pampinea desiluisse rate,
et tibi per mediam bene olentia flumina Diam,[1]
   unde tuum potant Naxia turba merum.
candida laxatis onerato colla corymbis
   cinget Bassaricas Lydia mitra comas,   30
levis odorato cervix manabit olivo,
   et feries nudos veste fluente pedes
mollia Dircaeae pulsabunt tympana Thebae,
   capripedes calamo Panes hiante canent,
vertice turrigero iuxta dea magna Cybelle
   tundet[2] ad Idaeos cymbala rauca choros.
ante fores templi crater antistitis auro
   libabit[3] fundens in tua sacra merum.
haec ego non humili referam memoranda coturno,
   qualis Pindarico spiritus ore tonat: 40
tu modo servitio vacuum me siste superbo,
   atque hoc sollicitum vince sopore caput.

XVIII

CLAVSVS ab umbroso qua alludit[4] pontus Averno
   umida Baiarum stagna tepentis aquae,
qua iacet et Troiae tubicen Misenus harena,
   et sonat Herculeo structa labore via;
hic, ubi, mortales dexter cum quaereret urbes,
   cymbala Thebano concrepuere deo :—

---

[1] Diam *Palmer*; Naxon *NFL*.
[2] tundet *Scaliger*: fundet *NFL*
[3] libabit *Foster*. libatum *NFL*.
[4] alludit *Lambinus*: ludit *NFL*.

to the three companies of Maenads, how the Tuscan sailors, turned to curved dolphin-shapes, leapt into the sea from the vine-clad ship, and how fragrant streams flowed for thee through Dia's midst and the folk of Naxos drank thy wine therefrom. While thy white neck bows beneath the trailing ivy-clusters, the Lydian turban shall crown thy hair, O Bassareus. Thy smooth throat shall stream with scented oil of olive, and thy flowing robe shall strike thy naked feet. Dircean Thebes shall beat the womanish timbrel for thee, and goat-footed Pans shall make music on the cloven reed. Hard by the great goddess, Cybelle, her head tower-crowned, shall clash the harsh cymbals to the Idaean dance. Before the temple gates shall stand the bowl, and the priest shall draw wine therefrom with golden ladle and pour it on thy sacrifice.

39 Of all this will I sing, things meet for no lowly accent, but with such voice as thundered from the lips of Pindar. Do thou only set me free from this haughty tyranny and vanquish mine anguished soul with slumber.

XVIII

WHERE the sea, shut out from dark-shadowed Avernus, beats with its laughing wave on Baiae's warm and steaming pools, where Misenus, trumpeter of Troy, lies in his sandy tomb, and the way built by the toil of Hercules is loud with the sea-billow; where the cymbals clashed in honour of the Theban god, when with kindly intent he visited the cities of men—but

SEXTI PROPERTI ELEGIARVM LIBER III

at nunc invisae magno cum crimine Baiae,
    quis deus in vestra constitit hostis aqua?—
hic[1] pressus Stygias vultum demisit in undas,
    errat et in vestro spiritus ille lacu.   10
quid genus aut virtus aut optima profuit illi
    mater, et amplexum Caesaris esse focos?
aut modo tam pleno fluitantia vela theatro,
    et per maternas omnia gesta manus?
occidit, et misero steterat vicesimus annus:
    tot bona tam parvo clausit in orbe dies.
i nunc, tolle animos et tecum finge triumphos,
    stantiaque in plausum tota theatra iuvent,
Attalicas supera vestes, atque omnia magnis
    gemmea sint ludis: ignibus ista dabis.   20
sed tamen huc omnes, huc[2] primus et ultimus
    ordo:
est mala, sed cunctis ista terenda via est;
exoranda canis tria sunt latrantia colla,
    scandenda est torvi[3] publica cumba senis.
ille licet ferro cautus se condat et aere,
    mors tamen inclusum protrahit inde caput.
Nirea non facies, non vis exemit Achillem,
    Croesum aut, Pactoli quas parit umor opes.
[hic olim ignaros luctus populavit Achivos,
    Atridae magno cum stetit alter amor.[4]]   30

---

[1] hic *Guyet*: his *NFL*.
[2] huc ... huc *f*: hoc ... huc *NFL*.
[3] torvi *f*. torti *FL*: -troci *N*.
[4] *This couplet is clearly alien to its present context. It is conceivable that it should be transposed to follow* II VI. 16.

THE ELEGIES OF PROPERTIUS BOOK III

now, ah, hateful Baiae, dark with deep guilt, what baleful god stands by your waters?—here he sank smitten down to the Stygian wave,[1] and that noble spirit wanders o'er your mere.

[11] What availed him birth or virtue or his mother's piety? What availed him his union with the house of Caesar, or the waving awnings of the theatre so thronged but yesterday, or all that his mother's hands had wrought for him? He is dead, cut short unhappy in his twentieth year. Such glory compassed in such narrow room!

[17] Go to now, exalt thy soul with pride and dream of triumphs, rejoice when whole theatres spring to their feet to cheer, outdo the cloth-of-gold of Attalus, at the great games let all be bright with gems! All these glories thou shalt yield up to the fires of death. And yet hither at last come all, come noble and come base; bitter is the way, but all must tread it; all must assuage the triple throat of the baying hound, and climb the boat of that grim greybeard that waits for all. Though a man seek to save himself by walls of iron and of brass, yet death shall drag forth his head from its sheltering place. Beauty saved not Nireus, nor might Achilles; nor was Croesus succoured by wealth born of Pactolus stream.

[[29] Such grief once wasted the perplexed Achivi, when Atrides' new passion cost them dear.]

---

[1] Marcellus, nephew of Augustus, died at Baiae 23 B.C.

SEXTI PROPERTI ELEGIARVM LIBER III

at tibi, nauta, pias hominum qui traicis umbras,
   hoc animae portent corpus inane suae : [1]
qua Siculae victor telluris Claudius et qua
   Caesar, ab humana cessit in astra via.

XIX

Obicitvr totiens a te mihi nostra libido :
   crede mihi, vobis imperat ista magis.
vos, ubi contempti rupistis frena pudoris,
   nescitis captae mentis habere modum.
flamma per incensas citius sedetur aristas,
   fluminaque ad fontis sint reditura caput,
et placidum Syrtes portum et bona litora nautis
   praebeat hospitio saeva Malea suo,
quam possit vestros quisquam reprehendere cursus
   et rapidae stimulos frangere nequitiae.   10
testis, Cretaei fastus quae passa iuvenci
   induit abiegnae cornua falsa bovis ;
testis Thessalico flagrans Salmonis Enipeo,
   quae voluit liquido tota subire deo.
crimen et illa fuit, patria succensa senecta
   arboris in frondes condita Myrrha novae.
nam quid Medeae referam, quo tempore matris
   iram natorum caede piavit amor ?
quidve Clytaemestrae, propter quam tota Mycenis
   infamis stupro stat Pelopea domus ?   20

[1] hoc *Lachmann*; huc *NFL*. suae *Markland*: tuae *NFL*.

[31] But to thee, O ferryman of pious souls, let them bear this body void of its spirit; his soul hath soared starward far from the paths of men by the road that Claudius and Caesar trod.

XIX

Oft thou reproachest me with the lust that rules us men. Believe me, 'tis rather of your womankind that lust is lord. Ye, when ye have burst the reins of despised modesty, ne'er set a limit to the frenzy of your heart. Sooner shall the flame be quenched amid the burning corn, and streams return to the fountain whence they sprang, sooner shall the Syrtes yield a calm haven and wild Malea give the mariner kindly welcome on its shores, than any man shall have power to check you in your course or break the goads of your headlong wantonness.

[11] Witness be she that suffered the scorn of the Cretan bull, and put on the false horns of the fir-wood cow. Witness Salmoneus' daughter that burned with passion for Thessalian Enipeus, and was ready to yield all her body to the watery god. Myrrha too is a reproach to your sex, that, fired with love for her aged sire, was transformed and hidden in the leaves of a strange tree. For why should I tell of Medea, when the mother, dearly though she loved her children, appeased her anger by their slaughter? Or why should I tell of Clytemestra, that in Mycenae brought shame on all the house of Pelops by her adultery?

SEXTI PROPERTI ELEGIARVM LIBER III

tuque, o Minoa venumdata Scylla figura,
  tondes[1] purpurea regna paterna coma.
hanc igitur dotem virgo desponderat hosti!
  Nise, tuas portas fraude reclusit amor.
at vos, innuptae, felicius urite taedas:
  pendet Cretaea tracta puella rate.
non tamen immerito Minos sedet arbiter Orci:
  victor erat quamvis, aequus in hoste fuit.

XX

Credis cum iam posse tuae meminisse figurae,
  vidisti a lecto quem dare vela tuo?
durus, qui lucro potuit mutare puellam!
  tantine, his[2] lacrimis, Africa tota fuit?
at tu, stulta, deos, tu fingis inania verba:
  forsitan ille alio pectus amore terat.
est tibi forma potens, sunt castae Palladis artes,
  splendidaque a docto fama refulget avo,
fortunata domus, modo sit tibi fidus amicus.
  fidus ero: in nostros curre, puella, toros!   10
nox mihi prima venit! primae date tempora
      noctis:[3]   13
  longius in primo, Luna, morare toro.   14
tu quoque, qui aestivos spatiosius exigis ignes,   11
  Phoebe, moraturae contrahe lucis iter.   12

[1] tondes *Keil*: tondens *NFL*.
[2] tantine his *Paldam*: tantisne in *N*: tantis in *FL*.
[3] *13, 14 transposed before 11, 12 by Scaliger.*

244

And thou, Scylla, that didst sell thyself for the beauty of Minos, thou didst shear away thy father's realm when thou shorest his purple lock. Such was the dower that the maiden pledged to the foe! Nisus, 'twas love that opened thy gates by guile. But may ye, unwedded maids, burn your marriage torches with happier omen: for, see, she hangs to the Cretan bark and is dragged through the sea. Yet Minos deserves his place as the judge of Hell: though victor he showed justice to his conquered foe.

XX

DEEMST thou that he whom thou hast seen set sail from thine embraces can give a thought to the remembrance of thy beauty? Cruel the man that had the heart to leave his mistress for the sake of gain! When such tears as thine were shed was all Africa worth the winning? But thou, foolish girl, dreamst of the gods by whom he swore, and of the light words he spake. Perchance e'en now he vexes his heart with another passion.

7 Thy beauty hath power, thine are the chaste arts of Pallas, and glorious is the renown shed on thee by thy learned grandsire.[1] Rich enough is thine house, if thy lover be but true! I will be true: do thou, my love, hasten to my couch!

13 The first night of love is come for me. Grant me, Moon and Sun, the full space of that first night. Moon, linger longer than thy wont o'er our first embraces. Thou too, Phoebus, that o'ermuch prolongst thy summer fires, shorten the course of thy

[1] It is possible that Cynthia (Hostia) claimed to be descended from the poet Hostius (*circa* 130), who wrote an epic on the Illyrian war of 178 B.C.

SEXTI PROPERTI ELEGIARVM LIBER III

foedera sunt ponenda prius signandaque iura
   et scribenda mihi lex in amore novo.
haec Amor ipse suo constringit pignora signo:
   testis sidereae torta corona deae.
quam multae ante meis cedent sermonibus horae,
   dulcia quam nobis concitet arma Venus!   20
namque ubi non certo vincitur foedere lectus,
   non habet ultores nox vigilata[1] deos,
et quibus imposuit, solvit mox vincla libido:
   contineant nobis omina[2] prima fidem.
ergo, qui pactas in foedera ruperit aras,
   pollueritque novo sacra marita toro,
illi sint quicumque solent in amore dolores,
   et caput argutae praebeat historiae,
nec flenti dominae patefiant nocte fenestrae:
   semper amet, fructu semper amoris egens.   30

XXI

Magnvm iter ad doctas proficisci cogor Athenas,
   ut me longa gravi solvat amore via.
crescit enim assidue spectando[3] cura puellae:
   ipse alimenta sibi maxima praebet amor.
omnia sunt temptata mihi, quacumque fugari
   possit: at ex omni me premit ipse deus.
vix tamen aut semel admittit, cum saepe negarit:
   seu venit, extremo dormit amicta[4] toro.

---

[1] vigilata *N*: vigilanda *FL*.
[2] omina *ς*: omnia *NFL*.
[3] spectando *FL*: spectandi *N*.
[4] amicta *Scaliger*: amica *NFL*.

laggard light. First must the terms be made, the pact be sealed, the contract written, that shall rule my new love. Love himself with his own signet seals up our troth; the whirling crown of the starry goddess[1] is witness. How many an hour shall first yield to my tale of love ere Venus spur us to her sweet warfare! For if Love's bed be not bound by compact sure the lover's nights of sleepless watching find no gods to avenge them, and lust soon breaks the fetters it imposed: but for us may our love's first omens keep fast our troth. Wherefore for him that breaks the pledge that he swore on heaven's altars, and pollutes the rites of wedlock by turning to other loves, for him be all the woes love knows so well, and let shrill-tongued gossip fasten on him, nor, though he weep, may the window of his mistress be unbarred to him by night; let him love without ceasing, yet ever lack the fruition of love.

XXI

I am constrained to set forth on a mighty journey to learned Athens, that long travel may free me from the burden of love. For my passion for my mistress grows with gazing on her: love itself is love's chief nourishment. I have tried all means whereby Love may be put to flight: but the god afflicts me from every side. Yet scarce ever, or only once and again, will she admit me, while oft she says me nay: or if she comes to me, she sleeps fully clad on the bed's

[1] Ariadne.

SEXTI PROPERTI ELEGIARVM LIBER III

unum erit auxilium : mutatis Cynthia terris
   quantum oculis, animo tam procul ibit amor.   10
nunc agite, o socii, propellite in aequora[1] navem,
   remorumque pares ducite sorte vices,
iungiteque extremo felicia lintea malo :
   iam liquidum nautis aura secundat iter.
Romanae turres et vos valeatis, amici,
   qualiscumque mihi tuque, puella, vale !
ergo ego nunc rudis Hadriaci vehar aequoris hospes,
   cogar et undisonos nunc prece adire deos.
deinde per Ionium vectus cum fessa Lechaeo
   sedarit placida vela phaselus aqua,   20
quod superest, sufferre pedes properate laborem,
   Isthmos qua terris arcet utrumque mare.
inde ubi Piraei capient me litora portus,
   scandam ego Theseae bracchia longa viae.
illic vel stadiis animum emendare Platonis
   incipiam aut hortis, docte Epicure, tuis ;
persequar aut studium linguae, Demosthenis arma,
   librorumque tuos, docte[2] Menandre, sales ;
aut certe tabulae capient mea lumina pictae,
   sive ebore exactae, seu magis aere, manus.   30
aut spatia annorum, aut longa intervalla profundi
   lenibunt tacito vulnera nostra sinu :
seu moriar, fato, non turpi fractus amore ;
   atque erit illa mihi mortis honesta dies.

---

[1] aequora *F:* aequore *NL.*
[2] docte *NFL ; the repetition of* docte *is scarcely defensible* scite *L. Müller.*

edge. There is no help but this: if I seek another land, love will fly as far from my soul as Cynthia from mine eyes.

11 Come now, my comrades, launch forth our ship to sea and draw lots in couples for your turn at the oar. Hoist the fair-omened sails to the mast's top, now the breeze forwards the mariner's course across the wave. Ye towers of Rome and ye my friends, farewell, and thou, my love, whate'er thou hast been for me, farewell!

17 Now therefore I shall be borne away, the Adriatic's unfamiliar guest, and now perforce approach with prayer gods of the roaring wave. Then when my bark has crossed the Ionian sea and lulled its sails in the calm waters of Lechaeum, for what remains of the journey hasten, my feet, to endure the toil where Isthmos with its fields beats back either sea. Then when the shores of Piraeus haven shall receive me I will climb the long arms[1] of Theseus' road. There I will begin to clear my soul of error in Plato's Academe,[2] or in thy gardens, learned Epicurus; or I will pursue the study of eloquence, the weapon of Demosthenes, and will cull the wit of thy books, learned Menander; or else bright pictures shall delight my eyes, or masterpieces wrought in ivory or bronze.

31 Either length of years or the wide-sundering spaces of the deep shall heal the wounds hidden in my silent breast, or, if I die, it shall be fate, not dishonouring love, shall lay me low; and the day of my death shall bring me no disgrace.

---

[1] The "long walls" of Athens.
[2] *stadiis* = gymnasium—*i.e.*, the Academia where Plato taught.

SEXTI PROPERTI ELEGIARVM LIBER III

XXII

Frigida tam multos placuit tibi Cyzicus annos,[1]
　　Tulle, Propontiaca quae fluit isthmos aqua,
Dindymus et secto fabricata in dente [2] Cybelle,
　　raptorisque tulit qua via Ditis equos?
si te forte iuvant Helles Athamantidos urbes,
　　at [3] desiderio, Tulle, movere meo,—
tu licet aspicias caelum omne Atlanta gerentem,
　　sectaque Persea Phorcidos ora manu,
Geryonis stabula et luctantum in pulvere signa
　　Herculis Antaeique, Hesperidumque choros;　　10
tuque tuo Colchum propellas remige Phasim,
　　Peliacaeque trabis totum iter ipse legas,
qua rudis Argea [4] natat inter saxa columba
　　in faciem prorae pinus adacta novae;
aut si qua Ortygie et [5] visenda est ora Caystri,
　　et qua septenas temperat unda vias;
omnia Romanae cedent miracula terrae:
　　natura hic posuit, quidquid ubique fuit.
armis apta magis tellus quam commoda noxae:
　　Famam, Roma, tuae non pudet historiae.　　20
nam quantum ferro tantum pietate potentes
　　stamus: victrices temperat ira manus.

[1] annos *fl*: annus *NFL*.
[2] secto ... in dente *Barton*: sacra ... inventa *NFL*; *the passage scarcely admits of certain correction.*
[3] at *Phillimore*: et *NFL*.　　[4] Argea *F*: Argoa *NL*.
[5] aut *Fonteine* et *N* at *FL*. Ortygie et *Haupt*: orige *NFL*.

THE ELEGIES OF PROPERTIUS BOOK III

XXII

Has cool Cyzicus, where the isthmus streams with wave of Propontis, and the goddess of Dindymus and Cybelle fashioned from carven tusks[1] and the path trodden by the steeds of Dis[2] the ravisher, have all these pleased thee for so many years, my Tullus? Though perchance the cities of Helle, daughter of Athamas, delight thee, yet, Tullus, be moved by my longing for thee.

[7] Though one gaze on Atlas supporting all the sky, and the head of Phorcys' daughter severed by Perseus' hand, the stalls of Geryon, the marks of Hercules and Antaeus wrestling in the dust, and the dances of the Hesperides; though another churn the waters of Colchian Phasis with his oarsmen and follow the whole course of the timbers hewn on Pelion, where the pine-tree, wrought into the shape of an unfamiliar ship and still strange to the sea, glided between the crags with Argos' dove for guide; though he must visit Ortygia and the shores of Cayster and the land where Nile's waters run in sevenfold channels; yet all these marvels shall yield to the land of Rome: here hath nature placed whate'er is best in all the world. 'Tis a land made for war rather than crime: Fame blushes not for thy story, O Rome. For we are stablished in power by loyal faith no less than by the sword: our anger restrains its conquering hands.

---

[1] At Cyzicus there was, according to Pausanias, a statue of Cybelle made of hippopotamus ivory.

[2] There seems to have been a legend which made Cyzicus, not Sicily, the place of Persephone's disappearance.

SEXTI PROPERTI ELEGIARVM LIBER III

hic Anio Tiburne fluis,[1] Clitumnus ab Vmbro
   tramite, et aeternum Marcius umor opus,
Albanus lacus et foliis Nemorensis abundans,[2]
   potaque Pollucis nympha salubris equo.
at non squamoso labuntur ventre cerastae,
   Itala portentis nec furit[3] unda novis;
non hic Andromedae resonant pro matre catenae,
   nec tremis Ausonias, Phoebe fugate, dapes,   30
nec cuiquam absentes arserunt in caput ignes
   exitium nato matre movente suo;
Penthea non saevae venantur in arbore Bacchae,
   nec solvit Danaas subdita cerva rates,
cornua nec valuit curvare in paelice Iuno
   aut faciem turpi dedecorare bove;

    .   .   .   .   .[4]

arboreasque cruces Sinis, et non hospita Grais
   saxa, et curvatas in sua fata trabes.
haec tibi, Tulle, parens, haec est pulcherrima sedes,
   hic tibi pro digna gente petendus honos,   40
hic tibi ad eloquium cives, hic ampla nepotum
   spes et venturae coniugis aptus amor.

[1] fluis ς. flues *NFL*.
[2] foliis *Housman*: sotii *FL* · socii *N*. abundans *Housman*: ab unda *NFL*
[3] furit ς : fuit *NFL*.
[4] *At least a couplet seems to have been lost.*

THE ELEGIES OF PROPERTIUS BOOK III

²³ Here flowest thou, Tibur's Anio, here is Clitumnus from his Umbrian path and the Marcian conduit that shall endure for ever. Here is Alba's lake and Nemi thick with leaves, and the healing spring whence drank the horse of Pollux. But here glide no horned asps with scaly bellies, nor are Italian waters wild with strange monsters. Here clang not Andromeda's fetters in payment for her mother's sin, nor, Phoebus, fliest thou in terror from Ausonian banquets;[1] here for no man's destruction hath burned far-distant fire when a mother compassed her own son's ruin.[2] No fierce Bacchanals hunt Pentheus in his tree, nor are Danaan fleets launched by the substitution of a doe.[3] Juno hath had no power to make curved horns to grow from her rival's[4] brow nor disfigure her features beneath the form of a cow. [*Here none tell of . . . nor of*] the trees where Sinis crucified strangers, nor of the rocks[5] that gave bitter welcome to the Greeks, nor of the ships built only to meet their doom.

³⁹ This, Tullus, is the land that bore thee, this thy fairest home; here shouldst thou seek honour that shall match thy lofty birth. Here are citizens for thine eloquence to sway, here is ample hope of offspring, and here awaits thee meet love from thy bride that shall be.

---

[1] The reference is to the banquet of Thyestes. Atreus prepared the flesh of Thyestes' children for their father to eat. The sun turned back his chariot in horror at the deed.

[2] Althaea brought about her son Meleager's death by burning a log, on the preservation of which his life depended.

[3] The sacrifice of Iphigenia.

[4] Io.

[5] See Caphareus, Index.

SEXTI PROPERTI ELEGIARVM LIBER III

XXIII

Ergo tam doctae nobis periere tabellae,
  scripta quibus pariter tot periere bona!
has quondam nostris manibus detriverat usus,
  qui non signatas iussit habere fidem.
illae iam sine me norant placare puellas,
  et quaedam sine me verba diserta loqui.
non illas fixum caras effecerat aurum:
  vulgari buxo sordida cera fuit.
qualescumque mihi semper mansere fideles,
  semper et effectus promeruere bonos. 10
forsitan haec illis fuerint mandata tabellis:
  " Irascor quoniam es, lente, moratus heri.
an tibi nescio quae visa est formosior? an tu
  non bona de nobis crimina ficta iacis?"
aut dixit: "Venies hodie, cessabimus una:
  hospitium tota nocte paravit Amor,"
et quaecumque volens[1] reperit non stulta puella
  garrula, cum blandis dicitur[2] hora dolis.
me miserum, his aliquis rationem scribit avarus[3]
  et ponit diras[4] inter ephemeridas! 20
quas si quis mihi rettulerit, donabitur auro:
  quis pro divitiis ligna[5] retenta velit?
i puer, et citus haec aliqua propone columna,
  et dominum Esquiliis scribe habitare tuum.

---

[1] volens *Broekhuyzen*: dolens *NFL*.
[2] dicitur ς. ducitur *NFL*. [3] avarus ς: avari *NFL*.
[4] diras *N*: duras *FL*. [5] ligna *Beroaldus*: signa *NFL*.

THE ELEGIES OF PROPERTIUS BOOK III

XXIII

So then my tablets, my learnèd tablets are lost, and with them many a gracious writing too is lost. Long usage at my hands had worn them down and bade them be believed without the warrant of a seal. They knew how to appease my loves, though I was not by, and, though I was not by, could speak in words of eloquence. No golden fittings made them precious; they were only dingy wax on common boxwood. Yet poor though they were, they were ever faithful to me and ever won deserved success. Sometimes, it may be, these were the words entrusted to their care: "I am angry, because thou didst tarry yestereve, thou sluggard. Didst thou deem thou hadst found a fairer love? Or dost thou spread some vile slander against me?" Or perchance she said: "Thou wilt come to-day and we will take our ease together: Love has made ready a welcome for thee all night long." These bare they, and all the words a chattering girl delights to find, when she appoints an hour for the stealthy joys of love. Alas! and now some greedy merchant writes his bill upon them and places them among his terrible ledgers! If any will return them to me he shall have gold for his reward: who would keep hard blocks of wood when he might have wealth for them? Go, boy, and with all speed set forth these lines upon some pillar, and write that thy master dwells upon the Esquiline.

SEXTI PROPERTI ELEGIARVM LIBER III

XXIV

Falsa est ista tuae, mulier, fiducia formae,
    olim oculis nimium facta superba meis.
noster amor tales tribuit tibi, Cynthia, laudes.
    versibus insignem te pudet esse meis ?
mixtam te varia laudavi saepe figura,
    ut, quod non esses, esse putaret amor ;
et color est totiens roseo collatus Eoo,
    cum tibi quaesitus candor in ore foret :
quod mihi non patrii poterant avertere amici,
    eluere aut vasto Thessala saga mari.   10
haec ego non ferro, non igne coactus, et ipsa
    naufragus Aegaea vera fatebar[1] aqua :
correptus saevo Veneris torrebar aeno ;
    vinctus eram versas in mea terga manus.
ecce coronatae portum tetigere carinae,
    traiectae Syrtes, ancora iacta mihi est.
nunc demum vasto fessi resipiscimus aestu,
    vulneraque ad sanum nunc coiere mea.
Mens Bona, si qua dea es, tua me in sacraria dono !
    exciderant surdo tot mea vota Iovi.   20

[1] vera *Passerat :* verba *NFL.* fatebar *ς* : fatebor *NFL.*

THE ELEGIES OF PROPERTIUS BOOK III

XXIV

False, woman, is the trust thou puttest in thy beauty; long since the partial judgment of mine eyes hath made thee overproud. Such praise of old my love bestowed on thee, and now it shames me that thou hast glory from my song. Oft did I praise the varied beauty of thy blending charms, and love deemed thee to be that which thou wert not. Oft was thy hue compared to the rosy star of dawn, though the splendour of thy face owed naught to nature. This madness my father's friends could not drive from me, nor any witch of Thessaly wash from me with the waves of the wild sea. All this—no fire or knife compelling—I confessed in utter truth, wrecked on a very ocean of trouble.[1] Venus caught me and seethed me in the caldron of her cruelty; my hands were twisted and bound behind my back. But lo! my ships have found haven and wear wreaths of thanksgiving, the Syrtes are crossed and mine anchor cast. Now at last my senses return to me, aweary of the wild sea-tides; my wounds have closed, my flesh is healed. Good Sense, if any such goddess there be, I dedicate myself to the service of thy shrine, for Jove was deaf and took no heed of all my vows.

[1] *Aegaea aqua* is metaphorical.

SEXTI PROPERTI ELEGIARVM LIBER III

XXV

Risvs eram positis inter convivia mensis,
    et de me poterat quilibet esse loquax.
quinque tibi potui servire fideliter annos:
    ungue meam morso saepe querere fidem.
nil moveor lacrimis: ista sum captus ab arte;
    semper ab insidiis, Cynthia, flere soles.
flebo ego discedens, sed fletum iniuria vincit:
    tu bene conveniens non sinis ire iugum.
limina iam nostris valeant lacrimantia verbis,
    nec tamen irata ianua fracta manu.   10
at te celatis aetas gravis urgeat annis,
    et veniat formae ruga sinistra tuae!
vellere tum cupias albos a stirpe capillos,
    a! speculo rugas increpitante tibi,
exclusa inque vicem fastus patiare superbos,
    et quae fecisti facta queraris anus!
has tibi fatales cecinit mea pagina diras:
    eventum formae disce timere tuae!

THE ELEGIES OF PROPERTIUS BOOK III

XXV

They made mock of me where the tables were set for feasting; the tongues of the vilest were suffered to make free with my name. For five years I had the heart to be thy faithful slave; oft shalt thou gnaw thy nails and mourn for my lost loyalty. Tears move me not a whit: 'twas tears ensnared me of old: Cynthia, thou never weepest save to deceive. I too shall weep as I depart, but my wrongs are stronger than grief; for thou lettest not the yoke sit easy on my shoulders. Farewell the threshold still weeping with my plaint, farewell that door ne'er broken by my hands for all its cruelty! But thee may weary age bow down with the years thou hast concealed,[1] and may ill-favoured wrinkles come to mar thy beauty! Then mayest thou desire to tear out thy white hairs by the root, when the mirror mocks thee with thy wrinkles; mayest thou in thy turn be shut out from bliss and endure another's haughty scorn! Turned to an ancient crone, mayest thou lament what thou hast done! Such curses fraught with doom are the burden of my song for thee: learn to dread the end that awaits thy beauty!

[1] Or perhaps "years that steal on unnoticed."

BOOK IV

LIBER QVARTVS

I

Hoc quodcumque vides, hospes, qua maxima Roma est,
    ante Phrygem Aenean collis et herba fuit;
atque ubi Navali stant sacra Palatia Phoebo,
    Euandri profugae concubuere boves.
fictilibus crevere deis haec aurea templa,
    nec fuit opprobrio facta sine arte casa;
Tarpeiusque pater nuda de rupe tonabat,
    et Tiberis nostris advena bubus erat.
qua gradibus domus ista Remi se sustulit, olim
    unus erat fratrum maxima regna focus. 10
Curia, praetexto quae nunc nitet alta senatu,
    pellitos habuit, rustica corda, Patres.
bucina cogebat priscos ad verba Quirites:
    centum illi in prato saepe senatus erat.
nec sinuosa cavo pendebant vela theatro,
    pulpita sollemnes non oluere crocos.
nulli cura fuit externos quaerere divos;
    cum tremeret patrio pendula turba sacro,

THE FOURTH BOOK

I

ALL that thou beholdest, stranger, where mighty Rome lies spread, was grass and hill before the coming of Phrygian Aeneas; and where stands the Palatine sacred to Phoebus of the Ships, there once lay the herd of Evander's exiled kine. From gods of clay sprang yonder golden temples; of old they spurned not to dwell in huts made by unskilled hands; the Tarpeian sire thundered from a bare crag, and Tiber still seemed strange to our cattle. Where Remus' house is perched yonder at the stairway's height [1] the brothers of old counted their tiny hearth a mighty realm. The Senate-house, that towers on high filled with a shining throng of senators clad in the robe with purple hem, once held a rustic company, the city fathers robed in skins of beasts. The trumpet summoned the olden Quirites to debate: a hundred gathered in a meadow oft made a senate. No rippling awnings hung o'er the hollow theatre, nor reeked the stage with saffron, as 'tis wont to-day. Then no man sought to bring in strange gods, when the folk trembled in suspense before the ritual of their sires; but greatly they cared to celebrate

---

[1] See p. 109, note 1. The stairway is the *Scala Cacia* leading from the Circus Maximus to the Palatine.

SEXTI PROPERTI ELEGIARVM LIBER IV

annua at[1] accenso celebrare Parilia faeno,
    qualia nunc curto lustra novantur equo.   20
Vesta coronatis pauper gaudebat asellis,
    ducebant macrae vilia sacra boves.
parva saginati lustrabant compita porci,
    pastor et ad calamos exta litabat ovis.
verbera pellitus saetosa movebat arator,
    unde licens Fabius sacra Lupercus habet.
nec rudis infestis miles radiabat in armis:
    miscebant usta proelia nuda sude.
prima galeritus posuit praetoria Lycmon,
    magnaque pars Tatio rerum erat inter oves.   30
hinc Titiens Ramnesque viri Luceresque Soloni,[2]
    quattuor hinc albos Romulus egit equos.
quippe suburbanae parva minus urbe Bovillae
    et, qui nunc nulli, maxima turba Gabi.
et stetit Alba potens, albae suis omine nata,
    hinc ubi Fidenas longa erat isse via.[3]

[1] annua at *Lachmann*: annuaque *NFL*.
[2] soloni *N*: coloni *FL*.
[3] hinc *Postgate*: hac *NFL*. longa . . via ⵎ: longe . . vias *NFL*.

the yearly feast of Pales with heaps of burning straw, making purification such as to-day we make with the blood of the maimed horse.[1] Vesta was poor, and necklaced asses[2] sufficed to make her glad, while lean kine dragged sacred emblems of little worth. The cross-roads,[3] small as yet, were sprinkled with the blood of fatted swine, and the shepherd to the sound of pipes of reed made acceptable sacrifice with the entrails of sheep. The ploughman girt with skins plied his shaggy scourge;[4] hence spring the rites of Fabian Lupercus. Their rude soldiers flashed not in threatening armour, but joined battle bare-breasted with stakes hardened in the fire. Lycmon wore but a wolf-skin helm when he pitched the first of general's tents, and the wealth of Tatius lay chiefly in his sheep. Thus rose the Titienses, the hero Ramnes, and the Luceres of Solonium; thus came it that Romulus drove the four white steeds of triumph. Of a truth Bovillae was less a suburb while Rome was yet so small, and Gabii, that now is naught, was then a crowded town. Then Alba, born of the white sow's omen, still stood in power, in the days when 'twas a long journey from Rome to Fidenae.

[1] On October 15 a horse known as the *October equus* was sacrificed to Mars. Its tail was cut off and the blood allowed to drop on the hearth of the *regia*, the ancient palace of Numa, near the temple of Vesta. The blood was preserved and formed part of a *suffimen*, or fumigatory powder, at the Parilia.

[2] The feast of Vesta took place on June 9, one of its chief features being a procession in which asses garlanded with strings of loaves took part.

[3] A reference to the *Compitalia*, or festival of the *Lares compitales*, which took place at the end of December.

[4] The reference is to the *Lupercalia* (February 15). Men girt with skins ran through the streets of Rome striking women with thongs of goat-skin. This was supposed to promote fertility.

SEXTI PROPERTI ELEGIARVM LIBER IV

nil patrium nisi nomen habet Romanus alumnus:
　sanguinis altricem non putet esse lupam.
huc melius profugos misisti, Troia, Penates.
　huc¹ quali vecta est Dardana puppis ave!　　　40
iam bene spondebant tunc omina, quod nihil illam
　laeserat abiegni venter apertus equi,
cum pater in nati trepidus cervice pependit,
　et verita est umeros urere flamma pios.
tunc animi venere Deci Brutique secures,
　vexit et ipsa sui Caesaris arma Venus,
arma resurgentis portans victricia Troiae:
　felix terra tuos cepit, Iule, deos,
si modo Avernalis tremulae cortina Sibyllae
　dixit Aventino rura pianda Remo,　　　50
aut si Pergameae sero rata carmina vatis
　longaevum ad Priami vera fuere caput:
"Vertite equum, Danai! male vincitis! Ilia tellus
　vivet, et huic cineri Iuppiter arma dabit!"
optima nutricum nostris lupa Martia rebus,
　qualia creverunt moenia lacte tuo!
moenia namque pio coner disponere versu:
　ei mihi, quod nostro est parvus in ore sonus;
sed tamen exiguo quodcumque e pectore rivi
　fluxerit, hoc patriae serviet omne meae.　　　60
Ennius hirsuta cingat sua dicta corona:
　mi folia ex hedera porrige, Bacche, tua,
ut nostris tumefacta superbiat Vmbria libris,
　Vmbria Romani patria Callimachi!

¹ huc *Baehrens*: heu *NFL*.

THE ELEGIES OF PROPERTIUS BOOK IV

The Roman of to-day has naught from his father save the name, nor would he deem that the she-wolf nurtured the blood from whence he sprang.

[39] Hither, O Troy, for happier destiny didst thou send thine exiled gods; with blessed augury came hither the Dardan bark; even then the omens boded her well, since the womb of the horse of fir-wood had done her no hurt in that day when the father hung trembling on his son's neck, and the flame feared to burn those pious shoulders. That day led hither the dauntless Decii and the consulship of Brutus, and Venus herself bore hither her Caesar's arms, even the victorious arms of Troy reborn; with blessing, Iulus, did the land receive thy gods, since the tripod of Avernus' trembling Sibyl bade Remus sanctify the fields of Aventine, and late in time the strains of the prophetess of Troy proved true concerning ancient Priam. "Turn your steeds, ye Danaans!" she cried "Ye conquer but in vain! Ilium's land shall live and Jove shall arm her ashes!"

[55] O wolf of Mars, thou best of nurses for our state, what walls have sprung from thy milk! Of those walls let me sing in order due—alas! how weak is the voice of my lips. Yet howsoever slender the stream of song that flows from my puny heart, yet all of it shall be given to the service of my country. Let Ennius crown his songs with rude, shaggy wreath! To me, O Bacchus, give of thine ivy's leaves, that my books may make Umbria swell with pride, Umbria the home of Rome's Callimachus!

SEXTI PROPERTI ELEGIARVM LIBER IV

scandentis qui Asis[1] cernit de vallibus arces,
   ingenio muros aestimet ille meo!
Roma, fave, tibi surgit opus, date candida cives
   omina, et inceptis dextera cantet avis!   68
dicam: "Troia cades, et Troica Roma resurges";   87.
   et maris et terrae longa pericla[2] canam.[3]   88
sacra diesque canam et cognomina prisca locorum: 69
   has meus ad metas sudet oportet equus.   70

Iᴀ[4]

Qvo ruis imprudens, vage, dicere fata, Properti?
   non sunt a dextro condita fila colo.
accersis lacrimas cantans;[5] aversus Apollo;
   poscis ab invita verba pigenda lyra.
certa feram certis auctoribus, aut ego vates
   nescius aerata signa movere pila.
me creat Archytae suboles Babylonius Orops
   Horon, et a proavo ducta Conone domus.
di mihi sunt testes non degenerasse propinquos,
   inque meis libris nil prius esse fide.   80
nunc pretium fecere deos et (fallitur auro
   Iuppiter) obliquae signa iterata rotae,

---

[1] qui Asis *Butler, following O. L. Richmond, who read* -que Asis cernit qui vallibus (asis μυf): quasuis *FL*: quisquis *N*.
[2] pericla ς: sepulcra *NFL*.
[3] *87, 88 transposed after 68 by Scaliger.*
[4] *No break in MSS The separation is due to early Renaissance scholars.*
[5] cantans *Baehrens*: cantas *NFL*.

THE ELEGIES OF PROPERTIUS BOOK IV

Let him that sees the towers of Asis climbing from the vale reckon the glory of its walls by the fame of my wit! Rome, smile on me! For thee my work is built. Ye citizens, give me fair omen, and from the right hand let some bird of augury sing me success. I will cry, "Troy, thou shalt fall, and thou, Trojan Rome, shalt arise anew!" and I will sing of all Rome's long perils by land and sea. Of holy rites and their days will I sing, and of the ancient names of places. This must be the goal toward which my foaming steed shall press.

I<small>A</small> [1]

W<small>HITHER</small> in heedless folly dost thou speed to sing the works of destiny, thou truant Propertius? The thread thou spinnest comes from no favouring distaff. Thy song shall bring thee sorrow; Apollo's face is turned from thee; thou askest of thine unwilling lyre such strains as thou shalt rue. I will tell thee sure truth with warrant sure; else am I a seer that knows not how to wheel the constellations on their orb of bronze.[2] Horos is my name, and Babylonian Orops, child of Archytas, begat me, and my house hath Conon for ancestor. The gods be witness that I have not shamed my kin and that in my books there is naught set down save truth. Now have men turned the gods to profit and Jupiter is fooled by their gold; to profit have they turned the oft-

---

[1] This elegy seems to be a sort of whimsical recantation of the previous poem. It takes the form of a soliloquy by an astrologer, named Horos.

[2] An orrery or planetarium.

SEXTI PROPERTI ELEGIARVM LIBER IV

felicesque Iovis stellas Martisque rapaces [1]
    et grave Saturni sidus in omne caput;
quid moveant Pisces animosaque signa Leonis,
    lotus et Hesperia quid Capricornus aqua.   86
dixi ego, cum geminos produceret Arria natos   89
    (illa dabat natis arma vetante deo):   90
non posse ad patrios sua pila referre Penates:
    nempe meam firmant nunc duo busta fidem.
quippe Lupercus, eques [2] dum saucia protegit ora,
    heu sibi prolapso non bene cavit equo;
Gallus at, in castris dum credita signa tuetur,
    concidit ante aquilae rostra cruenta suae:
fatales pueri, duo funera matris avarae!
    vera, sed invito, contigit ista fides.
idem ego, cum Cinarae traheret Lucina dolores,
    et facerent uteri pondera lenta moram,   100
" Iunonis facito [3] votum impetrabile" dixi:
    illa parit: libris est data palma meis!
hoc neque harenosum Libyae Iovis explicat antrum,
    aut sibi commissos fibra locuta deos,
aut si quis motas cornicis senserit alas,
    umbrave quae [4] magicis mortua prodit aquis.
aspicienda via est caeli verusque per astra
    trames, et ab zonis quinque petenda fides.

---

[1] rapaces *Livineius*. rapacis *NFL*.
[2] eques *Heinsius*: equi *NFL*.
[3] facito *Lachmann*: facite *NFL*.
[4] umbrave quae *Turnebus*: umbrane quae *N*: umbraque ne *FL*.

scanned constellations of the slanting zodiac, the blessed star of Jove, the greedy star of Mars, the sign of Saturn that brings woe to one and all, the purport of the Fish and the fierce constellation of the Lion and Capricorn, bathed in the waters of the West.

[89] When Arria was in travail with her twin sons I foretold—for she destined her sons for arms, though a god forbade—that they should never bring home their spears to the gods of their father's home, and now lo! two tombs prove that my words were true. For the horseman Lupercus, as he shielded his wounded face, guarded himself but ill, alas! for his steed had fallen: while Gallus, as in the camp he defended the standards entrusted to his charge, fell dead before his eagle's beak and bathed it in his blood. Doomed boys, both brought to your death by your mother's greed, my words found true fulfilment—ah! would that they had not! I, too, when Lucina prolonged Cinara's pains, and the slow burden of her womb delayed, cried: "Let her make a vow to Juno that shall win the ear of the goddess!" She was delivered: my books won the day. Such truth is not unfolded by the cave of Libyan Jove amid the desert sands,[1] nor by entrails that speak forth the will of heaven entrusted to their care; such truth he cannot tell that marks the crow's beating wings, nor the spirit of the dead that rises from magic waters. The seer must gaze upon the path of heaven, on the road of truth that lies among the stars, and from the five zones seek

[1] Jupiter Ammon.

SEXTI PROPERTI ELEGIARVM LIBER IV

exemplum grave erit Calchas: namque Aulide solvit
   ille bene haerentes ad pia saxa rates;   110
idem Agamemnoniae ferrum cervice puellae
   tinxit, et Atrides vela cruenta dedit;
nec rediere tamen Danai: tu, diruta, fletum
   supprime et Euboicos respice, Troia, sinus!
Nauplius ultores sub noctem porrigit ignes,
   et natat exuviis Graecia pressa suis.
victor Oiliade, rape nunc et dilige vatem,
   quam vetat avelli veste Minerva sua!
hactenus historiae: nunc ad tua devehar astra;
   incipe tu lacrimis aequus adesse novis.   120
Vmbria te notis antiqua Penatibus edit:
   mentior? an patriae tangitur ora tuae?
qua[1] nebulosa cavo rorat Mevania campo,
   et lacus aestivis intepet Vmber aquis,
scandentisque Asis consurgit vertice murus,
   murus ab ingenio notior ille tuo?
ossaque legisti non illa aetate legenda
   patris et in tenues cogeris ipse lares:
nam tua cum multi versarent rura iuvenci,
   abstulit excultas pertica tristis opes.   130
mox ubi bulla rudi demissa est aurea collo,
   matris et ante deos libera sumpta toga,

[1] qua ϛ: quam *NFL*.

assurance.[1] Calchas bears grievous witness; for he loosed from Aulis the ships that clung to the kindly rocks, as still they should have clung; 'twas Calchas, too, that embrued the steel in the blood of Agamemnon's daughter and launched Atrides with blood upon his sails; yet never did the Danaans return; fallen Troy, check thy weeping and behold Euboea's bays! Nauplius uplifts his vengeful fires by night, and Greece swims sunken by the weight of her spoils. Victorious son of Oileus, go, ravish thy prophetess and take her to thy love, though Minerva forbid thee to tear her from her robe!

[119] Thus far shall history witness; now to thy stars I turn; prepare to lend patient hearing to a new tale of tears. Ancient Umbria bore thee in a home of high renown—do I lie? or do I touch thy country's borders?—where misty Mevania sheds its dews on the hollow plain and the waters of Umbria's lake send forth their summer steam, and the wall rises from the peak of climbing Asis, that wall made yet more glorious by thy wit. And all too young thou didst gather to thy bosom thy father's bones and wert driven to a poorer home. Many were the steers that tilled thy fields, but the pitiless measuring-rod[2] robbed thee of thy wealth of plough-land. Thereafter when the ball of gold[3] was cast from thy young neck and the robe of manhood's freedom[4] was

---

[1] Heaven was divided into five zones: on either side of the central or torrid lay the two temperate zones, and beyond them two zones of cold. See Vergil, *Georg.* I. 233.

[2] A reference to the confiscation of lands for distribution among the soldiers of Caesar. See Introduction.

[3] A locket worn by the sons of senators or knights. It contained a charm against the evil eye, and was laid aside on reaching puberty.

[4] See p. 229, note.

SEXTI PROPERTI ELEGIARVM LIBER IV

tum tibi pauca suo de carmine dictat Apollo
　et vetat insano verba tonare Foro.
at tu finge elegos, fallax opus:—haec tua castra!—
　scribat ut exemplo cetera turba tuo.
militiam Veneris blandis patiere sub armis,
　et Veneris pueris utilis hostis eris.
nam tibi victrices quascumque labore parasti,
　eludit palmas una puella tuas:　　　　　　　140
et bene confixum mento discusseris[1] uncum,
　nil erit hoc: rostro te premet ansa suo.[2]
illius arbitrio noctem lucemque videbis:
　gutta quoque ex oculis non nisi iussa cadet.
nec mille excubiae nec te signata iuvabunt
　limina: persuasae fallere rima[3] sat est.
nunc tua vel mediis puppis luctetur in undis,
　vel licet armatis hostis inermis eas,
vel tremefacta cavum tellus diducat[4] hiatum:
　octipedis Cancri terga sinistra time!　　　　150

II

Qvid mirare meas tot in uno corpore formas?
　accipe Vertumni signa paterna dei.
Tuscus ego Tuscis orior, nec paenitet inter
　proelia Volsinios deseruisse focos.

---

[1] discusseris ς: discusserit *NFL.*
[2] rostro *Dom. Calderinus:* nostro *NFL.* ansa *Dom. Calderinus:* ausa *NFL.* suo *FL:* tuo *N.*
[3] limina ς: lumina *NFL.* rima *Beroaldus·* prima *NFL.*
[4] cavum *f:* cavo *NFL.* diducat *N* deducat *FL.*

donned before thy mother's gods, then did Apollo teach thee some little of his song and forbid thee to thunder forth thy speech in the mad tumult of the Forum. Nay then, be elegy thy task, a work full of guile—here lies thy warfare!—that other bards may write inspired by thee. Thou shalt endure the alluring strife of Venus' wars and shalt be a foeman meet for the shafts of Venus' boys. For whatever victories thy toil may win thee, there is one girl shall baffle thee ever; and though thou shake from thy mouth the hook that is fast therein, it will avail thee naught; the rod shall keep thee captive with its barb. Her whim shall order thy waking and thy sleeping, and the tear shall not fall from thine eyes save at her command. Nor shall a thousand guards aid thee, nor a thousand seals set on her doors; if she be resolved to cheat thee, a chink in the door will suffice her. And now whether thy bark be tossed in mid tempest or thou goest unarmed amid an armoured foe, or earth tremble and yawn for thee with gaping chasm, fear thou the ill-omened back of the eight-footed Crab![1]

II

WHY marvellest thou that my one body should have so many shapes? Learn the tokens of the god Vertumnus' birth. A Tuscan I from Tuscans sprung, nor do I repent me that I left Volsinii's hearths

---

[1] Those born under the constellation of the Crab were supposed to be avaricious. The allusion is to Cynthia's avarice; *cp.* II. XVI., and III. XIII.

SEXTI PROPERTI ELEGIARVM LIBER IV

haec mea turba iuvat, nec templo laetor eburno:
    Romanum satis est posse videre Forum.
hac quondam Tiberinus iter faciebat, at aiunt
    remorum auditos per vada pulsa sonos:
at postquam ille suis tantum concessit alumnis,
    Vertumnus verso dicor ab amne deus.   10
seu, quia vertentis fructum praecepimus anni,
    Vertumni rursus credis id[1] esse sacrum.
prima mihi variat liventibus uva racemis,
    et coma lactenti spicea fruge tumet;
hic dulces cerasos, hic autumnalia pruna
    cernis et aestivo mora rubere die;
insitor hic solvit pomosa vota corona,
    cum pirus invito stipite mala tulit.
mendax fama vaces:[2] alius mihi nominis index:
    de se narranti tu modo crede deo.   20
opportuna mea est cunctis natura figuris:
    in quamcumque voles verte, decorus ero.
indue me Cois, fiam non dura puella:
    meque virum sumpta quis neget esse toga?
da falcem et torto frontem mihi comprime faeno:
    iurabis nostra gramina secta manu.
arma tuli quondam et, memini, laudabar in illis:
    corbis at[3] imposito pondere messor eram.
sobrius ad lites: at cum est imposta corona,
    clamabis capiti vina subisse meo.   30

---

[1] credis id *Postgate*. credidit *O*.
[2] vaces *ς*: voces *FL* : noces *N*.
[3] at *Butler*. in *N* om. *FL*.

amid the din of battle. This throng that is ever round me is my joy; I need no ivory temple for my delight; enough that I can see the Roman Forum.

⁷ There once the Tiber went, and they say that the sound of oars [1] was heard across the smitten shallows. But after he had yielded thus much ground to his nurslings I was called the god Vertumnus from the turning of the river. Or else because I receive the first-fruits of the year as it turns its round, for this reason also thou deemest that offering to be Vertumnus' due. For me the first grape changes colour with darkening cluster, and the spiked ear of corn swells with its milky fruit. There thou seest sweet cherries glow, here autumn plums and summer mulberries. Here the grafter pays his vows with garland of fruit, when the pear's unwilling stock hath borne him apples.

¹⁹ Lying rumour be silent; another warrant is there for my name; believe the god that tells his own tale. My nature suits with every form: turn me to what thou wilt, I shall still be comely. Clothe me in silks of Cos, I shall prove a graceful girl; and when I wear the toga who shall deny me to be a man? Give me a sickle and bind my brow with twisted hay, thou wilt swear that grass has been cut by my hands. Once I bore arms and, I mind me, won praise in war; but when the heavy basket was placed upon my back I was a reaper. Sober am I when law-suits call, yet when the wreath is on my brow thou wilt cry that the wine has stolen to my head. Gird my head with

---

[1] See Velabrum, Index.

SEXTI PROPERTI ELEGIARVM LIBER IV

cinge caput mitra, speciem furabor Iacchi;[1]
  furabor Phoebi, si modo plectra dabis.
cassibus impositis venor: sed harundine sumpta
  fautor[2] plumoso sum deus aucupio.
est etiam aurigae species Vertumnus et eius,
  traicit alterno qui leve pondus equo.
suppetat hoc, pisces calamo praedabor, et ibo
  mundus demissis institor in tunicis.
pastor me ad baculum possum curvare[3] vel idem
  sirpiculis medio pulvere ferre rosam.   40
nam quid ego adiciam, de quo mihi maxima fama est,
  hortorum in manibus dona probata meis?
caeruleus cucumis tumidoque cucurbita ventre
  me notat et iunco brassica vincta levi;
nec flos ullus hiat pratis, quin ille decenter
  impositus fronti langueat ante meae.
at mihi, quod formas unus vertebar in omnes,
  nomen ab eventu patria lingua dedit.
et tu, Roma, meis tribuisti praemia Tuscis,
  (unde hodie Vicus nomina Tuscus habet,)   50
tempore quo sociis venit Lycomedius armis
  atque Sabina feri contudit arma Tati.
vidi ego labentes acies et tela caduca,
  atque hostes turpi terga dedisse fugae.
sed facias, divum Sator, ut Romana per aevum
  transeat ante meos turba togata pedes.

[1] Iacchi *early Renaissance scholars*: achei *NFL*.
[2] fautor *Rossberg*: fauor *N*. faunor *FL*.
[3] pastor me *Ayrmann*: pastorem *NFL*. curvare ς. curare *NFL*.

a turban, I will steal for me the semblance of Iacchus; I will steal the semblance of Phoebus if thou wilt but give me his lyre. With nets on my shoulder I go hunting; but when the fowler's reed is in my hand I am that god who speeds the snaring of feathered fowl. Vertumnus takes also the guise of a charioteer, and of him who transfers his nimble weight from horse to horse. Supply me and with a rod I will take spoil of fish, or will go my way a spruce pedlar with trailing tunic. I can stoop like a shepherd o'er his crook; I too can bring roses in baskets through the midst of summer's dust. For why should I add, since there lies my greatest fame, that the garden's choice gifts may be seen in my hands? The dark-green cucumber and the gourd with swelling belly and the cabbage tied with light rushes mark me out. Nor grows there any flower in the fields but is placed upon my brow and droops in comely fashion before my face. Nay, my name sprang from my deeds; 'twas because I turned to every shape that my native tongue bestowed it on me.

[49] And thou, Rome, thou didst reward my Tuscan kin—from whom to-day the Tuscan street is named—what time the Lycomedian came with succouring host and crushed the Sabine warriors of fierce Tatius. I saw the breaking ranks, the weapons cast to earth, I saw the foe turn his back in base flight.

[55] But do thou, O Father of the gods, grant that the toga-clad throng of Rome may pass for ever before my feet.

SEXTI PROPERTI ELEGIARVM LIBER IV

sex superant versus: te, qui ad vadimonia curris,
   non moror: haec spatiis ultima creta meis.
stipes acernus eram, properanti falce dolatus,
   ante Numam grata pauper in urbe deus.   60
at tibi, Mamurri, formae caelator aenae,
   tellus artifices ne terat Osca manus,
qui me tam dociles potuisti fundere in usus.
   unum opus est, operi non datur unus honos.

III

Haec Arethusa suo mittit mandata Lycotae,
   cum totiens absis, si potes esse meus.
si qua tamen tibi lecturo pars oblita derit,
   haec erit e lacrimis facta litura meis:
aut si qua incerto fallet te littera tractu,
   signa meae dextrae iam morientis erunt.
te modo viderunt iteratos Bactra per ortus,
   te modo munito Neuricus[1] hostis equo,
hibernique Getae, pictoque Britannia curru,
   tunsus[2] et Eoa discolor Indus aqua.   10
haecne marita fides et pactae in savia noctes,[3]
   cum rudis urgenti bracchia victa dedi?
quae mihi deductae fax omen praetulit, illa
   traxit ab everso lumina nigra rogo;

---

[1] munito *Beroaldus*: munitus *NFL*. Neuricus *Jacob* hericus *NFL*.

[2] tunsus *Housman*. ustus *NFL*.

[3] pactae in savia noctes *Haupt*: et parce avia noctes *N*: et pacatae mihi noctes *FL*.

THE ELEGIES OF PROPERTIUS BOOK IV

⁵⁷ Six lines remain; I would not delay you that hurry to answer your bail; this is the ending of my course.

⁵⁹ Once I was a maple stock, rough-hewn with hurried sickle; 'twas before Numa's days I dwelt, no wealthy god, in the city of my love. But may the rude earth ne'er bruise thy cunning hands, Mamurius, that didst grave my form in bronze and hadst the skill to cast me to such changeful use. Thy work is but one, yet manifold the honour that it wins.

III

This charge doth Arethusa send to her Lycotas, if I may call thee mine who art so often far from me. Yet if any part thou wouldst read be lost and blotted, the blot will have been made by my tears; or if any letter baffle thee with uncertain outline, 'twill be the token of my right hand that now faints in death.

⁷ Thee now did Bactra behold in the twice-visited East, now the Neuric foe with armoured steed, the wintry Getans, and Britain of the painted car and the swart Indian washed by the Eastern wave.

¹¹ Was this the meaning of thy wedded troth, of the night pledged to our kisses, when a stranger in love's warfare I yielded to thine onset? The torch that burned with ominous light before me as they led me to thy house drew its baleful flame from the ruins of some pyre; I was sprinkled with water from the

SEXTI PROPERTI ELEGIARVM LIBER IV

et Stygio sum sparsa lacu, nec recta capillis
    vitta data est: nupsi non comitante deo.
omnibus heu portis pendent mea noxia vota:
    texitur haec castris quarta lacerna tuis
occidat, immerita qui carpsit ab arbore vallum
    et struxit querulas rauca per ossa tubas,   20
dignior obliquo funem qui torqueat Ocno,
    aeternusque tuam pascat, aselle, famem!
dic mihi, num[1] teneros urit lorica lacertos?
    num gravis imbelles atterit hasta manus?
haec noceant potius, quam dentibus ulla puella
    det mihi plorandas per tua colla notas!
diceris et macie vultum tenuasse: sed opto,
    e desiderio sit color iste meo.
at mihi cum noctes induxit vesper amaras,
    si qua relicta iacent, osculor arma tua;   30
tum queror in toto non sidere pallia lecto,
    lucis et auctores non dare carmen aves.
noctibus hibernis castrensia pensa laboro
    et Tyria in gladios vellera secta suo;
et disco, qua parte fluat vincendus Araxes,
    quot sine aqua Parthus milia currat equus;
cogor et e tabula pictos ediscere mundos,
    qualis et educti sit positura Dai,[2]
quae tellus sit lenta gelu, quae putris ab aestu,
    ventus in Italiam qui bene vela ferat.   40
assidet una soror curis, et pallida nutrix
    peierat hiberni temporis esse moras.

[1] num ς. dum *NFL*.
[2] educti ... Dai *Ellis:* haec docti ... dei *NFL*.

pool of Styx, the wreath was set awry upon my hair: Hymen was not with me when I wedded. On every gate, alas! are hung my vows for thy safety, vows that bring naught save woe, and 'tis now the fourth cloak I am weaving for thy warfare. Perish the man first plucked the soldier's stake from some unoffending tree, and wrought mournful trumpets from hoarse-echoing bones! Worthier he than Ocnus to twist the rope, sitting slantwise at the task, and to feed thy hungry maw, poor ass, to all eternity!

[23] Tell me, does the breastplate gall thy soft arms? does the heavy spear chafe thy hands that were not meant for war? Sooner let spear and breastplate hurt thee than that any girl should mar thy neck with the marks of her teeth, marks that must bring me tears to weep! They say, too, that thy face is lean and drawn: only I pray that thy pallor spring but from longing for me.

[29] Meanwhile I, when evening brings round for me the bitter night, kiss whatever of thy weapons lie left at home. Then I complain that the coverlet will never stay upon my couch, and that the birds that herald dawn are slow to sing. Through the nights of winter I toil to weave thee raiment for thy life in camp, and sew lengths of woollen cloth purple with Tyrian dye, only to meet the sword. I learn where flows the Araxes thou must conquer, and how many miles the Parthian charger can run without slaking his thirst. I am driven also to study from a map the painted world and to learn what is the position of the far-northern Dahan, what lands are stiff with frost, what crumbling with heat, and what is the wind that may waft thy sails safe home to Italy.

[41] My sister only waits on my sorrows, and my nurse, turning pale, swears falsely 'tis winter's season that

SEXTI PROPERTI ELEGIARVM LIBER IV

felix Hippolyte! nuda tulit arma papilla
  et texit galea barbara molle caput.
Romanis utinam patuissent castra puellis!
  essem militiae sarcina fida tuae,
nec me tardarent Scythiae iuga, cum pater altas
  acrius[1] in glaciem frigore nectit aquas.
omnis amor magnus, sed aperto in coniuge maior:
  hanc Venus, ut vivat, ventilat ipsa facem.   50
nam mihi quo Poenis nunc[2] purpura fulgeat ostris
  crystallusque meas ornet aquosa manus?
omnia surda tacent, rarisque assueta kalendis
  vix aperit clausos una puella Lares,
Craugidos et catulae vox est mihi grata querentis:
  illa tui partem vindicat una toro.
flore sacella tego, verbenis compita velo,
  et crepat ad veteres herba Sabina focos.
sive in finitimo gemuit stans noctua tigno,
  seu voluit tangi parca lucerna mero,   60
illa dies hornis caedem denuntiat agnis,
  succinctique calent ad nova lucra popae
ne, precor, ascensis tanti sit gloria Bactris,
  raptave odorato carbasa lina duci,
plumbea cum tortae sparguntur pondera fundae,
  subdolus et versis increpat arcus equis!
sed (tua sic domitis Parthae telluris alumnis
  pura triumphantis hasta sequatur equos)

[1] acrius *Postgate*: africus *NFL*.
[2] nunc *Housman*: tibi *FL*: te *N*.

THE ELEGIES OF PROPERTIUS BOOK IV

delays thee. Happy Hippolyte! bare-breasted she bore arms and savage-hearted hid her soft locks beneath the helm. Would that the camps of Rome had opened their gates to women; then had I been the faithful burden of thy warfare. Nor would Scythia's hills delay me when Father Jove binds the deep waters to ice with keener cold. Love is mighty ever, but mightier far for an acknowledged husband; this flame Venus herself fans that it may live.

51 To what purpose now should robes of purple shine for me or clear crystal adorn my fingers? All things are silent and deaf, the Lares' closed shrine is opened on the Kalends, that come so seldom, and scarce even then by one solitary handmaid on her accustomed round. Dear to me is the whine of the little dog Craugis: she only claims thy place in my bed. I cover shrines with flowers, I wreathe the crossroads with sacred branches, and the herb Sabine [1] crackles for me on ancient altars. If the owl perched on some neighbouring bough makes moan, or the lamp, as it burns low, needs the sprinkling of wine,[2] that day orders sacrifice of this year's lambs, and the high-girt priests busy themselves to win fresh profit.

63 Count not, I pray, too high the glory of scaling Bactra's walls, or the spoil of fine linen torn from some perfumed chief, in that hour when the bolts of the twisted sling are scattered abroad and the crafty bow twangs from the flying steed! But—so when Parthia's nurslings are tamed may the headless

---

[1] There were two kinds of herb Sabine, one resembling a cypress in leaf, the other identical with *amaracus*, or marjoram. It was used as incense.

[2] The sputtering of a lamp was a good omen. The wine was dropped on the flame to ratify the omen.

SEXTI PROPERTI ELEGIARVM LIBER IV

incorrupta mei conserva foedera lecti!
    hac ego te sola lege redisse velim: 70
armaque cum tulero portae votiva Capenae,
    subscribam SALVO GRATA PVELLA VIRO.

IV

TARPEIVM nemus et Tarpeiae turpe sepulcrum
    fabor et antiqui limina capta Iovis.
hunc Tatius montem[1] vallo praecingit acerno,   7
    fidaque suggesta castra coronat humo.
quid tum Roma fuit, tubicen vicina Curetis
    cum quateret lento murmure saxa Iovis,   10
atque ubi nunc terris dicuntur iura subactis,
    stabant Romano pila Sabina Foro?[2]
murus erant montes: ubi nunc est Curia saepta,
    bellicus exili[3] fonte bibebat equus.   14
lucus erat felix hederoso conditus antro,   3
    multaque nativis obstrepit arbor aquis,   4
Silvani ramosa domus, quo dulcis ab aestu   5
    fistula poturas ire iubebat oves.[4]   6
hinc Tarpeia deae fontem libavit: at illi   15
    urgebat medium fictilis urna caput.
et satis una malae potuit mors esse puellae,
    quae voluit flammas fallere, Vesta, tuas?

---

[1] montem *Heinsius*: fontem *NFL*.
[2] foro *f*. foco *NFL*.   [3] exili *Postgate*. ex illo *NFL*.
[4] 3-6 and 7-14 *transposed by Baehrens*.

spear-shaft[1] follow thy triumphant steeds!—do thou keep unsullied the pact that binds thee to my bed! 'Tis the sole condition on which I would have thee return! Then when I shall have carried thine armour and votive offering to the Capene gate I will write beneath it: THE THANKOFFERING OF A GRATEFUL WIFE FOR HER HUSBAND'S SAFETY.

IV

I WILL tell of the Tarpeian grove, of Tarpeia's shameful tomb, and of the capture of the house of ancient Jove. This mount did Tatius gird with palisade of maple and ringed his camp securely with circling mound. What was Rome in those days when the trumpeter of Cures made the neighbouring cliffs, where Jove sits throned, tremble before his long-drawn blast, and when Sabine javelins stood in the Roman Forum, where now laws are given to the conquered world? Rome had no ramparts save her hills. Where now stands the Senate-house hedged in by walls, once the war-horse drank from a slender spring.

[3] A goodly grove there was, hidden in a rocky, ivy-mantled glen, and many a tree made answering murmur to its native springs. 'Twas the branching home of Sylvanus, whither the sweet pipe would call the sheep from the hot sun to drink. From this spring Tarpeia drew water for her goddess, and the urn of earthenware bowed down her head whereon 'twas poised.

[17] Ah! could one death alone suffice for doom of that accursed maid that had the heart to betray thy sacred

---

[1] A spear-shaft without a head was a reward for distinguished military service.

SEXTI PROPERTI ELEGIARVM LIBER IV

vidit harenosis Tatium proludere campis
   pictaque per flavas arma levare iubas: 20
obstipuit regis facie et regalibus armis,
   interque oblitas excidit urna manus.
saepe illa immeritae causata est omina lunae,
   et sibi tingendas dixit in amne comas:
saepe tulit blandis argentea lilia Nymphis,
   Romula ne faciem laederet hasta Tati:
dumque subit primo Capitolia nubila fumo,
   rettulit hirsutis bracchia secta rubis,
et sua Tarpeia residens ita flevit ab arce
   vulnera, vicino non patienda Iovi: 30
"Ignes castrorum et Tatiae praetoria turmae
   et formosa[1] oculis arma Sabina meis,
o utinam ad vestros sedeam captiva Penates,
   dum captiva mei conspicer ora[2] Tati!
Romani montes, et montibus addita Roma,
   et valeat probro Vesta pudenda meo!
ille equus, ille meos in castra reponet amores,
   cui Tatius dextras collocat ipse iubas!
quid mirum in patrios Scyllam saevisse capillos,
   candidaque in saevos inguina versa canes?   40
prodita quid mirum fraterni cornua monstri,
   cum patuit lecto stamine torta via?
quantum ego sum Ausoniis crimen factura puellis,
   improba virgineo lecta ministra foco!
Pallados exstinctos si quis mirabitur ignes,
   ignoscat: lacrimis spargitur ara meis.

[1] formosa ς: famosa *NFL*.   [2] ora ς · esse *NFL*

THE ELEGIES OF PROPERTIUS BOOK IV

fire, O Vesta? She saw Tatius practise for battle on the sandy plain and lift his flashing spear amid the yellow helmet-plumes. Dumbstruck she marvelled at the king's face and at the kingly armour, and the urn fell from her forgetful hands. Often did she plead that the moon boded ill—yet the moon was guiltless—and said that she must bathe her locks in the running stream. Often she offered silvery lilies to the kindly nymphs, that the spear of Romulus might not wound the face of Tatius; and while she climbed the Capitol clouded with the first smoke of morning she came home with arms torn by rough brambles. And thus as she sate on the Tarpeian height she bewailed the wounds that Jove in his dwelling hard by might not forgive:

31 "Watchfires of the camp and thou, royal tent amidst the host of Tatius, and Sabine armour so lovely to mine eyes, would that I might sit a captive before your household gods, if so I might behold the face of Tatius! Farewell, ye hills of Rome, and Rome that crowns the hills, and Vesta brought to shame by my sin! That horse, o'er whose right shoulder Tatius smooths the mane, that horse and none other shall bear me love-maddened to his camp, my home.

39 "What marvel if Scylla waxed fierce against her father's locks and her white waist was transformed to fierce hounds? What marvel that the horns of the monstrous brother [1] were betrayed, when the path was revealed by the gathering of the thread? What reproach I shall bring upon Ausonia's maids, I the traitress that was chosen to be the handmaid of the virgin hearth! If any shall marvel that the fires of Pallas [2] are extinguished, let him pardon me! The altar is sprinkled with my tears!

[1] The Minotaur.   [2] An image of Minerva was kept in the temple of Vesta and reputed to be the Palladium of Troy.

SEXTI PROPERTI ELEGIARVM LIBER IV

cras, ut rumor ait, tota purgabitur[1] urbe:
    tu cape spinosi rorida terga iugi.
lubrica tota via est et perfida: quippe tacentes
    fallaci celat limite semper aquas.   50
o utinam magicae nossem cantamina Musae!
    haec quoque formoso lingua tulisset opem.
te toga picta decet, non quem sine matris honore
    nutrit inhumanae dura papilla lupae
sic hospes pariamne tua regina sub aula?
    dos tibi non humilis prodita Roma venit.
si minus, at raptae ne sint impune Sabinae,
    me rape et alterna lege repende vices!
commissas acies ego possum solvere: nuptae,
    vos medium palla foedus inite mea.   60
adde Hymenaee modos, tubicen fera murmura conde:
    credite, vestra meus molliet arma torus.
et iam quarta canit venturam bucina lucem,
    ipsaque in Oceanum sidera lapsa cadunt
experiar somnum, de te mihi somnia quaeram:
    fac venias oculis umbra benigna meis."
dixit, et incerto permisit bracchia somno,
    nescia vae furiis[2] accubuisse novis.
nam Vesta, Iliacae felix tutela favillae,
    culpam alit et plures condit in ossa faces   70
illa ruit, qualis celerem prope Thermodonta
    Strymonis abscisso pectus[3] aperta sinu.

---

[1] purgabitur *codd. Cantab., Voss. 81, Berolin. Diez. B. 41*;
pugnabitur *NFL*.
[2] vae furiis *Itali* nefariis *NFL*.
[3] pectus *Hertzberg*· fertur *NFL*.

⁴⁷ "To-morrow, so rumour tells, there shall be a purification through all the city; do thou take the dewy ridge of the thorn-clad hill. The path is slippery and treacherous through all its length: for alway it hides silent waters on its deceitful track. Would that I knew the charms of the magic Muse! Then had my tongue also brought thee succour, my beauteous lover! The royal robe beseems thee rather than that motherless wight, whom the rude teat of the savage she-wolf suckled.

⁵⁵ "Wilt thou make me thy queen on these terms, O stranger, and shall I bear thee children in thy halls? With me comes Rome betrayed, no puny dower! If thou wilt not have me thus, ravish me and have thy vengeance in turn, that the Sabine maids be not ravished unavenged! I have the power to part the hosts when locked in battle: enter, ye brides, on reconciling peace! My robe of marriage shows the way! And do thou, Hymenaeus, sound thy strain: trumpeter, hush thy wild blasts; believe me, my marriage-bed shall assuage your warfare.

⁶³ "Now the fourth bugle sings the approach of dawn, and the stars themselves sink to their rest in Ocean. I will try sleep and will seek for dreams of thee: grant that thy semblance may come to cheer mine eyes."

⁶⁷ She spake, and let fall her arms in uneasy slumber: she knew not, alas! that she had laid her down to be the prey of fresh furies. For Vesta, the blessed guardian of the Trojan embers, fed her sin with fuel and hid more firebrands in her bones. She rushed away, like the Strymonian Amazon by swift Thermodon's bank, with raiment torn and bosom bared to view.

SEXTI PROPERTI ELEGIARVM LIBER IV

urbi festus erat (dixere Parilia Patres),
 hic primus coepit moenibus esse dies,
annua pastorum convivia, lusus in urbe,
 cum pagana madent fercula divitiis,
cumque super raros faeni flammantis acervos
 traicit immundos ebria turba pedes.[1]
Romulus excubias decrevit in otia solvi
 atque intermissa castra silere tuba.   80
hoc Tarpeia suum tempus rata convenit hostem:
 pacta ligat, pactis ipsa futura comes.
mons erat ascensu dubius festoque remissus:[2]
 nec mora, vocales occupat ense canes.
omnia praebebant somnos: sed Iuppiter unus
 decrevit poenis invigilare tuis.
prodiderat portaeque fidem patriamque iacentem,
 nubendique petit, quem velit, ipsa diem.
at Tatius (neque enim sceleri dedit hostis
  honorem)
 "Nube" ait "et regni scande cubile mei!"   90
dixit, et ingestis comitum super obruit armis.
 haec, virgo, officiis dos erat apta tuis.
a duce Tarpeia mons est cognomen adeptus:
 o vigil, iniuste[3] praemia sortis habes.

[1] immundos . . . pedes *Itali* · immundas . . . dapes *NFL*.
[2] remissus *N* · remissis *FL*.   [3] iniuste *FL* · iniustae *N*.

THE ELEGIES OF PROPERTIUS BOOK IV

⁷³ 'Twas a feast-day in the city—the Fathers named it Parilia—the birthday of the walls of Rome, the yearly banquet of the shepherds, when the city makes merry, when country platters are moistened with rich fare, and the drunken crowd flings dust-stained feet o'er heaps of burning hay placed here and there. Romulus decreed that the watchmen should take their ease in rest, that the trumpet should be laid aside and the camp have silence Tarpeia deemed her hour had come and met the foeman: she made her pact, herself a part thereof.

⁸³ The hill was treacherous of ascent, but unguarded by reason of the feast; of a sudden with his sword he cuts down the noisy watchdogs. All was slumber: only Jove had resolved to wake that he might work thy doom. She had betrayed the secret of the gate, betrayed her prostrate country, and asked for marriage on the day of her own choice. But Tatius—for even the foe gave no honour to crime—answered: "Marry then, and climb thus my royal bed." He spake and bade his comrades crush her beneath their piled shields. Such, Vestal, was thy dower, meet guerdon of thy services.

⁹³ The hill took its name from Tarpeia, the foeman's guide. O watcher, unjustly hast thou won this recompense for thy doom.[1]

---

[1] *I.e.*, such was Tarpeia's crime that she did not deserve to have the rock called after her.

SEXTI PROPERTI ELEGIARVM LIBER IV

V

Terra tuum spinis obducat, lena, sepulcrum,
  et tua, quod non vis, sentiat umbra sitim;
nec sedeant cineri Manes, et Cerberus ultor
  turpia ieiuno terreat ossa sono!
docta vel Hippolytum Veneri mollire negantem,
  concordique toro pessima semper avis,
Penelopen quoque neglecto rumore mariti
  nubere lascivo cogeret Antinoo.
illa velit, poterit magnes non ducere ferrum,
  et volucris nidis esse noverca suis.   10
quippe et, Collinas ad fossam moverit herbas,
  stantia currenti diluerentur aqua :
audax cantatae leges imponere lunae
  et sua nocturno fallere terga lupo,
posset ut[1] intentos astu caecare maritos,
  cornicum immeritas eruit ungue genas,
consuluitque striges nostro de sanguine, et in me
  hippomanes fetae semina legit equae.
exercebat opus verbis heu blanda perinde
  saxosam atque forat sedula talpa[2] viam: 20
" Si te Eoa †Dorozantum[3] iuvat aurea ripa,
  et quae sub Tyria concha superbit aqua,

---

[1] ut ς : et *NFL*.
[2] exercebat . . . heu blanda perinde saxosam atque *Housman*: exorabat . . . ceu blanda perure saxosamque *NFL*. forat *Rossberg*: ferat *NFL*. talpa *v*. culpa *NFL*.
[3] dorozantum *N* derorantum *FL*; *probably corrupt*.

THE ELEGIES OF PROPERTIUS BOOK IV

V

May the earth cover thy tomb with thorns, thou bawd, and may thy shade be parched with thirst, for thirst thou hatest. May thy ghost find no rest among thine ashes, and may vengeful Cerberus fright thy dishonoured bones with hungry howl.

[5] Skilled to win even Hippolytus that said "Nay" to love, and ever worst of omens to lovers' peace, she could force even Penelope to be deaf to rumours of her husband's safety and to wed with wanton Antinous. Should she will it, the magnet will refuse to draw the steel, and the bird prove a stepmother to her nestlings. Nay, did she bring herbs from the Colline field to the magic trench, things solid would dissolve into running water. She dared put spells upon the moon to do her bidding and to disguise her shape beneath the form of the night-prowling wolf, that by her cunning she might blind jealous husbands, and with her nails she tore out the undeserving eyes of crows; she consulted owls how she might have my blood, and gathered for my destruction the charm that drips from the pregnant mare.[1]

[19] She plied her task, alas! with flattering words, even as the persistent mole bores out its stony path. Thus would she speak. "If the golden shores of the Dorozantes delight thee, or the shell that flaunts its purple in the Tyrian sea, if Eurypylus' weft of

---

[1] *Cp.* Vergil, *Georg.* III. 280: *hippomanes vero quod nomine dicunt | pastores, lentum distillat ab inguine virus | hippomanes, quod saepe malae legere novercae.*

SEXTI PROPERTI ELEGIARVM LIBER IV

Eurypylique placet Coae textura Minervae,
   sectaque ab Attalicis putria signa toris,
seu quae palmiferae mittunt venalia Thebae,
   murreaque in Parthis pocula cocta focis;
sperne fidem, provolve deos, mendacia vincant,
   frange et¹ damnosae iura pudicitiae!
et simulare virum pretium facit: utere causis!
   maior dilata nocte recurret amor.   30
si tibi forte comas vexaverit, utilis ira:
   postmodo mercata pace premendus erit.
denique ubi amplexu Venerem promiseris empto,
   fac simules puros Isidis esse dies.
ingerat Apriles Iole tibi, tundat Amycle
   natalem Mais Idibus esse tuum.
supplex ille sedet—posita tu scribe cathedra
   quidlibet: has artes si pavet ille, tenes!
semper habe morsus circa tua colla recentes,
   litibus alternis quos putet esse datos   40
nec te Medeae delectent probra sequacis
   (nempe tulit fastus ausa rogare prior),
sed potius mundi Thais pretiosa Menandri,
   cum ferit astutos comica moecha Getas.
in mores te verte viri: si cantica iactat,
   i comes et voces ebria iunge tuas.
ianitor ad dantes vigilet: si pulset inanis,
   surdus in obductam somniet usque seram.²

---

¹ frange et ς : frangent *NFL*
² *This couplet is found in a Pompeian wall-inscription, see C.I.L. 4, 1894. The inscription gives* dantis *and* pulsat.

Coan silk please thee or crumbling figures cut from coverlets of gold, or the wares sent from palm-bearing Thebes and myrrhine [1] goblets baked in Parthian kilns, then spurn thine oath, and down with the gods! Let lies win the day! Break all the laws of chastity; they bring but loss! Feign that thou hast a husband; 'twill heighten thy price! Use every excuse! Love will return with added fire after a night's delay. If perchance he be angry and tear thy hair, his anger shall bring thee profit; after that thou must torment him till he purchase peace. Then when he has bought thine embraces and thou hast promised him enjoyment of thy love, see that thou feign that the days of Isis are come, enjoining abstinence. Let Iole thrust on thy notice that April's Kalends are near, let Amycle din into thine ears that thy birthday falls on the Ides of May. He sits in supplication before thee. Take thy chair and write somewhat: if he trembles at these tricks thou hast him fast! Ever have fresh bites about thy throat, that he may deem to have been given in the strife of love. But delight not thou in the railing of importunate Medea—she was cast off that had dared be first to ask for love. But rather be costly Thais thy pattern, of whom Menander's wit hath told, when the harlot of the stage tricks the shrewd Scythian slaves.

45 "Change thy ways to suit thy man. If he boasts his powers of song, accompany him and join thy drunken voice to his. Let thy porter be open-eyed for them that bring gifts; if he that knocks be empty-handed, let him sleep on, propped on the bar

---

[1] It is not certain what *murra* was. Some take it to be Chinese porcelain, others hold it to be fluor-spar. Propertius seems to describe it as baked in kilns. Pliny, however, speaks of it as a natural product caused by the heat of the earth.

SEXTI PROPERTI ELEGIARVM LIBER IV

nec tibi displiceat miles non factus amori,
    nauta nec attrita si ferat aera manu,   50
aut quorum titulus per barbara colla pependit,
    cretati[1] medio cum saluere foro.
aurum spectato, non quae manus afferat aurum!
    versibus auditis quid nisi verba feres?
 Quid iuvat ornato procedere, vita, capillo
    et tenuis Coa veste movere sinus?'
qui versus, Coae dederit nec munera vestis,
    ipsius tibi sit surda sine aere[2] lyra.
dum vernat sanguis, dum rugis integer annus,
    utere, ne quid cras libet ab ore dies!   60
vidi ego odorati victura rosaria Paesti
    sub matutino cocta iacere Noto.''
his animum nostrae dum versat Acanthis amicae,
    per tenuem ossa mihi sunt numerata cutem.[3]
sed cape torquatae, Venus o regina, columbae
    ob meritum ante tuos guttura secta focos.
vidi ego rugoso tussim concrescere collo,
    sputaque per dentes ire cruenta cavos,
atque animam in tegetes putrem exspirare paternas:
    horruit algenti pergula curta[4] foco.   70
exsequiae fuerant rari furtiva capilli
    vincula et immundo pallida mitra situ,
et canis, in nostros nimis experrecta dolores,
    cum fallenda meo pollice clatra forent.

---

[1] cretati *Passerat* caelati *NFL*.   [2] aere *N*: arte *FL*.
[3] tenuem ossa mihi ... cutem *Jacob.* tenues ossa ... cutes *NFL*.
[4] pergula *Beroaldus* percula *NL*: parvula *F*. curta *ς*. curva *NFL*.

that is drawn across the door. Nor would I have thee spurn soldiers not made for love, nor sailors, if their horny hands bring coin, nor yet one of those on whose barbarian necks the salesman's bill has hung, when with whitened feet they danced in the market-place [1] Look to the gold, not to the hand that brings it. Though thou give ear to their verse, what will be thine save empty words? 'What boots it, light of my life, to go forth with locks adorned, and to rustle in slender folds of Coan silk?' [2] Who brings thee verse yet never a gift of Coan raiment, let his lyre meet with deaf ears, since it brings no pelf. While spring is in the blood and thy years know not wrinkles, use thy time, lest the morrow take toll of thy beauty! I have seen the rose-beds of perfumed Paestum that should have lived lie blasted at morn by the Scirocco's breath."

63 While thus Acanthis plied my mistress' soul, all my bones might be counted beneath the shrunken skin. But do thou, Queen Venus, receive my thank-offering, a ring-dove's throat cut before thine altar. I saw the cough clot in her wrinkled throat, and the bloodstained spittle trickle through her hollow teeth. I saw her breathe out her plague-struck spirit on the blankets that were once her father's: the hearth was chill and the broken shed where she lay shivered for cold. For pomp of funeral she had but the stolen bands that bound her scanty hair, a mutch with colour dimmed by foul neglect; and the dog that of old was over-wakeful for my woes, when with stealthy fingers I had to slip the bolts that

---

[1] It was customary to whiten the feet of slaves put up for sale. They were made to dance to show their physical vigour.

[2] A quotation from I. II. 1, 2.

SEXTI PROPERTI ELEGIARVM LIBER IV

sit tumulus lenae curto vetus amphora collo:
  urgeat hunc supra vis, caprifice, tua.
quisquis amas, scabris hoc bustum caedite saxis,
  mixtaque cum saxis addite verba mala!

VI

Sacra facit vates: sint ora faventia sacris,
  et cadat ante meos icta iuvenca focos.
serta[1] Philetaeis certet Romana corymbis,
  et Cyrenaeas urna ministret aquas.
costum molle date et blandi mihi turis honores,
  terque focum circa laneus orbis eat.
spargite me lymphis, carmenque recentibus aris
  tibia Mygdoniis libet eburna cadis.
ite procul fraudes, alio sint aere noxae:
  pura novum vati laurea mollit iter.   10
Musa, Palatini referemus Apollinis aedem:
  res est, Calliope, digna favore tuo.
Caesaris in nomen ducuntur carmina: Caesar
  dum canitur, quaeso, Iuppiter ipse vaces.
est Phoebi fugiens Athamana ad litora portus,
  qua sinus Ioniae murmura condit aquae,
Actia Iuleae pelagus monumenta carinae,
  nautarum votis non operosa via.
huc mundi coiere manus: stetit aequore moles
  pinea, nec remis aequa favebat avis.   20

---

[1] serta *Scaliger*: cera *NFL*.

barred the door. Let the bawd's tomb be an old wine-jar with broken neck, and over it, wild fig-tree, put thou forth thy might. Whoe'er thou art that lovest, batter this grave with jagged stones, and mingled with the stones add words of cursing!

VI

The priest doth sacrifice; be silent all that his sacrifice may prosper, and let the heifer fall smitten before mine altar-hearths. Let the garland of Rome vie with the ivy-clusters of Philetas, and let the urn serve me with water of Cyrene. Give me soft nard and offerings of appeasing incense, and thrice about the hearth be the woollen fillet twined. Sprinkle me with water, and by the new-built altar let the ivory pipe make libation of song from Phrygian vessels. Fly hence afar all guile, and beneath other skies let mischief dwell; new is the path the priest must tread, but the pure laurel-branch doth make it smooth for him.

11 My Muse, we will tell of the temple of Palatine Apollo; Calliope, the theme is worthy of thy favour. My songs are spun for the glory of Caesar: while Caesar is the theme of song, do thou, Jupiter, even thou, rest from thy labours and give ear.

15 By the Athamanian shores where Phoebus dwells there lies a haven, whose bay hushes the roar of the Ionian sea, Actium's wide water that guards the memory of the Julian bark, and gives easy entrance to the mariner's prayer. Here met the hosts of all the world: motionless on the deep stood the huge ships of pine, yet smiled not fortune alike on all their

SEXTI PROPERTI ELEGIARVM LIBER IV

altera classis erat Teucro damnata Quirino,
 pilaque femineae turpiter apta manu:
hinc Augusta ratis plenis Iovis omine velis,
 signaque iam patriae vincere docta suae.
tandem acies geminos Nereus lunarat in arcus,
 armorum et radiis picta tremebat aqua,
cum Phoebus linquens stantem se vindice Delon
 (nam tulit iratos mobilis una[1] Notos)
astitit Augusti puppim super, et nova flamma
 luxit in obliquam ter sinuata facem.   30
non ille attulerat crines in colla solutos
 aut testudineae carmen inerme lyrae,
sed quali aspexit Pelopeum Agamemnona vultu,
 egessitque avidis Dorica castra rogis,
aut qualis flexos solvit Pythona per orbes
 serpentem, imbelles quem timuere deae[2]
mox ait "O longa mundi servator ab Alba,
 Auguste, Hectoreis cognite maior avis,
vince mari: iam terra tua est: tibi militat arcus
 et favet ex umeris hoc onus omne meis.   40
solve metu patriam, quae nunc te vindice freta
 imposuit prorae publica vota tuae.
quam nisi defendes, murorum Romulus augur
 ire Palatinas non bene vidit aves.
et nimium remis audent prope: turpe Latinos[3]
 principe te fluctus regia vela pati.

[1] una ϛ unda *NFL*
[2] deae *ed. Etonensis* · lyrae *NFL*
[3] Latinos *Markland*. latinis *NFL*.

oars. There stood one fleet, doomed by Trojan Quirinus, and Roman javelins—ah! shame!—were grasped in a woman's hand. And there stood the ship of Augustus, its sails filled by the blessing of Jove, its standards long since taught to conquer for their country's sake. And now Nereus had bent the lines to twin crescent curves and the water quivered bright with the flash of arms, when Phoebus, leaving Delos, that abides firmly rooted now beneath his protection—for once alone of isles it was the sport of the South Wind's anger—took his stand above Augustus' ship, and thrice a strange flame shone forth, bent like the slant lightning-flash. He came not with hair streaming o'er his neck or with peaceful music of the tortoise lyre; but his face was as when he looked on Agamemnon Pelops' son, and carried forth the warriors of the Dorian camp to the greedy funeral pyre;[1] or as when he slew the serpent Python, the terror of the peaceful Muses, and relaxed its coils in death.

37 Then he spake: "O saviour of the world, Augustus, sprung from Alba Longa and known for greater than thy Trojan sires, conquer now by sea! Already the land is thine. My bow fights for thee, and every arrow that burdens my shoulders wishes thee well. Free thy country from fear, thy country that, relying on thy protection, hath freighted thy bark with a nation's prayers. If thou defend her not, 'twas in evil hour that Romulus, as he sought omens for the founding of his walls, beheld the birds fly forth from the Palatine Aye! and too near they venture with their oars! Shame that Latium's waves, while thou art prince, should bear the sails of a queen! Nor let it

---

[1] A reference to the plague sent by Apollo to punish Agamemnon for the rape of Chryseis. See *Iliad*, I.

SEXTI PROPERTI ELEGIARVM LIBER IV

nec te, quod classis centenis remiget alis,
　　terreat: invito labitur illa mari:
quodque vehunt prorae Centaurica saxa minantes,
　　tigna cava et pictos experiere metus.　　　　50
frangit et attollit vires in milite causa;
　　quae nisi iusta subest, excutit arma pudor.
tempus adest, committe rates: ego temporis auctor
　　ducam laurigera Iulia rostra manu."
dixerat, et pharetrae pondus consumit in arcus:
　　proxima post arcus Caesaris hasta fuit.
vincit Roma fide Phoebi: dat femina poenas:
　　sceptra per Ionias fracta vehuntur aquas.
at pater Idalio miratur Caesar ab astro:
　　"Sum deus; est nostri sanguinis ista fides."　　60
prosequitur cantu Triton, omnesque marinae
　　plauserunt circa libera signa deae.
illa petit Nilum cumba male nixa fugaci,
　　hoc unum, iusso non moritura die
di melius! quantus mulier foret una triumphus,
　　ductus erat per quas ante Iugurtha vias!
Actius hinc traxit Phoebus monumenta, quod eius
　　una decem vicit missa sagitta rates.
bella satis cecini: citharam iam poscit Apollo
　　victor et ad placidos exuit arma choros.　　　　70
candida nunc molli subeant convivia luco;
　　blanditiaeque fluant per mea colla rosae,

fright thee that their fleet is winged, each ship, with an hundred oars. The sea whereon it sails will have none of it. And though the prows bear figures threatening to cast rocks such as centaurs throw, thou shalt find them but hollow planks and painted terrors. 'Tis his cause that makes or mars a soldier's strength. If the cause be not just, shame strikes the weapon from his hands. The time is come! Launch thy ships upon the foe! 'Tis I appoint the hour of battle and will guide the Julian prows with laurel-bearing hand."

⁵⁵ He spake and gave his quiver's burden to the bow; after his shafts the spear of Caesar was first to fly. Phoebus kept troth and Rome conquered; the woman met her doom, and broken sceptres floated on Ionia's waves. But his sire Caesar gazed marvelling from his Idalian star:[1] "I am a god, and thy victory gives proof that thou art sprung from our blood." Triton hailed the victor with his song, and all the sea-goddesses clapped their hands around the standards of liberty. But she, vainly trusting in her flying sloop, sought the Nile; this only did she win, death at the hour of her own choice. Heaven willed it and 'twas better so; how mean a triumph would one woman make in those streets through which Jugurtha once was led!

⁶⁷ Hence Actian Phoebus won his temple. Each arrow sped from his bow vanquished ten vessels of the foe.

⁶⁹ I have sung enough of war: victorious Apollo now demands my lyre, and doffs his armour for the dances of peace. Let white-robed banqueters enter the luxuriant grove, and winsome roses stream about

---

[1] The star of Caesar was a comet which appeared shortly after his death. It is called Idalian because the *gens Iulia* traced their descent from Venus through Aeneas.

SEXTI PROPERTI ELEGIARVM LIBER IV

vinaque fundantur prelis elisa Falernis,
  terque[1] lavet nostras spica Cilissa comas.
ingenium potis[2] irritet Musa poetis:
  Bacche, soles Phoebo fertilis esse tuo.
ille paludosos memoret servire Sycambros,
  Cepheam hic Meroen fuscaque regna canat,
hic referat sero confessum foedere Parthum:
  " Reddat signa Remi, mox dabit ipse sua: 80
sive aliquid pharetris Augustus parcet Eois,
  differat in pueros ista tropaea suos.
gaude, Crasse, nigras si quid sapis inter harenas:
  ire per Euphraten ad tua busta licet."
sic noctem patera, sic ducam carmine, donec
  iniciat radios in mea vina dies.

VII

Svnt aliquid Manes: letum non omnia finit,
  luridaque evictos[3] effugit umbra rogos.
Cynthia namque meo visa est incumbere fulcro,
  murmur ad extremae nuper humata viae,
cum mihi somnus ab exsequiis penderet amoris,
  et quererer lecti frigida regna mei.
eosdem habuit secum quibus est elata capillis,
  eosdem oculos: lateri vestis adusta fuit,
et solitum digito beryllon adederat ignis,
  summaque Lethaeus triverat ora liquor.   10
spirantisque animos et vocem misit: at illi
  pollicibus fragiles increpuere manus:

[1] terque ϛ: perque *NFL*.   [2] potis ϛ: positis *NFL*.
[3] evictos ϛ: eiunctos *N* evinctos *FL*.

my neck. Be wine outpoured crushed in Falernian presses, and thrice let Cilician saffron bathe my locks. Let the Muse stir poets that now are fired with wine; Bacchus, 'tis thy wont to inspire Phoebus whom thou lovest. Let one tell how the Sycambri of the marsh have bowed to slavery, another sing of the dusky realms of Cephean Meroe; let another record how late in time the Parthian hath made truce and owned defeat. "Let him return the standards of Remus; soon shall he yield up his own. Or if Augustus spare for a little the quivers of the East, let him put off those trophies that his boys [1] may win them. Rejoice, Crassus, if thou knowest aught in the darkness of the sands where thou liest: now may we cross Euphrates to thy grave." Thus will I pass the night with drink and thus with song, till dawn shall cast its rays upon my wine.

VII

THE Shades are no fable: death is not the end of all, and the pale ghost escapes the vanquished pyre. For Cynthia seemed to bend o'er my couch's head, Cynthia so lately buried beside the roaring road, as fresh from love's entombment I slept a broken sleep and mourned that the bed that was my kingdom was void and cold. Her hair, her eyes were the same as when she was borne to the grave: her raiment was charred against her side, and the fire had eaten away the beryl ring her finger wore, and the water of Lethe had withered her lips. Spirit and voice yet lived, but the thumb-bones rattled on her brittle hands.

[1] The grandsons of Augustus, Lucius and Caius Caesar.

SEXTI PROPERTI ELEGIARVM LIBER IV

"Perfide nec cuiquam melior sperande puellae,
   in te iam vires somnus habere potest?
iamne tibi exciderant vigilacis furta Suburae
   et mea nocturnis trita fenestra dolis?
per quam demisso quotiens tibi fune pependi,
   alterna veniens in tua colla manu!
saepe Venus trivio commissa[1] est, pectore mixto
   fecerunt tepidas pallia nostra vias.   20
foederis heu taciti, cuius fallacia verba
   non audituri diripuere Noti!
at mihi non oculos quisquam inclamavit euntis:
   unum impetrassem te revocante diem:
nec crepuit fissa me propter harundine custos,
   laesit et obiectum tegula curta caput
denique quis nostro curvum te funere vidit,
   atram quis lacrimis incaluisse togam?
si piguit portas ultra procedere, at illuc
   iussisses lectum lentius ire meum.   30
cur ventos non ipse rogis, ingrate, petisti?
   cur nardo flammae non oluere meae?
hoc etiam grave erat, nulla mercede hyacinthos
   inicere et fracto busta piare cado.
Lygdamus uratur, candescat lammina vernae:
   sensi ego, cum insidiis pallida vina bibi.
aut Nomas arcanas tollat versuta salivas:
   dicet damnatas ignea testa manus.

---

[1] commissa ς : commixta *NFL*.

THE ELEGIES OF PROPERTIUS BOOK IV

13 "False heart!" she cried, "—yet ne'er may woman hope for truer—can sleep have power on thee so soon? So soon hast thou forgotten the guile we practised in the sleepless Subura and my window worn by our cunning in the night?—that window from which so oft for thy sake I let down the rope and hung in mid air, as with alternate hand descending I came to thine embrace. Oft at the cross-roads were our rites accomplished and the street grew warm beneath our cloaks. Alas for that wordless bond whose cheating terms the deaf wind of the South-West has swept away! Yet no man called upon my name as I passed and mine eyelids closed: surely hadst thou recalled me, I had been granted one more day. No watchman rattled his cleft reed for my sake, and a broken tile wounded my defenceless brow.[1] Aye, and who saw thee bowed with grief at my graveside? who saw thy robe of mourning grow hot with thy tears? If it vexed thee to go further than my portal, yet thus far thou mightest have bidden my bier be borne more slowly. Why, ungrateful, prayedst thou not for winds to fan my pyre? Why were the flames wherein I burned not fragrant with nard? Was this also a burden, to cast hyacinths —no costly gift—upon me and to appease mine ashes with wine from the shattered jar?

35 " Let Lygdamus be burned, let the branding-iron glow white for the slave of mine house! I knew his guilt when I drank the wine that struck me pale. And as for Nomas, let her hide her secret poisons if she will! The burning potsherd shall convict her

[1] The meaning of this line is uncertain. It may mean (1) that her head was propped on the bier by a broken tile, or (2) that on the way to burial her head was cut by a falling tile.

SEXTI PROPERTI ELEGIARVM LIBER IV

quae modo per viles inspecta est publica noctes,
   haec nunc aurata cyclade signat humum,   40
et graviora rependit iniquis pensa quasillis,
   garrula de facie si qua locuta mea est ;
nostraque quod Petale tulit ad monumenta coronas,
   codicis immundi vincula sentit anus ;
caeditur et Lalage tortis suspensa capillis,
   per nomen quoniam est ausa rogare meum ;
te patiente meae conflavit imaginis aurum,
   ardente e nostro dotem habitura rogo.
non tamen insector, quamvis mereare, Properti :
   longa mea in libris regna fuere tuis.   50
iuro ego Fatorum nulli revolubile carmen,
   tergeminusque canis sic mihi molle sonet,
me servasse fidem. si fallo, vipera nostris
   sibilet in tumulis et super ossa cubet.
nam gemina est sedes turpem sortita per amnem,
   turbaque diversa remigat omnis aqua :
una Clytaemestrae stuprum vehit, altera Cressae
   portat mentitae lignea monstra bovis :
ecce coronato pars altera rapta[1] phaselo,
   mulcet ubi Elysias aura beata rosas,   60
qua numerosa fides, quaque aera rotunda[2] Cybelles
   mitratisque sonant Lydia plectra choris.
Andromedeque et Hypermestre sine fraude maritae
   narrant historias, pectora nota, suas :[3]
haec sua maternis[4] queritur livere catenis
   bracchia nec meritas frigida saxa manus ;

[1] rapta *Palmer*   parta *NFL*.
[2] quaque aera rotunda *Turnebus*: qua quaerar ut unda *N*, *and similar corruptions in FL*.
[3] historias . . . suas *Markland*. historiae . . . suae *NFL*.
[4] sua maternis *μ*: suma eternis *L* · summa eternis *NF*.

THE ELEGIES OF PROPERTIUS BOOK IV

hands of guilt. She that of old was public to all men's gaze and asked so little for her love, now marks the dust with her train's golden hem, and if some chattering slave hath praised my beauty, requites her unjustly with heavier tasks of wool. For bearing wreaths to my sepulchre aged Petale is shackled to a foul clog of wood, while Lalage is hung by her twisted hair for daring to ask a boon in my name.

47 "And thou didst suffer *her* to melt mine image of gold, that so she might win her dowry from the flame that consumed me. Yet I chide thee not, Propertius, though thou deservest my chiding: long did I reign supreme in thy songs. I swear by the chant of the Fates that none may make unsung (and may the three-headed hound lull his baying for me, as I speak true), I swear that I kept faith to thee. If I lie, may the adder hiss on my tomb and couch above my bones.

55 "Two mansions are there allotted beside the foul stream of Hell, and all the dead must ply the oar this way or that. One bark bears the adultery of Clytemestra, another the monstrous timber of the feigned Cretan cow;[1] but lo! yet others are swept away in wreathèd boat, where blessed airs fan the roses of Elysium, where the harp makes music and the round cymbals of Cybelle, and turbaned dancers strike the Lydian lyre. Andromede and Hypermestra, souls renowned, wives without blame, tell forth their story. The one complains that her arms are bruised with the chains brought on her by her mother's pride, and that her hands deserved not to

[1] See Pasiphae, Index.

SEXTI PROPERTI ELEGIARVM LIBER IV

narrat Hypermestre magnum ausas esse sorores,
   in scelus hoc animum non valuisse suum.
sic mortis lacrimis vitae sanamus amores:
   celo ego perfidiae crimina multa tuae   70
sed tibi nunc mandata damus, si forte moveris
   si te non totum Chloridos herba tenet:
nutrix in tremulis ne quid desideret annis
   Parthenie: patuit,[1] nec tibi avara fuit:
deliciaeque meae Latris, cui nomen ab usu est,
   ne speculum dominae porrigat illa novae:
et quoscumque meo fecisti nomine versus,
   ure mihi: laudes desine habere meas.
pelle hederam tumulo, mihi quae pugnante corymbo
   mollia[2] contortis alligat ossa comis;   80
ramosis Anio qua pomifer incubat arvis,
   et numquam Herculeo numine pallet ebur;
hic carmen media dignum me scribe columna,
   sed breve, quod currens vector ab urbe legat:
HIC TIBVRTINA IACET AVREA CYNTHIA TERRA:
   ACCESSIT RIPAE LAVS, ANIENE, TVAE.
nec tu sperne piis venientia somnia portis:
   cum pia venerunt somnia, pondus habent.
nocte vagae ferimur, nox clausas liberat umbras,
   errat et abiecta Cerberus ipse sera.   90
luce iubent leges Lethaea ad stagna reverti:
   nos vehimur, vectum nauta recenset onus.

[1] patuit ς: potuit *NFL*.
[2] mollia ς molli *NFL*.

be bound to icy crags. Hypermestra tells how her sisters dared a mighty deed, and how she had not heart for such a crime. Thus with the tears of death we heal the passions of life; I hide in silence the many sins of thy faithlessness.

71 "But now I charge thee, if perchance my words move thee, and the spells[1] of Chloris hold not all thy soul: let my nurse Parthenie lack naught in her years of palsied eld; she was kind to thee and clutched not at thy gold. And let not my darling Latris, whose name came from her service,[2] hold up the mirror for another mistress. And all the verses thou didst make in mine honour, burn them, I pray thee; cease to win praise through me. Drive the ivy from my tomb, that with grappling cluster and twining leaves binds my frail bones, where apple-bearing Anio broods o'er its orchard meadows and by the favour of Hercules the ivory ne'er grows yellow.[3] And write these verses on a pillar's midst; they shall be worthy of me, but brief, that the traveller may read them as he hastens by: HERE GOLDEN CYNTHIA LIES IN THE FIELDS OF TIBUR. ANIO, NEW PRAISE IS ADDED TO THY BANK.

87 "Nor spurn thou visions that come through holy portals; when dreams are holy they have the weight of truth. By night we range in wandering flight; night frees the prisoned shades, and Cerberus himself strays at will, the bar that chains him cast aside. At dawn Hell's ordinance bids us return to the pools of Lethe: we are ferried over and the mariner tells o'er his freight.

---

[1] Lit "herbs" = love-philtre.
[2] *Latris*, from λατρεύειν, "to serve."
[3] The air of Tibur was supposed to preserve ivory. Hercules was specially worshipped there.

SEXTI PROPERTI ELEGIARVM LIBER IV

nunc [1] te possideant aliae: mox sola tenebo:
  mecum eris, et mixtis ossibus ossa teram."
haec postquam querula mecum sub lite peregit,
  inter complexus excidit umbra meos.

VIII

Disce, quid Esquilias hac nocte fugarit aquosas,
  cum vicina Novis turba cucurrit Agris.
Lanuvium annosi vetus est tutela draconis:
  hic tibi [2] tam rarae non perit hora morae;
qua sacer abripitur caeco descensus hiatu,
  qua penetrat (virgo, tale iter omne cave!)
ieiuni serpentis honos, cum pabula poscit
  annua et ex ima sibila torquet humo.
talia demissae pallent ad sacra puellae,
  cum temere anguino creditur ore manus.   10
ille sibi admotas a virgine corripit escas:
  virginis in palmis ipsa canistra tremunt.
si fuerint castae, redeunt in colla parentum,
  clamantque agricolae " Fertilis annus erit."
huc mea detonsis avecta est Cynthia mannis: [3]
  causa fuit Iuno, sed mage causa Venus.
Appia, dic quaeso, quantum te teste triumphum
  egerit effusis per tua saxa rotis,
[turpis in arcana sonuit cum rixa taberna;
  si sine me, famae non sine labe meae.[4]]   20

---

[1] nunc *N*   nec *FL*.   [2] hic tibi *ς*.   hic ubi *NFL*.
[3] mannis *Beroaldus*   ab annis *NFL*.
[4] *This couplet is clearly alien to the context: Lutjohann would place it after line 2, perhaps rightly.*

THE ELEGIES OF PROPERTIUS BOOK IV

93 "Now let others possess thee! Soon shalt thou be mine alone; with me shalt thou be, and I will grind bone with mingled bone."

95 When thus in querulous plaint she had brought her tale to a close, her spirit vanished from my embrace.

VIII

Learn what this night struck panic through the watery Esquiline, when all the neighbours ran headlong through the New Fields

3 Lanuvium is from of old under the guard of an ancient serpent; thou shalt not count it wasted time if thou give an hour to so wondrous a visit. Here down a dark chasm plunges a sacred path, where penetrates the offering of the hungry snake—beware, O maid, of all such paths as this!—when he demands his yearly tribute of food and sends forth loud hisses from the depths of earth. Maids that are sent down to rites such as this turn pale when their hand is rashly trusted in the serpent's mouth. He seizes the morsels that the virgin holds toward him: even the baskets tremble in the virgin's hands. If they have been chaste, they return to embrace their parents, and farmers cry: "'Twill be a fertile year."

15 Hither was my Cynthia drawn by close-clipped ponies. She pleaded Juno's worship; more truly had she pleaded rites of Venus. Tell forth, prithee, thou Appian Way, what a triumphal journey she made before thine eyes, as her wheels whirled madly over thy paving-stones, [when a noisy brawl broke out in a secret tavern and brought shame on my fair

315

SEXTI PROPERTI ELEGIARVM LIBER IV

spectaclum ipsa sedens primo temone pependit,
   ausa per impuros frena movere locos.
Serica nam taceo vulsi carpenta nepotis [1]
   atque armillatos colla Molossa canes,
qui dabit immundae venalia fata saginae,
   vincet ubi erasas barba pudenda genas.
cum fieret nostro totiens iniuria lecto,
   mutato volui [2] castra movere toro.
Phyllis Aventinae quaedam est vicina Dianae,
   sobria grata parum: cum bibit, omne decet.   30
altera Tarpeios est inter Teia lucos,
   candida, sed potae non satis unus erit.
his ego constitui noctem lenire vocatis,
   et Venere ignota furta novare mea.
unus erat tribus in secreta lectulus herba.
   quaeris concubitus? inter utramque fui.
Lygdamus ad cyathos, vitrique [3] aestiva supellex
   et Methymnaei Graeca saliva meri.
Nile, tuus tibicen erat, crotalistria [4] Phyllis,
   et facilis spargi munda sine arte rosa,   40
Magnus et ipse suos breviter concretus in artus
   iactabat truncas ad cava buxa manus.
sed neque suppletis constabat flamma lucernis,
   reccidit inque suos mensa supina pedes.

---

[1] Serica nam taceo *Beroaldus*: si riganam tacto *NFL*. nepotis ϛ : nepoti *NFL*.

[2] mutato ϛ. mulctato *NFL*. volui *Beroaldus* voluit *NFL*.

[3] vitrique *Scaliger* · utrique *N*. uterque *FL*.

[4] crotalistria *Turnebus* eboralistria *N*: colistria *F*: coralistria *L*.

THE ELEGIES OF PROPERTIUS BOOK IV

name, though I was not there]. She was a sight to see as she sat there bending over the pole's end and daring to drive amain through rough places. For I say naught of the silk-hung chariot of the close-shaven fop, nor of the dogs with rich collars about their Molossian necks; some day he will sell his doomed body to feed on the foul fare of a gladiator, when the beard whereof he is now ashamed shall master those close-shaven cheeks.

[27] Since so oft she wronged our bed, I resolved to change my couch and pitch my camp elsewhere. There is a certain Phyllis, that dwells nigh Diana on the Aventine. Sober she pleases me little; when she drinks all is charm. Another there is, one Teia, that dwells 'twixt the Tarpeian groves; fair is she, but when the wine is on her, one lover will be all too few. These two I resolved to summon to make night pass less sadly, and to renew my amorous adventures with love still strange to me. One little couch there was for three on a secret lawn. Dost ask how we lay? I was between the two. Lygdamus had charge of our cups; we had a service of glass to suit the summer with Greek wine that smacked of Methymna. Thou, Nile, didst provide us with a piper, while Phyllis played the castanets, and, fair in her artless beauty, was right content to be pelted with roses. Magnus himself, with short and shrunken limbs, clapped his deformed hands to the sound of the hollow boxwood flute. But, though their bowls were full, the lamp-flames flickered, and the table's top fell upside down on the feet that had supported

SEXTI PROPERTI ELEGIARVM LIBER IV

me quoque per talos Venerum quaerente secundos
   semper damnosi subsiluere canes.
cantabant surdo, nudabant pectora caeco:
   Lanuvii ad portas, ei mihi, solus eram;
cum subito rauci sonuerunt cardine postes,
   et levia ad primos murmura facta Lares.   50
nec mora, cum totas resupinat Cynthia valvas,
   non operosa comis, sed furibunda decens.
pocula mi digitos inter cecidere remissos,
   pallueruntque ipso labra soluta mero.
fulminat illa oculis et quantum femina saevit,
   spectaclum capta nec minus urbe fuit.
Phyllidos iratos in vultum conicit ungues:
   territa vicinas Teia clamat aquas.
lumina sopitos turbant elata Quirites,
   omnis et insana semita nocte sonat.   60
illas direptisque comis tunicisque solutis
   excipit obscurae prima taberna viae.
Cynthia gaudet in exuviis victrixque recurrit
   et mea perversa sauciat ora manu,
imponitque notam collo morsuque cruentat,
   praecipueque oculos, qui meruere, ferit.
atque ubi iam nostris lassavit bracchia plagis,
   Lygdamus ad plutei fulcra[1] sinistra latens
eruitur, geniumque meum protractus adorat.
   Lygdame, nil potui: tecum ego captus eram.   70
supplicibus palmis tum demum ad foedera veni,[2]
   cum vix tangendos praebuit illa pedes,

---

[1] fulcra *Beroaldus*: fusca *NFL*.   [2] veni ς: venit *NFL*.

it. And as for me, while I sought for sixes from the favouring dice, ever the ruinous aces leapt to light. They sang to me, but I was deaf. They bared their bosoms, but I was blind. Alas! I stood alone at Lanuvium's gates.

[49] And lo! of a sudden the door-posts groaned harsh with turning hinge, and a light sound was heard at the entrance of the house. Straightway Cynthia hurled back the folding portals, Cynthia with hair disordered, yet lovely in her fury. My fingers loosed their grasp and dropped the cup; my lips turned pale though drunken with wine. Her eyes flashed fire: she raged with all a woman's fury. The sight was fearful as a city's sack. She dashed her angry nails in Phyllis' face: Teia calls out in terror on all the watery neighbourhood. The brandished lights awakened the slumbering citizens, and all the street rang loud with the madness of the night. The girls fled with dishevelled raiment and tresses torn, and the first tavern in the street received them.

[63] Cynthia rejoiced in her spoils and hastened back to me victorious, and bruised my face with cruel hands, and marked my neck with her teeth, till her bite drew blood, and above all smote mine eyes that had deserved her blows. Then when her arms were tired with beating me she routed forth Lygdamus, who lay hid on our left crouched beneath the couch's head at its very feet. Dragged forth to light, he implored protection from my guardian spirit. Lygdamus, I was powerless; I was thy fellow-captive.

[71] At last I yielded to her terms, my hands outstretched in suppliant wise; but scarce would she let me so much as touch her feet, and said: "If thou

SEXTI PROPERTI ELEGIARVM LIBER IV

atque ait "Admissae si vis me ignoscere culpae,
 accipe, quae nostrae formula legis erit.
tu neque Pompeia spatiabere cultus in umbra,
 nec cum lascivum sternet harena Forum.
colla cave inflectas ad summum obliqua theatrum,
 aut lectica tuae se det¹ aperta morae.
Lygdamus in primis, omnis mihi causa querelae,
 veneat et pedibus vincula bina trahat." 80
indixit legem: respondi ego "Legibus utar."
 riserat imperio facta superba dato.
dein quemcumque locum externae tetigere puellae,
 suffiit,² ac pura limina tergit aqua,
imperat et totas iterum mutare lacernas,
 terque meum tetigit sulpuris igne caput.
atque ita mutato per singula pallia lecto
 respondi, et noto³ solvimus arma toro.

IX

Amphitryoniades qua tempestate iuvencos
 egerat a stabulis, o Erythea, tuis,
venit ad invictos pecorosa Palatia montes,
 et statuit fessos fessus et ipse boves,
qua Velabra suo stagnabant flumine quaque⁴
 nauta per urbanas velificabat aquas.

¹ se det *Gruter*: sudet *NFL*
² suffiit *Beroaldus*, ac *Baehrens* sufficat *NFL*.
³ respondi *NFL, perhaps corrupt* escendi *Postgate*. noto *Heinsius*· toto *NFL* ⁴ quaque ς: quoque *NFL*.

wouldst have me pardon the sin thou hast done, hear the conditions of the law that I impose. Never shalt thou walk abroad in rich attire in the shade of Pompey's colonnade, nor when the sand is strewn in the wanton Forum.[1] Beware that thou bend not thy neck awry to gaze at the theatre's topmost ring; let never a litter yield itself uncurtained to thy loitering gaze. And above all let Lygdamus, chief cause of my complaint, be sold and trail double shackles on his feet."

[81] Such were the terms she imposed. I replied: "I accept the terms." She laughed, exulting in the dominion I had given her over me. Then she purified with fire each place that the foreign girls had touched, and cleansed the threshold with pure water; she bade me change all my raiment anew, and thrice touched my head with burning sulphur. Then when every covering of the bed had been changed, I bowed to her will and we made up our quarrel on the couch we knew so well.

IX

What time Amphitryon's son drove the oxen from thy stalls, O Erythea, he came to that hill untamed by man, the sheep-grazed Palatine, and there, himself aweary, halted his weary kine, where the Velabrum spread its stagnant stream and the mariner sailed over waters in the city's midst. But the kine

---

[1] *I.e.*, for gladiatorial shows, which were sometimes given in the Forum.

SEXTI PROPERTI ELEGIARVM LIBER IV

sed non infido manserunt hospite Caco
  incolumes: furto polluit ille Iovem.
incola Cacus erat, metuendo raptor ab antro,
  per tria partitos qui dabat ora sonos.   10
hic, ne certa forent manifestae signa rapinae,
  aversos cauda traxit in antra boves,
nec sine teste deo: furem sonuere iuvenci,
  furis et implacidas diruit ira fores.
Maenalio iacuit pulsus tria tempora ramo
  Cacus, et Alcides sic ait: " Ite boves,
Herculis ite boves, nostrae labor ultime clavae,
  bis mihi quaesitae, bis mea praeda, boves,
arvaque mugitu sancite Bovaria longo:
  nobile erit Romae pascua vestra Forum."   20
dixerat, et sicco torquet sitis ora palato,
  terraque non ullas[1] feta ministrat aquas.
sed procul inclusas audit ridere puellas,
  lucus ubi[2] umbroso fecerat orbe nemus,
femineae loca clausa deae fontesque piandos,
  impune et nullis sacra retecta viris.
devia puniceae velabant limina vittae,
  putris odorato luxerat igne casa,
populus et longis ornabat frondibus aedem,
  multaque cantantes umbra tegebat aves.   30
huc ruit in siccam congesta pulvere barbam,
  et iacit ante fores verba minora deo:
" Vos precor, o luci sacro quae luditis antro,
  pandite defessis hospita fana[3] viris.

---

[1] ullas ς: nullas *NFL.*   [2] ubi *Heinsius* ab *NFL*
[3] fana *Scaliger* vana *NFL.*

THE ELEGIES OF PROPERTIUS BOOK IV

remained not safe, since Cacus proved a disloyal host, and outraged Jove with theft. Cacus was a dweller in the place, a robber issuing from his dreaded cave, who spake with threefold utterance from three several mouths. He, that there might be no sure token to betray his theft, dragged the cattle tail foremost to his cave. But the god beheld him: the lowing steers revealed the thief, and wrath beat down the thief's cruel [1] doors.

[15] Cacus lay low, thrice smitten on the brow with the Maenalian club, and thus spake Alcides: "Go, ye oxen, go, oxen of Hercules, the last labour of my club. Twice, oxen, did I seek ye, and twice ye were my prey. Go ye and with your long-drawn lowing hallow the Place of Oxen; your pasture shall in times to come be the far-famed Forum of Rome." He spake, and thirst tortured his parched palate, while teeming earth supplied no water.

[23] But far off he heard the laughter of cloistered maids, where a sacred grove made a dark encircling wood, the secret place of the Goddess of Women,[2] with holy fountains and rites ne'er revealed to men save to their cost. Wreaths of purple veiled its portals far-withdrawn and a ruinous hovel shone with sweet fire of incense. A poplar decked the shrine with its long leaves, and its deep foliage shielded singing birds.

[31] Hither he rushed, the dust thick-clotted on his parched beard, and before the portal spake wild words unworthy of a god. "Ye, that make merry in the sacred dells of the grove, I pray you, open your hospitable shrine to a weary man Athirst for water

[1] Probably because they were decorated with trophies of human bones, &c. *Cp.* Ovid. *Fasti*, I. 557; Vergil, *Aeneid*, VIII. 196. [2] The Bona Dea

SEXTI PROPERTI ELEGIARVM LIBER IV

fontis egens erro circaque sonantia lymphis,
 et cava suscepto flumine palma sat est.
audistisne aliquem, tergo qui sustulit orbem?
 ille ego sum: Alciden terra recepta vocat.
quis facta Herculeae non audit fortia clavae
 et numquam ad nocuas[1] irrita tela feras, 40
atque uni Stygias homini luxisse tenebras?
 accipite: haec[2] fesso vix mihi terra patet.
quodsi Iunoni sacrum faceretis amarae,
 non clausisset aquas ipsa noverca suas.
sin aliquem vultusque meus saetaeque leonis
 terrent et Libyco sole perusta coma,
idem ego Sidonia feci servilia palla
 officia et Lydo pensa diurna colo,
mollis et hirsutum cepit mihi fascia pectus,
 et manibus duris apta puella fui." 50
talibus Alcides; at talibus alma sacerdos,
 puniceo canas stamine vincta comas:
" Parce oculis, hospes, lucoque abscede verendo
 cede agedum et tuta limina linque fuga.
interdicta viris metuenda lege piatur,
 quae se summota vindicat ara casa.
magno[3] Tiresias aspexit Pallada vates,
 fortia dum posita Gorgone membra lavat.
di tibi dent alios fontes: haec lympha puellis
 avia secreti limitis una fluit." 60

[1] nocuas *Santen*: vatas *N* · natas *FL*.
[2] accipite *ς*: accipit *NFL*. haec *f*: et *N*: hic *FL*. *The whole line is perhaps interpolated: compare l. 66.*
[3] magno *Passerat*: magnam *NFL*.

I wander, while all the place is loud with the sound of streams. Enough for me were a draught of the running brook caught in the hollow of my hand. Have ye heard of one that bore the globe on his back? I am he; the world I carried calls me Alcides. Who has not heard of the mighty deeds of Hercules' club, and of those shafts that ne'er were spent in vain on ravening beasts? Who has not heard how for me alone of mortals the darkness of Hell [1] was not dark? Receive me; this land is all but closed to me and I am aweary. Nay, though ye were sacrificing to Juno, that is my bane, even my stepdame had not closed her waters to me. But if some one of you be frighted by my visage and the lion's mane and my locks burnt by the Libyan sun, I also have performed servile tasks, clad in Sidonian cloak, and wrought the day's tale of wool with Lydian distaff. My shaggy breast was girt by the soft breast-band, and though my hands were horny I proved a nimble girl."

[51] So spake Alcides; but thus replied the kindly priestess, her white hair bound in a purple band: "Forbear to gaze, O stranger, and leave this dreaded grove. Come, leave it, depart from its threshold and seek safety in flight. The altar that guards its sanctity in this secret hut is forbidden to men, and dire is the doom that avenges its pollution. At great cost did the seer Tiresias behold Pallas, while she bathed her mighty limbs, the Gorgon breastplate laid aside. The gods give thee other fountains! This one stream flows for maidens only in secret channel far from the paths of men." So spake the aged

---

[1] He broke into Hades to rescue Theseus and carried off Cerberus.

SEXTI PROPERTI ELEGIARVM LIBER IV

sic anus : ille umeris postes concussit opacos,
   nec tulit iratam ianua clausa sitim.
at postquam exhausto iam flumine vicerat aestum,
   ponit vix siccis tristia iura labris :
" Angulus hic mundi nunc me mea fata trahentem
   accipit : haec fesso vix mihi terra patet.
Maxima quae gregibus devota est Ara repertis,
   ara per has " inquit " maxima facta manus,
haec nullis umquam pateat veneranda puellis,
   Herculis aeternum ne sit[1] inulta sitis."   70
Sancte pater salve, cui iam favet aspera Iuno :
   Sancte, velis libro dexter inesse meo.
hunc, quoniam manibus purgatum sanxerat orbem,
   sic Sanctum Tatiae composuere Cures.

X

Nvnc Iovis incipiam causas aperire Feretri
   armaque de ducibus trina recepta tribus.
magnum iter ascendo, sed dat mihi gloria vires :
   non iuvat e facili lecta corona iugo.
imbuis exemplum primae tu, Romule, palmae
   huius, et exuvio plenus ab hoste redis,
tempore quo portas Caeninum Acronta petentem
   victor in eversum cuspide fundis equum.
Acron Herculeus Caenina ductor ab arce,
   Roma, tuis quondam finibus horror erat.   10

[1] Herculis aeternum *Housman*   Hercule exterminium *NFL*.
ne sit *ς*   nascit *NFL*

dame. He with his shoulders shattered the doorposts that barred his sight, nor could the closed gate endure the fury of his thirst.

⁶³ But after he had quenched his burning and drained the stream to naught, with lips scarce dry he pronounced this stern decree: "This corner of the world hath now received me as I drag out my doom: weary though I be this land is all but closed to me. May that Mightiest of Altars dedicated for the finding of my flocks, this altar made Mightiest by mine hands, never be open to women's worship, that the thirst of Hercules be avenged to all eternity"

⁷¹ Hail, Holy Sire, on whom now cruel Juno smiles. Holy one, I pray thee to take thy place in my book with blessing. This hero of old, for that he had cleansed the world with his hands and made it holy, Tatian Cures established in his temple as the Holy one.

X

Now will I begin to show forth the origins of Feretrian Jupiter and to tell of the triple spoils of armour[1] won from three several chiefs. Great are the heights I must scale, but glory lends me strength; crowns plucked from easy summits please me not.

⁵ Thou, Romulus, first didst win this prize and camest home laden with the spoil of thy foe, what time thou didst vanquish Caeninian Acron, as he sought the gates of Rome, and with thy spear didst hurl him dead upon his fallen steed. Acron, the chieftain from Caenina's citadel, sprung from the seed of Hercules, was once the terror of thy lands, O Rome.

[1] Spoils won by a Roman general from a general of the enemy were known as *spolia opima*.

SEXTI PROPERTI ELEGIARVM LIBER IV

hic spolia ex umeris ausus sperare Quirini
   ipse dedit, sed non sanguine sicca suo.
hunc videt ante cavas librantem spicula turres
   Romulus et votis occupat ante ratis:
" Iuppiter, haec hodie tibi victima corruet Acron."
   voverat, et spolium corruit ille Iovi.
Vrbis virtutumque[1] parens sic vincere suevit,
   qui tulit a parco frigida castra lare.
idem eques et frenis, idem fuit aptus aratris,
   et galea hirsuta compta lupina iuba;   20
picta neque inducto fulgebat parma pyropo:
   praebebant caesi baltea lenta boves;
necdum ultra Tiberim belli sonus, ultima praeda   25
   Nomentum et captae iugera terna[2] Corae.   26
Cossus at insequitur Veientis caede Tolumni,   23
   vincere cum Veios posse laboris erat,[3]   24
heu Vei veteres! et vos tum regna fuistis,
   et vestro posita est aurea sella foro:
nunc intra muros pastoris bucina lenti
   cantat, et in vestris ossibus arva metunt.   30
forte super portae dux Veius astitit arcem
   colloquiumque sua fretus ab urbe dedit:
dumque aries murum cornu pulsabat aeno,
   vinea qua ductum longa tegebat opus,
Cossus ait " Forti melius concurrere campo."
   nec mora fit, plano sistit uterque gradum.

---

[1] virtutumque ⵏ · virtutemque *FL*. virtutis *N*.
[2] terna ⵏ. terra *NFL*.
[3] 25, 26 and 23, 24 transposed by *Passerat*.

He dared to hope for spoil from Quirinus' shoulders, but himself gave up his own, spoil dripping with his own life-blood. Him Romulus espied, as he poised his javelin against the hollow towers, and forestalled him with a vow that heaven approved: "Jupiter, behold thy victim; to-day shall Acron fall in thine honour." The vow was made, and Acron fell to be the spoil of Jupiter. Thus was he wont to conquer, the father of Rome and the Virtues, who from homes of thrift led forth an unluxurious host. The knight was ready alike to guide the war-horse or the plough; his helm was of wolf-skin decked with shaggy plume, his shield shone not with gaudy inlay of golden bronze, and his tough belt was but the hide of slaughtered kine. Not yet was the sound of war heard beyond Tiber's bank, and Nomentum and the three acres of captured Cora were Rome's furthest prey.

[23] Cossus comes next with the slaughter of Tolumnius, Veii's lord, in the days when even to have power for Veii's conquest was a mighty task. Alas! Veii, thou ancient city, thou too wert then a kingdom and the throne of gold was set in thy market-place: now within thy walls is heard the horn of the idle shepherd, and they reap the cornfields amid thy people's bones. It chanced that Veii's chief stood on the tower above the gate and parleyed without fear from his own city: and while the ram shook the walls with brazen horn, where the long mantlet shielded the siege-works' line, Cossus cried: "'Twere better for the brave to meet in open field." No tarrying then, but both stood forth on the level plain. The

SEXTI PROPERTI ELEGIARVM LIBER IV

di Latias iuvere manus, desecta Tolumni
   cervix Romanos sanguine lavit equos.
Claudius a Rhodano [1] traiectos arcuit hostes,
   Belgica cum vasti parma relata ducis   40
Virdomari. genus hic Rheno iactabat ab ipso,
   mobilis e rectis [2] fundere gaesa rotis.
illi virgatis iaculantis ab [3] agmine bracis
   torquis ab incisa decidit unca gula.
nunc spolia in templo tria condita · causa Feretri,
   omine quod certo dux ferit ense ducem;
seu quia victa suis umeris haec arma ferebant,
   hinc Feretri dicta est ara superba Iovis.

XI

Desine, Paulle, meum lacrimis urgere sepulcrum:
   panditur ad nullas ianua nigra preces;
cum semel infernas intrarunt funera leges,
   non exorato stant adamante viae.
te licet orantem fuscae deus audiat aulae:
   nempe tuas lacrimas litora surda bibent.
vota movent superos: ubi portitor aera recepit,
   obserat umbrosos lurida porta locos. [4]
sic maestae cecinere tubae, cum subdita nostrum
   detraheret lecto fax inimica caput.   10

---

[1] a Rhodano *Postgate*: a Rheno *NFL*.
[2] e rectis *Passerat* erecti *N* effecti *FL*
[3] ut . . . iaculans it *Postgate* iaculantis *NFL*.
[4] umbrosos ς. herbosos *NL* erbosos *F*. locos *Markland* · rogos *NFL*.

THE ELEGIES OF PROPERTIUS BOOK IV

gods aided the Latin's hands, and Tolumnius' severed neck bathed Roman steeds with blood.

[39] Claudius beat back the foe that had crossed from the banks of Rhone, when the Belgic shield of the giant chief Virdomarus was brought back to Rome. He boasted to be sprung from Rhine himself, and nimble was he to hurl the Gallic spear from unswerving chariot. Even as in striped breeches he went forth before his host, the bent torque fell from his severed throat.

[45] These triple spoils are stored in the temple. Hence comes Feretrius' name, because with heaven's sure favour chief smote[1] chief with the sword: or else the proud altar of Feretrian Jupiter hath won its name because the victor bore[1] the armour of the vanquished on his shoulders.

XI

CEASE, Paullus, to burden my grave with tears: no prayers may open the gate of darkness; when once the dead have passed beneath the rule of Hell the ways are barred with inexorable adamant. Though thine entreaty reach the ears of the god that reigns in the house of gloom, the shores of Styx shall drink thy tears unmoved. Heaven only is won by supplication: when the ferryman has received his toll, the pale portal closes on the world of shadows. Such was the burden of the trumpets' strain, when the loathed torch was placed beneath my pyre and the flames engulfed my head.

[1] The pun on *ferire, fero*, and *Feretrius* is untranslatable.

SEXTI PROPERTI ELEGIARVM LIBER IV

quid mihi coniugium Paulli, quid currus avorum
    profuit aut famae pignora tanta meae?
non minus immites habuit Cornelia Parcas:
    et sum, quod digitis quinque legatur, onus.
damnatae noctes et vos vada lenta paludes,
    et quaecumque meos implicat unda pedes,
immatura licet, tamen huc non noxia veni:
    det pater hic umbrae mollia iura meae.
aut si quis posita iudex sedet Aeacus urna,
    in mea sortita vindicet ossa pila: 20
assideant fratres, iuxta et Minoida sellam [1]
    Eumenidum intento turba severa foro.
Sisyphe, mole vaces; taceant Ixionis orbes;
    fallax Tantaleo corripere [2] ore liquor;
Cerberus et nullas hodie petat improbus
    umbras;
    et iaceat tacita laxa catena sera.
ipsa loquor pro me: si fallo, poena sororum
    infelix umeros urgeat urna meos.
si cui fama fuit per avita tropaea decori,
    nostra Numantinos signa [3] loquuntur avos: 30
altera maternos exaequat turba Libones,
    et domus est titulis utraque fulta suis.
mox, ubi iam facibus cessit praetexta maritis,
    vinxit et acceptas altera vitta comas,

---

[1] iuxta et *Itali*. iuxta *FL*. Minoida ς. Minoia *FL*. sellam ς. sella et μυ. sella *FL*.

[2] corripere ore *Auratus:* corripiare *FL*.

[3] nostra ... signa *Bochrens:* et ... regna *L:* aera ... regna μυ. omitted by *F*.

THE ELEGIES OF PROPERTIUS BOOK IV

¹¹ What availed me the wedded love of Paullus? what the triumphal chariot of mine ancestors, or those that live to bear witness to their mother's glory? Cornelia found not therefore the Fates less cruel, and lo! I am now but one little handful of dust. Dark night of doom, and ye, O shallow, stagnant meres, and every stream that winds about my feet, guiltless, though untimely, am I come hither, and may Father Dis deal gentle judgment to my soul. Else, if there be an Aeacus who sits in judgment with the urn at his side, let him punish my shade when the lot bearing my name is drawn. Let the two brothers [1] sit by him, and near the seat of Minos let the stern band of Furies stand, while all the court is hushed to hear my doom. Sisyphus, be thou freed awhile from thy huge stone! Hushed be Ixion's wheel! And thou, baffling water, be thou caught by the lips of Tantalus! To-day let cruel Cerberus attack no shade, let his chain hang slack from its silent bar! Myself I plead my cause. If I plead falsely, let the woeful urn that is the Danaid sisters' doom bow down my shoulders!

²⁹ If ancestral trophies have e'er won glory for any, why, then, the statues of my house tell of Numantine [2] ancestry, while yonder is gathered a not less glorious band, the Libones of my mother's line: on either side my house is pillared with glory. Such was my birth; thereafter when the maid's robe of purple was laid aside before the torch of marriage, and a new wreath caught up and bound my hair, I was

---
[1] Minos and Rhadamanthus.
[2] Scipio Africanus.

SEXTI PROPERTI ELEGIARVM LIBER IV

iungor, Paulle, tuo sic discessura cubili:
  in lapide hoc uni nupta fuisse legar.
testor maiorum cineres tibi, Roma, verendos,
  sub quorum titulis, Africa, tunsa iaces,
      .   .   .   .[1]

et Persen proavo stimulantem pectus Achille,
  quique tuas proavo fregit, Averne,[2] domos,   40
me neque censurae legem mollisse neque ulla
  labe mea nostros erubuisse focos.
non fuit exuviis tantis Cornelia damnum:
  quin et erat magnae pars imitanda domus
nec mea mutata est aetas, sine crimine tota est:
  viximus insignes inter utramque facem.
mi natura dedit leges a sanguine ductas,
  ne possem melior iudicis esse metu.
quaelibet austeras de me ferat urna tabellas:
  turpior assessu[3] non erit ulla meo,   50
vel tu, quae tardam movisti fune Cybellen,
  Claudia, turritae rara ministra deae,
vel cui, iuratos[4] cum Vesta reposceret ignes,
  exhibuit vivos carbasus alba focos
nec te, dulce caput, mater Scribonia, laesi:
  in me mutatum quid nisi fata velis?

---

[1] *Munro pointed out that at least a couplet must be lost here. he suggested, e.g.*, et qui contuderunt animos pugnacis Hiberi, | Hannibalemque armis Antiochumque suis.

[2] Averne *Munro* Achille *FL*.

[3] assessu *ς*: assensu *FL*.

[4] cui iuratos *Butler* cuius rasos *FL*.

THE ELEGIES OF PROPERTIUS BOOK IV

wedded to thy couch, my Paullus, doomed, alas! to leave it thus. Behold the legend on this stone: "To one and one alone was she espoused." I call to witness the ashes of my sires, revered, O Rome, by thee; beneath their glory's record thou, Africa, liest beaten to the dust. . . . [*I call the chiefs of Carthage and the East*] and Perseus, whose soul was spurred by the thought that he came of Achilles' line and of his [1] that shattered thy halls, Avernus, to witness that the censor's [2] ordinance was ne'er relaxed for me and that my hearth ne'er blushed for sin of mine. Cornelia ne'er dimmed the lustre of such spoils of war; nay, even in that great house she was a pattern to be followed.

45 My life was changeless; through all its days it knew no slander: 'twixt torch of marriage and torch of death ours was a life of high renown. The laws I followed sprang from pride of blood: 'twas nature gave me them, that no fear of judgment might lead me toward virtue. I care not who the judges be that pass stern sentence on me; no woman shall be shamed by sitting at my side, not thou, Claudia, the peerless servant of the tower-crowned goddess, that didst lay hold of the cable and move Cybelle's lagging image, nor thou [3] whose white linen robe showed that the hearth still lived, when Vesta demanded the fire thou hadst sworn to keep. Nor yet in aught have I wronged thee, sweet mother mine, Scribonia: what wouldst thou have me change save only my doom? My

[1] Hercules. See p 325, note.
[2] Paullus was censor in 22 B.C
[3] Aemilia, a Vestal virgin, was accused of having allowed the sacred fire of Vesta to be extinguished. She vindicated herself by placing a portion of her dress upon the hearth, and the fire straightway blazed up. *iuratos* lit. = "by which she had sworn." She swore by the sacred fire that she would keep it alight.

SEXTI PROPERTI ELEGIARVM LIBER IV

maternis laudor lacrimis urbisque querelis,
   defensa et gemitu Caesaris ossa mea.
ille sua nata dignam vixisse sororem
   increpat, et lacrimas vidimus ire deo.   60
et tamen emerui generosos vestis honores,
   nec mea de sterili facta rapina domo.
tu, Lepide, et tu, Paulle, meum post fata levamen;
   condita sunt vestro lumina nostra sinu.
vidimus et fratrem sellam geminasse curulem,
   consule quo, festo[1] tempore rapta soror.
filia, tu specimen[2] censurae nata paternae,
   fac teneas unum nos imitata virum.
et serie fulcite genus: mihi cumba volenti
   solvitur aucturis tot mea facta meis.[3]   70
haec est feminei merces extrema triumphi,
   laudat ubi emeritum libera fama rogum.
nunc tibi commendo communia pignora natos:
   haec cura et cineri spirat inusta meo.
fungere maternis vicibus, pater. illa meorum
   omnis erit collo turba ferenda tuo.
oscula cum dederis tua flentibus, adice matris:
   tota domus coepit nunc onus esse tuum.
et si quid doliturus eris, sine testibus illis!
   cum venient, siccis oscula falle genis!   80

[1] festo *Koppiers*. facto *FL*.
[2] specimen ς: speciem *FL*.
[3] aucturis ς · uncturis *L* nupturis *F*. facta ς: fata *FL*. meis *Paulmier*. malis *FL*.

mother's tears and the laments of Rome give glory to my name and mine ashes are championed by the grief of Caesar. Moaning he cries that in me his daughter [1] had a worthy sister, and we saw that even a god may weep.

61 Yet well did I merit the robe of honour,[2] nor childless was the household whence I was snatched away. Thou, Lepidus, and thou, Paullus, are my comfort even in death; in your bosom were mine eyelids closed. My brother also I saw twice throned in the curule chair, and 'twas in the very hour of rejoicing, when they chose him consul,[3] that I his sister was rapt away. And thou, my daughter, born to be the mirror of thy father's censorship, see thou follow mine example and wed one and one only. My children, get you children also to be pillars of the house: I grudge not now to put forth in the boat of death, since so many of my blood shall add fresh lustre to my deeds. This is the supreme honour of a woman's triumph, that outspoken rumour should praise her dead ashes.

73 And now to thee, Paullus, I commend our children, the common pledges of our love: this care yet lives deep-burned even into mine ashes Father, 'tis thine to fill the mother's room; thy neck alone must bear all my children's throng. When thou dost kiss their tears away, add thereto their mother's kisses; henceforth the whole house must be thy burden. And if thou must weep at all, weep when they are not by; when they come to thee, cheat their kisses with tearless eye. Enough

---

[1] Iulia, Augustus' daughter, was half-sister to Cornelia.
[2] The *stola* of honour awarded to the wife that had borne three children.
[3] P. Cornelius Scipio, consul 16 B.C.

SEXTI PROPERTI ELEGIARVM LIBER IV

sat tibi sint noctes, quas de me, Paulle, fatiges,
    somniaque in faciem credita saepe meam:
atque ubi secreto nostra ad simulacra loqueris,
    ut responsurae singula verba iace.
seu tamen adversum mutarit ianua lectum,
    sederit et nostro cauta noverca toro,
coniugium, pueri, laudate et ferte paternum
    capta dabit vestris moribus illa manus.
nec matrem laudate nimis: collata priori
    vertet in offensas libera verba suas.   90
seu memor ille mea contentus manserit umbra
    et tanti cineres duxerit esse meos,
discite venturam iam nunc sentire senectam,
    caelibis ad curas nec vacet ulla via
quod mihi detractum est, vestros accedat ad annos:
    prole mea Paullum sic iuvet esse senem.
et bene habet: numquam mater lugubria sumpsi;[1]
    venit in exsequias tota caterva meas.
causa perorata est. flentes me surgite, testes,
    dum pretium vitae grata rependit humus.   100
moribus et caelum patuit: sim digna merendo,
    cuius honoratis ossa vehantur avis.[2]

[1] lugubria sumpsi ς : lubrigia sumptum *N*: lubrica sumptum *FL*.
[2] avis *Heinsius* · aquis *NFL*.

for thee, Paullus, be the nights thou wearest out with memories of me, enough the dreams wherein so oft thou thinkest to see my very self: and when in secret thou shalt speak unto mine image, breathe every word as though to one that should reply.

85 Yet if another couch [1] shall front the portals of our hall, and a wary stepdame usurp my bed, my sons, praise and endure your father's spouse; your virtues shall win her heart to yield. Nor praise your mother overmuch: she will be angered if in unguarded speech ye compare her with her that was. Or if he forget me not, if my shade sufficeth him and he still doth prize mine ashes, learn even now to note how old age steals upon him, and leave no path for grief to assail his widowed heart. May the years that were snatched from me be added to your years; thus may my children's presence sweeten old age for Paullus. Aye, and 'tis well: ne'er did I don a mother's mourning weeds; all, all my children came to my graveside.

99 My pleading is accomplished; rise, ye my witnesses that weep my loss, and wait Earth's kindly sentence that shall give the reward my life hath earned. Even heaven hath unbarred its gates to virtue; may my merit win its guerdon and mine ashes be borne to dwell with my glorious ancestors.

[1] The *lectus genialis*, dedicated to the *genii* of the married pair, was placed in the *atrium* facing the door.

INDEX

ACANTHIS, IV. v. 63 A procuress who instructs Cynthia in the "art of love"

Achaea, II xxviii 53

Achaemenius, II xiii 1. = Persian.

Achelous, II xxxiv 33. A river of Aetolia which contended with Hercules for the love of Deianira

Acheron, III v. 13.

Achilles, II. i. 37, iii 39, viii 29, ix 9, 13, xxii 29, III. xviii. 27, IV xi 39.

Achivus, II viii 31; III xviii 29

Acron, IV. x 7, 9, 15. King of Caenina.

Actiacus, II xv 44 Actius, II i. 34, xvi 38, xxxiv 61; IV. vi 17, 67 Adj from Actium, a bay on the coast of Epirus, the scene of Augustus' final victory over Antonius.

Admetus, II vi 23 Husband of Alcestis, who died to prolong his life

Adonis, II xiii 53

Adrastus, II xxxiv 37 Leader of the Seven against Thebes

Adryas, I xx 12. = Dryas

Aeacus, II xx 30, III iv 20; IV xi 19. A judge among the dead.

Aeaeus, II xxxii 4, III xii. 31 Adj from Aeaea, the island of Circe, or of Calypso

Aegaeus, I vi 2; III vii. 57, xxiv 12

Aegyptus, II i 31, xxxiii 15

Aelia Galla, III xii 1, 4, 15, 19, 22, 38 A Roman lady, wife of Postumus, perhaps sister of Aelius Gallus, Prefect of Egypt

Aemilius, III iii 8. A reference to Aemilius Paulus, who defeated Demetrius of Pherae in 219 B C

Aeneas, II xxxiv 63; III iv 20

Aeolus, II iii 19 A reference to the Aeolic school of lyric poets, of whom Sappho was pre-eminent

Aeschyleus, II xxxiv 41

Aesonides, I xv 17. Aesonius, III. xi 12. Jason, the son of Aeson.

Agamemnon, IV. vi 33.

Agamemnonius, III vii 21; IV. i 111

Aganippeus, II iii. 20 Aganippe, the fountain of the Muses on Mount Helicon

Alba, III iii 3; IV. i 35, vi. 37.

Albanus, III xxii. 25 The Alban Lake.

Alcides, I. xx. 49; II xxiv 34; IV ix. 16, 38, 51 Hercules

Alcinous, I xiv 24 King of Phaeacia; gave rich gifts to Ulysses

Alcmaeonius, III. v 41. Alcmaeon slew his mother, Eriphyla, and was pursued by Furies

Alcmene, II xxii 25. Mother of Hercules

Ales (Amor), II xxx 31.

Alexandria, III xi 33

Alexis, II xxxiv 73 A Vergilian shepherd

z   341

INDEX

Alphesiboea, I xv. 15 Wife of Alcmaeon Alcmaeon left her for Callirrhoe, but on returning home to Arcadia was killed by Alphesiboea. She avenged her faithless husband by killing her brothers

Amazonis, III xiv 13

Amor, I. i 4, 17, 34, ii. 8, iii. 14, v 24, vii 20, 26, ix. 12, 23, 28, x 20, xii 16, xiv 8, 15, xvii. 27, xix 22; II ii 2, iii 24, vi 22, viii 40, x 26, xii 1, xiii 2, xxix 18, xxx 2, 7, 24, xxxiii 42, xxxiv 1, III i 11, v 1, xvi 16, xx. 17, xxiii. 16

Amphiaraus, III xiii 58 Amphiareus (adj), II. xxxiv. 39 Amphiaraus, one of the Seven against Thebes, was swallowed up with his chariot in a chasm.

Amphion, III. xv. 29, 42. Amphionius, I x 10 Son of Antiopa With his lyre he caused stones to gather themselves together and form the walls of Thebes.

Amphitryoniades, IV. ix 1 Hercules

Amycle, IV v 35. A slave of Cynthia

Amymone, II xxvi. 47. Daughter of Danaus, yielded herself to Poseidon, on condition of his causing a spring to burst forth in time of drought

Amythaonius, II iii 54 Amythaon, father of Melampus (q v)

Androgeon, II i. 62. Son of Minos, killed in Attica, and, according to Propertius, restored to life by Asclepius, the god of healing, whose chief temple was at Epidaurus

Andromacha, II xx 2, xxii 31

Andromede, I iii 4, II xxviii 21; III xxii 29, IV. vii. 63

Amenus, I. xx. 8; III. xvi 4, IV. vii. 86, Anio, III xxii 23, IV vii. 81. The river on which Tibur stands.

Antaeus, III xxii. 10. A Libyan giant slain by Hercules

Antigone, II. viii 21

Antilochus, II. xiii 49. The son of Nestor, killed during the siege of Troy

Antimachus, II. xxxiv 45 A poet of Colophon, wrote an epic on the Seven against Thebes and love elegies in memory of his mistress Lyde

Antinous, IV. v 8 The leader of Penelope's suitors

Antiope, I. iv. 5, III. xv 12, 19, 22, 39 Daughter of Nycteus and wife of Lycus, King of Thebes Lycus put her away and married Dirce Dirce tormented Antiope, who took refuge on the mountains with Amphion and Zethus, sons whom she in earlier years had borne to Jupiter.

Antonius (M.), III. ix. 56.

Anubis, III xi 41. A dog-headed god of Egypt.

Aonius, I. ii. 28; III iii. 42 Aonia was a district of Boeotia round Mount Helicon.

Apelles, III ix 11 Apelleus, I. ii 22 A famous Greek painter, fourth century B C

Apidanus, I. iii. 6 A river of Thessaly.

Apollo, I. viii 41; II i 3; III ii 9, ix 39, xi 69; IV. i. 73, 133, vi. 11, 69.

Appia, Via, II. xxxii. 6; IV. viii 17 The "Great South Road" of Rome

Aprilis, IV v. 35 The Kalends of April were specially associated with courtesans, who on that day sacrificed to Venus and Fortuna virilis

Aquilo, II v. 11; III vii. 13, 71.

Aquilonius, I xx. 25.

342

INDEX

Ara Maxima, IV. ix 67 An altar situated in the Forum Boarium

Arabia, II x. 16 Augustus sent an army under Aelius Gallus to invade Arabia in 24 B C The expedition was a failure.

Arabius, I xiv 19; II. iii. 15

Arabs, II xxix 17; III xiii 8

Aracynthus, III xv 42 Part of the Cithaeron range, on the borders of Attica and Boeotia

Araxes, III xii 8, IV iii 35. A river of Armenia flowing into the Caspian

Arcadius, I i 14, xviii. 20; II. xxviii 23. The Arcadian god is Pan

Archemorus, II xxxiv 38 Infant son of Eurydice and Lycurgus, King of Nemea, was killed by a serpent during the absence of his nurse Hypsipyle, who had gone to point out a spring to the Seven against Thebes Funeral games were celebrated in his honour, from which sprang the Nemean games

Archytas, IV i 77 The famous mathematician of Tarentum *Floruit* fourth century B C

Arctos, II. xxii. 25.

Arethusa, IV iii. 1 Pseudonym of a Roman lady, perhaps Aelia Galla

Arganthus, I. xx 33. A mountain in Mysia

Argeus, III xxii 13. Adj from Argus, the steersman of the Argo

Argivus, I xv 22, xix 14; II xxv 43

Argus, I iii 20 The many-eyed guardian of Io

Argus, I xx 17, II xxvi 39. *See* Argeus

Argynnus, III vii 22 A youth beloved by Agamemnon, and drowned

Ariadna, II iii 18, III xvii 8

Arion, II xxxiv 37. The horse of Adrastus, gifted with human speech.

Arionius, II xxvi 18 Adj from Arion, the musician.

Armenius, I. ix. 19.

Arria, IV. i 89. A friend or kinswoman of Propertius. Perhaps the mother of the Gallus of I xx.

Artacius, I viii 25. Adj from Artacia, a mythical fountain in the land of the Laestrygones

Ascanius, I. xx 4, 16 A river in Mysia

Ascraeus, II x 25, xiii 4, xxxiv 77 Ascra, in Boeotia, was the birthplace of Hesiod

Asia, I vi 14, II iii 36.

Asis, IV i 65, 125 Assisi, or the hill on which Assisi stands

Asopus, III. xv 27 A river in Boeotia

Athamanus, IV vi 15. The Athamanes were a people of Epirus

Athamantis, I xx 19, III xxii 5 Helle, daughter of Athamas

Athenae, I vi 13; III. xxi 1.

Atlas, III xxii 7

Atrida, II xiv. 1 Atrides, III vii. 23; xviii 30; IV. i. 112. Agamemnon.

Attalicus, II xiii. 22, xxxii 12; III xviii 19, IV. v. 24 Attalus, King of Pergamum, was said to have invented cloth-of-gold

Atticus, II. xx 6.

Augustus, II. x 15, III. xi 50, xii 2, IV. vi. 22, 29, 38, 81

Aulis, IV i. 109

Aurora, II. xviii. 7; III xiii. 16

Ausonius, I. xx 12; II. xxxiii 4 III iv 5, xxii. 30, IV iv 43. Italian

Auster, II xvi 56, xxvi 36

Aventinus, IV i. 50, viii 29.

Avernalis, IV. i. 49.

343

INDEX

Avernus, III XVIII 1; IV XI 40 A lake north of Naples, reputed to be the gate of Hades, and often synonymous with Hades

BABYLON, III. XI. 21
Babylonius, IV I 77.
Baccha, III. XXII 33.
Bacchus, I III 9, II XXX 38, III. II 9, XVII 1, 6, 13, 20; IV I. 62, VI 76
Bactra, III I 16, XI 26, IV III. 7, 63 A town in Persia, the modern Balkh.
Baiae, I XI. 1, 27, 30; III. XVIII. 2 Baia, a watering place at the north of the Bay of Naples
Bassaricus, III XVII. 30 Adj from Bassareus, a name of Bacchus
Bassus, I IV. 1, 12 A friend of Propertius and writer of *iambi*
Belgicus, II XVIII 26; IV X. 40
Bellerophonteus, III. III 2 The horse of Bellerophon is Pegasus, a blow from whose hoof called forth the spring Hippocrene
Bistonius, II XXX 36 The Bistones were a people of Thrace.
Boebeis, II II 11 A Thessalian lake
Boeotius, II VIII 21
Bootes, III V 35. The star Arcturus
Boreas, II XXVI 51, XXVII 12
Borysthenidae, II VII 18 Dwellers on the Borysthenes, the modern Dnieper
Bosporus, III XI 68 The town of Panticapaeum, in the Crimea, where Mithridates committed suicide
Bovaria, IV. IX 19 The cattle market at Rome, more commonly called Boarium
Bovillae, IV I 33 A small town near Rome.

Brennus, III XIII 51 Leader of the Gauls who attacked Delphi in 278 B C.
Brimo, II II 12 Hecate
Briseis, II VIII. 35, IX. 9, XX 1, XXII 29
Britannia, IV III. 9
Britannus, II. I 76, XVIII 23, XXVII. 5.
Brintus, IV I 45

CACUS, IV IX 7, 9, 16 A robber living on the Aventine, and slain by Hercules for stealing his cattle.
Cadmeus, I VII 1; III XIII 7
Cadmus, III IX 38 The founder of Thebes.
Caeninus, IV X 7, 9 Caenina was a small town in Latium which went to war with Rome on account of the rape of the Sabine women
Caesar (Augustus), I XXI 7, II I. 25, 26, 42, VII. 5, XVI. 41, XXXI 2, XXXIV 62, III. IV. 1, 13, IX 27 33, XI 66, 72, XVIII 12, IV I. 46, VI 13, 56, XI 58
Caesar (Julius), III XVIII 34; IV VI. 59.
Calais, I XX 26 A winged son of Boreas
Calamis, III IX 10 A sculptor of the fifth century B.C, particularly famous as a sculptor of horses
Calchas, IV. I 109. The prophet of the Greek army who decreed the sacrifice of Iphigeneia at Aulis
Callimachus, II I 40, XXXIV 32, III. I. 1, IX. 43; IV I 64
Calliope, II I 3, III III. 51; IV. VI 12. Calliopea, I II 28; III II 16. III 38
Callisto, II XXVIII 23. A nymph of Arcadia transformed into the constellation of the Little Bear
Calpe, III. XII. 25. Gibraltar.

344

INDEX

Calvus, II xxv 4, xxxiv. 89. G Licinius Calvus, the friend of Catullus, a poet of the learned Alexandrian school

Calypso, I xv 9; II xxi. 13

Cambyses, II xxvi 23 King of Persia, conqueror of Egypt.

Camena, III x 1.

Camillus, III ix 31, xi 67 The conqueror of the Gauls after the sack of Rome

Campania, III. v. 5.

Campus (Martius), II xvi. 34.

Cancer, IV i 150

Canis, II. xxviii 4.

Cannensis, III iii 10

Canopus, III xi 39. A luxurious town in Egypt some twelve miles from Alexandria

Capaneus, II xxxiv 40. Capaneus, one of the Seven against Thebes, boasted that he would sack Thebes in despite of Jove Jove therefore blasted him with his thunderbolt.

Capena (Porta), IV iii 71. The gate through which the Via Appia entered Rome, the natural gate for the entry of one who, like Lycotas, had been campaigning in the East, and would return by Brundisium or Naples

Caphareus, III vii 39 A headland of Euboea on which Nauplius burned false beacons, thereby causing the Greek fleet returning from Troy to be wrecked He did this to avenge the death of his son, Palamedes, put to death on a false charge by the Greeks

Capitolia, IV iv. 27

Capricornus, IV i 86.

Carpathius, II v. 11, III vii 12. The southern portion of the Aegean, Carpathus being an island between Crete and Rhodes

Carthago, II. i. 23.

Cassiope, I xvii 3 A port in the north of Corcyra

Castalius, III iii 13 The Castalian spring was on Parnassus, though in this poem the scene is laid on Helicon

Castor, I ii 15; II. vii 16, xxvi. 9, III xiv 17.

Catullus, II. xxv. 4, xxxiv 87.

Caucasius, II i 69, xxv 14.

Caucasus, I xiv 6.

Cayster, III xxii 15 A river of Asia Minor on which Ephesus is situated

Cecropius, II. xx. 6, xxxiii 29 Athenian, from Cecrops, an ancient King of Attica

Centauricus, IV. vi. 49.

Centaurus, II. ii. 10, vi. 17, xxxiii. 31.

Cepheus, I iii 3 Cepheus, IV vi 78 Adj from Cepheus, the father of Andromeda

Ceraunia, I. viii 19 Ceraunus, II xvi 3 Ceraunia, or Acroceraunia, was a dangerous headland in Epirus

Cerberus, III v. 44, IV. v 3, vii 90, xi. 25

Chaonius, I. ix 5 The Chaones were a tribe of Epirus dwelling near Dodona Here = Dodonean

Charybdis, II xxvi 54, III xii 28

Chiron, II. i. 60. A centaur, son of Jupiter and Phillyra

Chius, III vii 49

Chloris, IV. vii. 72 Mistress of Propertius after Cynthia's death

Cicones, III xii 25 A Thracian tribe defeated by Ulysses (Od ix 40)

Cilissa, IV vi 74

Cimbri, II i. 24 A Germanic tribe defeated by Marius

Cinara, IV i 99 A friend or relative of Propertius

Circaeus, II i 53

Circe, III. xii. 27.

345

INDEX

Cithaeron, III. ii. 5, xv. 25. A mountain between Attica and Boeotia

Claudia, IV. xi. 52 Claudia Quinta, when the mysteries of Cybele were introduced into Rome (205 B.C.), and the ship bearing the image, &c., stuck on a shoal in the Tiber, pulled it off single-handed, and thereby cleared herself of the suspicion of unchastity

Claudius (M Marcellus Maior), III. xviii 33; IV x 39. The conqueror of Syracuse in the second Punic war, and ancestor of the "young Marcellus." *See also* Virdomarus

Clitumnus, II xix. 25; III. xxii. 23 A river of Umbria

Clytemestra, III xix 19.

Cocles (Horatius), III xi 63

Coeus, III ix 48 A giant

Colchis, II i. 54, xxi 11, xxxiv. 8; III xi 9 The home of Medea, east of the Black Sea

Colchus, III xxii 11

Collinus, IV. v 11 Near the Colline gate was the *campus sceleratus*, where Vestal virgins unfaithful to their vows were buried alive.

Conon, IV. i. 78. A Greek astronomer of Samos (*flor*. 250 B C)

Cora, IV x 26 An ancient town of the Volsci

Corinna, II iii 21 A famous Boeotian poetess, contemporary with Pindar

Corinthus, III v 6

Cornelia, IV xi. 13, 43 The daughter of Cornelius Scipio and Scribonia, and the wife of L Aemilius Paullus

Corydon, II xxxiv 73 A Vergilian shepherd

Cossus (Aulus Cornelius Cossus), IV. x. 23, 35 Consul 428 B.C.

Cous, I ii 2; II i 5, 6, III. i 1, IV ii 23, v. 23, 56, 57

Crassus, II x 14, III iv 9, v 48; IV vi 83

Craugis, IV iii 55 A dog, so called from the Greek κραυγή, "baying"

Cressus, II i 61, IV vii 57 *Cressae herbae* probably refers to the miraculous herb called *dictamnus*

Cretaeus, III. xix 11, 26.

Creusa, II xvi 30, xxi 12 Daughter of Creon, King of Corinth Jason deserted Medea to marry her Medea took her revenge by sending Creusa a poisoned robe which consumed Creusa and Creon with fire

Croesus, II xxvi 23; III v. 17, xviii 28

Cumaeus, II ii. 16 The Sibyl of Cumae (north of Bay of Naples) was reputed to be fabulously old.

Cupido, II xviii 21.

Cures IV ix 74 The ancient capital of the Sabines

Curetis, IV iv 9 Adj from Cures *See above*

Curia, IV i 11, iv 13

Curius, III iii 7 The Curiatii who fought against the Horatii

Curtius, III xi 61. Curtius threw himself into a chasm in the Forum 360 B C., thereby causing it to be miraculously closed

Cybele, Cybelle, III xvii 35, xxii 3; IV. vii. 61, xi 51.

Cydonium, III xiii 27. A quince, from Cydonia, the modern Canea, in Crete.

Cymothoe, II xxvi. 16 A Nereid

Cynthia, I i 1, iii 8, 22, iv. 8, 19, 25, v 31, vi 16, viii 8, 30, 42, x 19, xi 1, 8, 23, 26, xii 6, 20, xv. 2, 26, xvii 5, xviii 5, 6, 22, 31, xix. 1, 15, 21; II. v 1, 4, 28, 30, vi 40, vii 1, 19, xiii. 7,

346

INDEX

57, XVI. 1, 11, XIX. 1, 7, XXIV 2, 5, XXIX. 24, XXX 25, XXXII. 3, 8, XXXIII 2, XXXIV 93; III XXI. 9, XXIV. 3, XXV 6; IV VII. 2, 85, VIII. 15, 51, 53

Cynthius, II xxxiv. 80 Apollo.

Cyrenaeus, IV vi 4 Adj from Cyrene, the birthplace of Callimachus

Cytaeine, I. i. 24 Cytaeis, II iv 7 A woman of Cyta, in Colchis—*i e*, Medea

Cytherea, II. xiv 25.

Cyzicus, III. XXII. 1. A town on the south coast of the Propontis

DAEDALIUS, II. XIV 8 Adj from Daedalus, the builder of the Labyrinth.

Danae, II. xx 10, 12, xxxii 59

Danaus, II. xxxi 4 The brother of Aegyptus, father of fifty daughters who, with the exception of Hypermnestra, murdered their husbands at their father's command

Danaus (adj), II xxvi 38; III viii 31, ix 10, xi. 14, xxii 34; IV i 53, 113.

Daphnis, II xxxiv. 68 A Vergilian shepherd.

Dardanius, II xiv 1 Dardanus, I xix 14; IV i 40.

Decius, III. xi 62; IV. i 45 Three Decii, father, son, and grandson, generals of Roman armies, sacrificed their lives to win success for their country (336, 296, 279 B C respectively).

Deidamia, II. ix. 16 Daughter of Lycomedes, King of Scyros, beloved of Achilles, to whom she bore Neoptolemus

Deiphobus, III. I. 29 A son of Priam

Delos, IV vi. 27. Delos was once a floating island, but after the birth of Diana and Apollo upon it it became fixed

Demophoon, II. XXII 2, 13 The pseudonym of a friend of Propertius, perhaps the poet Tuscus, who was called Demophoon because his mistress was called Phyllis See below

Demophoon, II. xxiv 44. Demophoon, son of Theseus, loved Phyllis, daughter of Sithon, King of Thrace He deserted her and she killed herself

Demosthenes, III. xxi. 27.

Deucalion, II. xxxii. 53, 54 Deucalion and his wife Pyrrha were the sole survivors of the Greek "Deluge."

Dia, III XVII. 27. Naxos

Diana, II xix 17, xxviii 60; IV. viii 29

Dindymis, III xxii. 3 Cybele, so called because she had a famous shrine on Mount Dindymus near Cyzicus

Dircaeus, III xvii 33 Adj from Dirce, a fountain near Thebes

Dirce, III xv 11, 28, 39 See Antiope

Dis, III xxii 4.

Dodona, II xxi 3. A place in Epirus famous for its oracle

Doricus, II viii. 32; IV vi 34.

Doris, I xvii 25 A sea-goddess.

Dorozantes, IV v 21

Dorus, III ix 44 The "Dorian poet" is Philetas

Dryades, I xx 45.

Dulichia, II. xiv. 4 An island off the west coast of Greece, often treated by Latin poets as the home of Ulysses.

Dulichius, II ii 7, xxi. 13; III. v 17.

EDONIS, I III 5 A woman of the Edoni, a Thracian tribe

Electra, II xiv 5.

347

INDEX

Eleus, III. 11. 20, IX. 17. Elis, I. VIII. 36. Olympia was in Elis, hence the frequent mention of Elis in connection with (1) race-horses, (2) Jupiter. *See* Phidiacus.

Elysius, IV. VII. 60.

Enceladus, II. I. 39. A giant.

Endymion, II. XV. 15.

Enipeus, I. XIII. 21; III. XIX. 13. A river of Thessaly. Poseidon assumed the shape of the river-god when he ravished Tyro, daughter of Salmoneus.

Ennius, III. III. 6; IV. I. 61. The father of Roman poetry, flourished in the second century B.C. His chief work was the *Annales*, an epic poem on the history of Rome.

Eous, I. XV. 7, XVI. 24; II. III. 43, 44, XVIII. 8; III. XIII. 15, XXIV. 7, 8, III. 10, V. 21, VI. 81.

Ephyreus, II. VI. 1. Adj. from Ephyra, an ancient name of Corinth.

Epicurus, III. XXI. 26.

Epidaurius, II. I. 61. The Epidaurian god is Asclepius, whose chief temple was at Epidaurus, in the Peloponnese.

Erechtheus, II. XXXIV. 29. Adj. from Erechtheus, an ancient King of Athens. Here = Athenian. The allusion is to Aeschylus.

Erichthonius, II. VI. 4. Adj. from Erichthonius, an ancient King of Athens. Here = Athenian.

Eridanus, I. XII. 4. The Po.

Erinna, II. III. 22. A Lesbian poetess contemporary with Sappho.

Erinys, II. XX. 29.

Eriphyla, II. XVI. 29; III. XIII. 57. Eriphyla, wife of Amphiaraus, was bribed by Polynices with the gift of a golden necklace to persuade her husband to join the Seven against Thebes. He consented, though he knew he should never return.

Erycinus, III. XIII. 6. Adj. from Eryx, a Sicilian town famous for its shrine of Venus. The nautilus was known as *concha Venerea*, and is here called *concha Erycina*.

Erythea, IV. IX. 2. A mythical island in the far west, the home of Geryones.

Erythia, II. XIII. 1. A mythical king of the East.

Esquiliae, III. XXIII. 24; IV. VIII. 1. One of the seven hills of Rome.

Etruscus, I. XXI. 2, 10, XXII. 6; II. I. 29; III. IX. 1.

Euboicus II. XXVI. 38; IV. I. 114.

Eumenides, IV. XI. 22.

Euphrates, II. X. 13, XXIII. 21; III. IV. 4, XI. 25; IV. VI. 84.

Europa, II. III. 36.

Europe, II. XXVIII. 52. Daughter of Agenor and sister of Cadmus; loved by Jupiter in the form of a bull.

Eurotas, III. XIV. 17. The river of Sparta.

Eurus, II. XXVI. 35; III. V. 30; XV. 32.

Eurymedon, III. IX. 48. A giant.

Eurypylus, IV. V. 23. A king of Cos. *Eurypyli textura* = Coan silks.

Eurytion, II. XXXIII. 31. A centaur slain at the wedding of Pirithous.

Evadne, I. XV. 21; III. XIII. 24. Evadne, the wife of Capaneus, flung herself upon her husband's pyre.

Evander, IV. I. 4. Evander, an exiled Arcadian king, dwelt on the site of what was afterwards Rome. *See* Vergil, *Aen.* VIII. 333.

INDEX

Evenus, I. ii. 18. The father of Marpessa. *See* Idas.

FABIUS (Q. Maximus), III. iii. 9. The celebrated general of the second Punic war, known as Cunctator ("Delayer") from his tactics.

Fabius, IV. i. 26. The Luperci, priests of Pan, were divided into two colleges, the Fabii and the Quintilii.

Falernus, II. xxxiii. 39; IV. vi. 73. A district in Campania famous for its wine.

Fama, II. xxxiv. 94; III. i. 9, xxii. 2.

Feretrius, IV. x. 1, 45, 48. A title of Jupiter.

Fidenae, IV. i. 36. A town of Latium, near Rome.

Forum, IV. i. 134, ii. 6, iv. 12, viii. 75, ix. 20.

GABII, IV. i. 34. A town of Latium not far from Rome.

Galaesus, II. xxxiv. 67. A river near Tarentum.

Galatea, I. viii. 18; III. ii. 7. A sea-goddess.

Galla. *See* Aelia.

Galli, II. xxxi. 13.

Gallicus, II. xiii. 48. If the reading be correct here, Gallicus must mean Phrygian, and be an adjective from Gallus, a river of Phrygia.

Gallus, I. v. 31, x. 5, xiii. 2, 4, 16, xx. 1, 14, 51. A friend of Propertius, perhaps Aelius Gallus, Prefect of Egypt.

Gallus, I. xxi. 7. A soldier killed in the Perusine war. Perhaps a kinsman of Propertius.

Gallus, IV. i. 95. The son of Arria, killed in battle. Possibly identical with the foregoing.

Gallus (C. Cornelius), II. xxxiv. 91. The first Prefect of Egypt. Incurred Augustus' displeasure through his arrogance and committed suicide. He was the first of Rome's great elegiac poets. He wrote in honour of his mistress Lycoris.

Geryones, III. xxii. 9. A monster killed by Hercules, who carried off his oxen.

Geta, IV. iii. 9, v. 44. The Getae were a tribe of Scythia. In the latter passage the reference is to the Scythian slaves, who acted as police at Athens.

Gigantes, III. v. 39.

Giganteus, I. xx. 9. The *ora Gigantea* is the Phlegrean plain immediately north of Naples.

Glaucus, II. xxvi. 13. A sea-god.

Gnosius, I. iii. 2; II. xii. 10. Adj. from Gnosus (Cnossus), in Crete.

Gorgon, II. ii. 8, xxv. 13; IV. ix. 58.

Gorgoneus, III. iii. 32. Pegasus, the winged horse of Perseus, sprang from the Gorgon's blood. It was a blow from his hoof which called forth Hippocrene, which is therefore called the "Gorgon's spring."

Graecia, II. vi. 2, ix. 17; III. vii. 40; IV. i. 116.

Graecus, IV. viii. 38.

Graius, II. vi. 19, xxxii. 61, xxxiv. 65; III. i. 4, viii. 29, ix. 41, xxii. 37.

Gygaeus, III. xi. 18. A Lydian lake near Sardis.

HADRIA, I. vi. 1.

Hadriacus, III. xxi. 17.

Haedus, II. xxvi. 56.

Haemon, II. viii. 21. The son of Creon, betrothed to Antigone, committed suicide after her death.

349

INDEX

Haemonius, I. XIII 21, XV 20; II I. 63, VIII. 38, X. 2; III I 26. Thessalian, from a certain Haemon, son of Pelasgus and father of Thessalus

Hamadryades, I XX 32; II XXXII. 37, XXXIV 76.

Hannibal, III. III 11, XI. 59

Hebe, I XIII 23. The goddess of youth; became the bride of Hercules when he became a god

Hector, II VIII 38, XXII 31, 34; III I. 28, VIII 31

Hectoreus, II VIII 32, IV VI 38

Helena, II I. 50, II. III 32, XXXIV 88; III. VIII 32, XIV 19

Helenus, III I 29. Son of Priam and a prophet

Helicon, II X 1, III III. 1, V 19

Helle, II XXVI 5, III XXII 5. Daughter of Athamas; gave her name to the Hellespont into which she fell from the back of the golden ram

Hercules, I XIII 23, XX 16; II XXIII. 8; III. XXII. 10; IV. IX 17, 70

Herculeus, I. XI 2; II XXXII 5; III XVIII 4, IV VII 82, IX 39, X. 9. The *via Herculea* of I XI 2 and III XVIII 4 was a narrow spit of land dividing the Lucrine Lake from the sea. It was said to have been built by Hercules when he carried off the oxen of Geryon

Hermione, I IV. 6. Daughter of Menelaus and Helen. Neoptolemus and Orestes were rivals for her love

Hesperides, III XXII 10. Nymphs of a legendary garden in the far West, where grew apples of gold

Hesperius, II. III. 43, 41, XXIV. 26; IV. I 86. Western. In II XXIV. 26 the allusion is to the snake which guarded the golden apples in the garden of the Hesperides.

Hiberus, II III 11

Hilaira, I. II 16. Hilaira and Phoebe, daughters of Leucippus were betrothed to Idas and Lynceus, sons of Aphareus, but were carried off by Castor and Pollux.

Hippodamia, I II 20, VIII 35. Daughter of Oenomaus, King of Elis, who promised her to the man that could defeat him in a chariot race. Pelops succeeded in so doing by fraud, and won Hippodamia

Hippolyte, IV. III 43. Queen of the Amazons; conquered by Theseus, whose wife she became

Hippolytus, IV. V 5. The son of Theseus and Hippolyte, beloved by his stepmother Phaedra

Homerus, I. VII 3, IX 11, II. I. 21, XXXIV 45; III I 33

Horatius, III. III. 7. *Horatia pila* refers to the three Horatii who fought the Curiatii, called Curii by Propertius

Horos, IV I 78. An astrologer.

Hylaei, I VIII 26. The inhabitants of Hylaea, a land beyond Scythia

Hylaeus, I I. 13. A centaur who attacked Atalanta. Milanion defended her, and was wounded by Hylaeus

Hylas, I XX. 6, 32, 48, 52. Son of Theiodamas, beloved by Hercules

Hymenaeus, IV IV. 61

Hypanis, I XII 4. Either the river Bug or the river Kuban, in South Russia

Hypermestre, IV VII. 63, 67. The only one of the fifty daughters of Danaus who refused to kill her husband.

Hypsipyle, I XV 18, 19. Queen of Lemnos, beloved and deserted by Jason.

INDEX

Hyrcanus, II xxx 20 *Hyrcanum mare* is the Caspian.

IACCHUS, II. III. 17; IV II. 31. Bacchus
Iasis, I. I. 10 Atalanta, daughter of Iasus, beloved and won, according to this version of the legend, by Milanion.
Iason, II XXI 11, XXXIV 85.
Iasonius, II XXIV 45
Icariotis, III XIII 10 Penelope, daughter of Icarius
Icarius, II XXXIII 24 Icarus, II. XXXIII. 29 Icarus, or Icarius, learned from Dionysus the art of making wine He gave some to some Attic peasants, who became drunk Thinking that they were poisoned, they murdered him He became a star in the Great Bear, named Arcturus, or Bootes
Ida, II. XXXII 35. Mount Ida, above Troy
Idaeus, II II 14, XXXII 39 ; III I. 27, XVII 36
Idalius, II. XIII 54 , IV VI. 59. Adj from Idalium, a mountain in Cyprus, sacred to Venus.
Idas, I. II. 17. *See* Hilaira
Iliacus, II XIII 48 ; IV IV 69.
Ilias, II I. 14, 50, XXXIV 66
Ilion, III. I 31
Ilius, III XIII 61 ; IV I 53.
Illyria, I. VIII 2 , II XVI 10
Illyricus, II XVI 1
Inachus, I III 20 , II XXXIII 4 Io, daughter of Inachus.
Inachius, I XIII 31 , II XIII 8 Argive, Greek, from Inachus, King of Argos
India, II X 15.
Indicus, II XXII. 10; III XVII 22.
Indus, I. VIII 39 ; II IX 29, XVIII 11 ; III. IV. 1, XIII. 5 , IV III 10
Ino, II XXVIII 19 Ino, daughter of Cadmus and wife of Athamas, was smitten with madness by Hera She threw herself into the sea and became a sea-goddess named Leucothea, here called Leucothae
Io, II XXVIII 17, XXX. 29, XXXIII 7 Io, beloved of Jupiter, was turned into a cow by the jealousy of Juno, and was only restored to human shape after long wanderings In XXXIII she is identified with Isis.
Iolciacis, II I 54 Adj from Iolcus, the home of Jason
Iole, IV V 35 A slave of Cynthia
Ionia, I VI 31
Ionius, II XXVI 2, 14 , III XI. 72, XXI 19 , IV VI 16, 58
Iope, II XXVIII 51 There were two Iopes : (1) Daughter of Iphicles and wife of Theseus (2) Daughter of Aeolus and wife of Cepheus, the mother of Andromeda, more commonly called Cassiope
Iphiclus II III 52 *See* Melampus.
Iphigenia, III VII 24.
Irus, III. V 17 A beggar at the house of Ulysses, defeated by the disguised Ulysses in a boxing match.
Ischomache, II II. 9. The bride of Pirithous, carried off by centaurs from her wedding feast
Isis, IV. V. 34
Ismara, III XII 25 The home of the Cicones in Thrace Propertius speaks of it as a mountain, Homer as a town.
Ismarius, II XIII 6, XXXIII 32. Adj from the foregoing , = Thracian
Isthmos, III XXI 22. Isthmus of Corinth
Italia, I. XXII. 4 ; III. VII 63 ; IV III 40
Italus, III I 4 , XXII 28

351

INDEX

Ithacus, I. xv 9; III xii. 29
Itys, III x 10 The son of Philomela, slain by his mother to avenge the outrage done by Philomela's husband, Tereus, to her sister Procne
Iugurtha, III. v 16; IV vi 66
Iuleus, IV. vi 17.
Iulius, IV. vi 54
Iulus, IV i 48 The son of Aeneas
Iuno, II. v 17, xxviii. 11, 33, 34, xxxiii 9; III xxii 35; IV i 101, viii 16, ix 43, 71
Iuppiter, I xiii 29, 32; II i. 39, ii 4, 6, iii. 30, vii 4, xiii 16, xvi 16, 18, xxii 25, xxvi. 42, 46, xxviii 1, 14; xxx. 28, xxxii 60, xxxiii 7, 14, xxxiv 18, 40; III i 27; ii 20, iii 12, iv 6, ix. 15, 47, xi 28, 41, 66, xv 19, 22, 36, 39, xxiv 20; IV i 54, 82, 83, 103; iv 2, 10, 30, 85, vi. 14, 23, ix. 8, x 1, 15, 16, 48
Ixion, IV xi 23.
Ixionides, II i 38 Pirithous, the friend of Theseus

LACAENA, II xv 13.
Lacon, III xiv. 33
Lais, II vi 1 A courtesan
Lalage, IV. vii 45 A slave of Cynthia
Lampetie, III xii 29, 30 Daughter of Phoebus and guardian of his cattle
Lanuvium, II xxxii 6; IV viii 3, 18 A small town some miles to the south-east of Rome
Laomedon, II xiv 2 The father of Priam
Lapitha, II ii 9. An ancestor of Ischomache.
Lar, II xxx 22; III. iii. 11; IV. iii 54, viii 50
Latinus, II. xxxii 61; IV vi 45
Latius, III iv 6; IV x 37
Latris, IV vii 75 A slave of Cynthia.

Lavinus, II. xxxiv 64 Adj from Lavinium, a city of Latium founded by Aeneas
Lechaeum, III xxi 19 The western port of Corinth.
Leda, I xiii 29, 30 Mother of Castor, Pollux, and Helen by Jupiter.
Leo, IV. i. 85.
Lepidus, IV xi. 63 One of Cornelia's sons
Lerna, II xxvi 48 Lernaeus, II xxiv 25 The name of the fen where dwelt the hydra, the slaying of which formed the second labour of Hercules.
Lesbia, II xxxii 45, xxxiv 88 The pseudonym of Clodia, the mistress of Catullus.
Lesbius, I xiv 2
Lethaeus, IV. vii. 10, 91
Leucadia, II xxxiv 86 The mistress of Varro of Atax
Leucadius, III xi. 69 Adj from Leucas, a promontory overlooking the Bay of Actium, on which was built a temple of Apollo
Leucippis, I ii. 15 See Hilaira
Leucothoe, II xxvi 10, xxviii 20 See Ino More usually Leucothea
Liber, I. iii 14
Libones, IV. xi 31 Cornelia's family on her mother's side.
Liburnus, III. xi 44 A kind of light galley
Libya, IV i 103
Libycus, II. xxxi. 12; IV. ix. 46
Linus, II xiii 8 A mythical personage regarded as one of the earliest poets.
Luceres, IV i. 31. The Roman people after the Sabine war were composed of three tribes, the Ramnes, the original followers of Romulus, the Titienses, the followers of Titus Tatius, and the Luceres under Lucumo, or Lygmon, who is represented by

INDEX

Propertius and Dionysius of Halicarnassus as coming from Solonium, a town near Lanuvium

Lucifer, II xix 28

Lucina, IV i 99 A title of Juno, as the goddess of childbirth

Lucrinus, I xi 10 A lagoon on the Bay of Naples, near Baiae

Luna, I x 8; II xxviii. 37, xxxiv. 52; III xx 14

Lupercus, IV. i 26. A priest of Lupercus, the Roman equivalent of Pan Lukaios

Lupercus, IV i. 93. Son of Arria

Lyaeus, II. xxxiii 35; III. v 21. A title of Bacchus

Lycinna, III xv 6, 43 Propertius' first love

Lycius, III i 38. The 'Lycian god" is Apollo

Lycomedius, IV ii 51 The Etruscans under Lucumo (see Luceres) were called Lycomedii

Lycoris, II xxxiv 91 The mistress of Cornelius Gallus Her real name was Cytheris

Lycotas, IV iii. 1 The pseudonym of some noble Roman, perhaps identical with the Postumus of III xii.

Lycurgus, III xvii 23 Lycurgus, King of Thrace, disapproving of the Bacchic revels, seized Dionysus. The god smote him with madness, so that while he thought to hew down a vine he slew his own son

Lycus, III xv 12. See Antiope

Lydia, I. vi 32.

Lydius, III. xi. 18, xvii. 30; IV vii 62

Lydus, III v 17; IV ix 48

Lygdamus, III vi 2, 11, 19, 24, 31, 36, 42; IV vii 35, viii 37, 68, 70, 79 A slave of Cynthia

Lygmon, IV i 29 See Luceres

Lynceus, II xxxiv 9, 25 A poet and friend of Propertius

Lysippus, III ix 9 A great sculptor, born at Sicyon, who flourished during the latter portion of the fourth century B C

MACHAON, II i 59 A Greek physician at the siege of Troy

Maeander, II xxx 17. A Phrygian river

Maeandrius, II. xxxiv. 35

Maecenas, II i 17, 73; III ix. 1, 21, 34, 59

Maenalius, IV ix 15 Adj from Maenalus, a mountain in Arcadia, and here used loosely = Arcadian

Maenas, III viii 14, xiii 62

Maeonius, II xxviii 29 Maeonia was an ancient name of Lydia Here the word means Homeric, as according to some accounts Homer was born in Lydia

Maeoticus, II iii 11

Maeotis, III xi 14. Lake Maeotis is the modern Sea of Azof

Magnus, IV. viii. 41 The name of a dwarf

Maius, IV. v 36.

Malea, III xix 8 The most southerly promontory of the Peloponnese

Mamurius, IV. ii 61 Mamurius Veturius was a mythical worker in bronze of the reign of Numa

Marcius, III ii 14, xxii 24 The *aqua Marcia* was the water supplied by the aqueduct built by Quintus Marcius Rex in 144 B C. It was famous for its excellence

Marianus, III. iii 43 *Marianum signum* refers to the eagle which Marius is said to have first adopted as the Roman standard

Marius, II i 24; III v 16, xi 46 Caius Marius, the great Roman general who defeated the Teutones and Cimbri in 102 and 101 B C

INDEX

Maro, II xxxii 14 Maro was a companion of Bacchus, some say his son

Mars, II xxxii. 33, xxxiv 56; III iii 42, iv 11, xi 58; IV i 83

Martius, IV i. 55

Mausoleus, III ii 21 The Mausoleum was erected in memory of Mausolus, King of Caria, by his widow Artemisia He died 353 His monument was one of the "Wonders of the World" Its sculptures are now in the British Museum.

Mavors, II xxvii 8

Medea, II xxiv 45; III xix 17; IV. v. 41.

Medus, III ix 25, xii 11.

Melampus, II iii 51 Melampus, son of Amythaon, undertook to drive off the herd of Iphiclus for Neleus, that Bias, his own brother, might win the hand of Pero, the daughter of Neleus He was captured and imprisoned, but escaped, and eventually succeeded in his task Propertius seems to follow a different version, making Melampus himself the suitor of Pero

Memnon, II xviii 16 The son of the Dawn, and King of Ethiopia; came to aid the Trojans and was slain by Achilles.

Memnonius, I vi 4

Memphis, III xi. 34 A town of Egypt

Menandreus, II. vi. 3 Menander, the celebrated writer of comedy, wrote a comedy with Thais, a well-known courtesan, for heroine

Menandrus, III. xxi 28; IV. v 43

Menelaeus, II xv 14

Menelaus, II iii 37, xxxiv 7

Menoetiades, II i 38. Patroclus, the son of Menoetius

Mens Bona, III. xxiv 19 The Romans, following their custom of personifying abstract conceptions, erected a temple to "Good Sense" in 217 B C

Mentor, III ix. 13 A famous silversmith of the early portion of the fourth century B C.

Mentoreus, I xiv. 2

Mercurius, II. ii. 11, xxx 6

Meroe, IV. vi. 78. The capital of Aethiopia.

Merops, II xxxiv. 31 Merops was an early King of Cos Here Merops = Coan.

Methymnaeus, IV viii 38. Adj from Methymna, in Lesbos

Mevania, IV i 123. The modern Bevagna, near Assisi

Milanion, I. i. 9. The lover of Atalanta

Mimas, III vii 22 A mountain in Lydia, running into a headland called Argennum, which may have been connected with Argynnus (q v).

Mimnermus, I ix. 11 A famous erotic poet of Colophon, flourished about 630 B C

Minerva, I. ii 30; II ix. 5; IV i 118, v 23

Minois, II xiv 7, xxiv. 43 Ariadne, daughter of Minos

Minois (adj), IV xi 21

Minos, II. xxxii 57; III xix 27 Minos, King of Cnossus, in Crete After his death he became judge in Hades.

Minous, III xix 21

Minyae, I xx 4 The Argonauts, so called because mostly descended from Minyas.

Misenus, III xviii 3. The trumpeter of Aeneas, buried at Misenum, at the north end of the Bay of Naples, the modern Miseno.

Misenus (adj), I xi 4

INDEX

Molossus, IV. VII 24 The Molossi were a tribe in Epirus.

Musa, I VIII. 41, II. I. 35, X 10, XII 22, XIII 3, XXXIV 31, III I 10, 14, II 15, III 29, V. 20, IV. IV 51, VI XI 75

Mutina, II I 27. The modern Modena, where Octavian defeated Mark Antony and relieved Decimus Brutus, who was besieged (43 B C)

Mycenae, III XIX 19

Mycenaeus, II XXII 32

Mygdonius, IV. VI. 8 Phrygian The Mygdones were a tribe of Phrygia

Myron, II XXXI 7 A famous Athenian sculptor, flourished 430 B C

Myrrha, III XIX 16. Myrrha fell in love with her father, Cinyras She was transformed as a punishment into a myrrh-tree

Mys, III IX 14 A famous silversmith of the fifth century B C

Mysus, I XX 10, II. I 63 The *Mysus iuvenis* of the latter passage is Telephus, King of Mysia, wounded by the spear of Achilles, and healed by the rust from the same spear

Nais, II XXXII. 40

Nauplius, IV. I. 115. See Caphareus.

Navalis (Phoebus), IV I 3 The temple of Phoebus Navalis was the famous temple of Apollo on the Palatine, erected by Augustus as a memorial of his victory at Actium.

Naxius, III XVII 28

Nemorensis, III XXII 25. The Lake of Nemi, in the Alban hills.

Neptunius, III IX 41.

Neptunus, II XVI 4, XXVI 9, 45, 46; III VII 15, XI 42, 51

Nereides, II. XXVI 15

Nereus, III VII 67; IV VI 25

Nesaee, II. XXVI. 16. A sea-nymph.

Nestor, II XIII 46, XXV. 10 King of Pylos, lived through three generations of men.

Nilus, II I 31, XXVIII 18, XXXIII 3, 20; III XI. 42, 51, IV VI 63 VIII 39

Niobe, II XX 7, III X 8 Niobe boasted that her six sons and six daughters were fairer than Apollo and Artemis. The latter punished her by slaying her children, while she was turned into stone. See Sipylus

Nireus, III XVIII 27 The handsomest man in the Greek army before Troy

Nisus, III XIX 24 King of Megara. He had a purple lock of hair, on which his life depended. Minos the Cretan besieged Megara, and Scylla, the daughter of Nisus, fell in love with him, cut off the purple lock from her father's head, and betrayed the city. Minos rewarded her by tying her to the rudder of his ship and so drowning her.

Nomas, IV VII 37 A slave of Cynthia

Nomentum, IV X 26. A town some three miles from Rome

Notus, II V. 12, IX 34, III XV 32, IV V. 62, VI 28, VII 22

Novi Agri, IV VIII. 2 The gardens laid out by Maecenas on the Esquiline in place of an insanitary burial-ground

Numa, IV II. 60 Pompilius Numa, an early King of Rome

Numantinus, IV. XI 30 Adj. from Numantia, in Spain. *Numantinos avos* refers to Scipio Africanus, the conqueror of Numantia He was known also as Numantinus

Nycteis, I IV 5 Antiope, daughter of Nycteus

Nycteus, III. XV. 12

INDEX

Nymphae, I. xx 11, 34, 52 ; IV. iv 25

Nysaeus, III. xvii 22 Adj from Nysa, a legendary mountain or town, where Bacchus was brought up by the nymphs

OCEANUS, II ix 30, xvi 17 ; IV. iv 64

Ocnus, IV iii 21 Ocnus was an industrious man, whose hard-won earnings were continually consumed by the extravagance of his wife In Polygnotus' great picture of the underworld he was represented as being punished for his folly by having eternally to twist a rope of straw, which an ass devoured continually at the other end "To twist the rope of Ocnus" was a proverbial expression

Oeagrus, II. xxx 35 Oeagrus was the father of Orpheus by the Muse Calliope. The phrase *Oeagri lyra* suggests that Propertius followed a form of the legend which made Apollo the father of Orpheus, disguised as Oeagrus

Oetaeus, I xiii 24 ; III. i 32 Hercules died on Mount Oeta, was translated to heaven, and married Hebe

Oiliades, IV. i. 117. Ajax, the son of Oileus, ravished Cassandra, and was punished for his sin by the disaster which befell the Greek fleet off Caphareus, in which he met his death

Olympus, II i 19

Omphale, III xi 17 A queen of Lydia, whom Hercules loved, and served disguised as a woman.

Orcus, III xix. 27

Orestes, II xiv 5

Oricius, III vii 49. Oricus, I viii 20. A seaport in Illyria.

Orion, II xvi. 51, xxvi 56

Orithyia, I. xx 31 ; II xxvi 51 ; III vii 13 The daughter of Pandion, ravished by the North Wind

Orontes, II xxiii 21 Oronteus, I ii 3 A Syrian river, near Antioch

Orops, IV. i 77 A Babylonian astrologer

Orpheus, III ii 3

Orpheus (adj), I iii 42

Ortygia. II xxxi 10 ; III xxii 15 A mythical island, later identified with Delos.

Oscus, IV ii. 62. The Oscans were a people of Italy Here the adjective means "rude," "brutal"

Ossa, II i 19. Otus and Ephialtes, giants, wished to pile Mount Pelion on Mount Ossa, that they might storm heaven Ossa is in Thessaly

PACTOLUS, I vi. 32, xiv 11 ; III xviii 28 A Lydian river famous for its alluvial gold

Paestum, IV v 61 The modern Pesto, in South Italy, was in ancient times famous for its roses.

Paetus, III vii 5, 17, 26, 27, 47, 54, 66. A friend of Propertius, drowned at sea.

Pagasa, I xx 17 A seaport in Thessaly, where the Argo was launched

Palatinus, IV vi. 11, 41.

Palatium, IV i 3, ix 3 The Palatine.

Palladius, III. ix 42

Pallas, II ii 7, xxviii. 12, xxx. 18 ; III. xx. 7 ; IV. iv 45, ix. 57

Pan, III. iii 30, xiii 45, xvii 34

Pandionius, I. xx. 31. Pandion, King of Athens, was the father

INDEX

of Orithyia, the North Wind's bride.

Panthus, II. XXI 1, 2 A lover of Cynthia

Parcae, IV. XI. 13

Parilia, IV. I. 19, IV 73 The feast of Pales, the goddess of flocks, took place on April 21, the day of the foundation of Rome.

Paris, II. III 37, XV 13, XXXII. 35 ; III. I 30, VIII. 29, XIII. 63

Parnassus, II. XXXI. 13 ; III. XIII. 54.

Parrhasius, III. IX. 12. A painter of Ephesus, flourished at the end of the fifth century B C

Parthenie, IV. VII. 74. Cynthia's nurse

Parthenius, I. I. 11. Adj from Parthenium, a mountain in Arcadia.

Parthus, II. X. 14, XIV 23, XXVII 5 ; III IV. 6, IX 54, XII 3 ; IV III. 36, 67, V. 26, VI. 79.

Pasiphae, II XXVIII 52. The wife of Minos, King of Cnossus, and mother of the Minotaur. *See* II. XXXII 57

Patroclos, II VIII 33.

Paullus (L Aemilius), IV. XI 1, 11, 35, 81, 96 The husband of Cornelia, consul in 34 B C, and censor in 22 B C

Paullus, IV. XI. 63. Son of the above

Pegae, I XX 33 A Mysian fountain where Hylas perished

Pegaseus, II XXX 3

Pegasides, III I. 19 The Muses, so called from the fountain of Hippocrene, sometimes called Pegasis because caused by a blow from the hoof of Pegasus

Pelasgus, II. XXVIII. 11. Perhaps a learned epithet for Juno, who is styled Hera Pelasgis in Appollonius Rhodius. The Pelasgi were a primitive people of Greece.

Peleus, II IX. 15 The father of Achilles.

Peliacus, III. XXII. 12. Adj. from Pelion. The phrase *Peliacae trabes* refers to the Argo, the timbers for which were hewn from Mount Pelion, in Thessaly.

Pelides, II. XXII 34 Achilles.

Pelion, II. I. 20. *See* Peliacus *and* Ossa

Pelopeus, III. XIX. 20 ; IV. VI 33.

Pelusium, III. IX. 55. A fortress on the Pelusiac branch of the Nile, captured by Augustus

Penelope, II IX 3 ; III. XII 38 ; XIII 24 , IV. V. 7

Penthesilea, III XI. 14 Penthesilea, queen of the Amazons, came to Troy to help the Trojans. She was slain by Achilles, who was said to have fallen in love with her when her helmet was removed and he saw the beauty of her dead face

Pentheus, III. XVII. 24, XXII 33. The son of Echion and Agave, torn in pieces by his mother and her attendant Bacchanals while he spied upon their revels.

Pergama, II. I. 21, III. 35 ; III. IX. 39. The citadel of Troy.

Pergameus, III. XIII. 62 ; IV. I. 51. Adj. from the above *Pergamea vatis* (IV. I. 51) is Cassandra

Perillus, II. XXV 12. Perillus made a bull of bronze, so fashioned that a man might be placed inside and roasted over a fire Phalaris, Tyrant of Agrigentum, to whom Perillus offered the bull, caused its maker to be roasted in it.

Perimedeus, II. IV 8. Adj from Perimede, a legendary sorceress

Permessus, II. X. 26

Pero, II. III 53. *See* Melampus

INDEX

Perirhaebus, III. v. 33. The Perrhaebi were a people of Epirus dwelling on the slopes of Mount Pindus.

Persa, III. xi. 21.

Persephone, II. xiii. 26, xxviii. 47, 48.

Perses, IV. xi. 39. Perses, or Perseus, King of Macedonia, was defeated by Aemilius Paullus, Cornelia's ancestor, at Pydna in 168 B.C. He claimed to be descended both from Achilles and Hercules.

Perseus, II. xxviii. 22, xxx. 4.

Perseus (adj.), III. xxii. 8.

Perusinus, I. xxii. 3. Adj. from Perusia, the modern Perugia, where Octavian defeated Lucius Antonius in the Perusine war, 41 B.C.

Petale, IV. vii. 43. A slave of Cynthia.

Phaeacus, III. ii. 13. Adj. from Phaeacia. The allusion is to the famous orchard of Alcinous described in the *Odyssey*.

Phaedra, II. i. 51.

Pharius, III. vii. 5; Pharos, II. i. 30. Pharos was an island in the port of Alexandria.

Phasis, I. xv. 18; III. xxii. 11. A river of Colchis, in the Black Sea.

Phidiacus, III. ix. 15. A reference to the chryselephantine statue of Zeus made by Phidias for the temple at Olympia.

Philetaeus, III. iii. 52; IV. vi. 3. The most famous of the elegiac poets of the Alexandrian period.

Philetas, II. xxxiv. 31; III. i. 1. A Coan poet, after Callimachus.

Philippeus, III. xi. 10. The "blood of Philip" means the Ptolemaic dynasty, whose kings claimed descent from Philip of Macedon.

Philippi, II. i. 27.

Phillyrides, II. i. 60. *See* Chiron.

Philoctetes, II. i. 59. Philoctetes was bitten by a serpent on the way to Troy, and abandoned in the island of Lemnos. Later an oracle declared that without the aid of Philoctetes' bow Troy would not be taken. He was therefore brought to Troy, and healed of the serpent's bite which had crippled him.

Phineus, III. v. 41. Phineus, King of Bithynia, was blinded as a punishment for his sin in blinding his children, and was also plagued by Harpies, who defiled the meats upon his table, making them uneatable.

Phlegraeus, II. i. 39; III. ix. 48, xi. 37. The Phlegrean plains, the volcanic district immediately north of Naples, were reputed to have been the scene of the battle between the gods and giants.

Phoebe, I. ii. 15. *See* Hilaira.

Phoebus, I. ii. 17, 27; II. xv. 15, xxviii. 54, xxxi. 1, 5, 10, xxxii. 28, xxxiv. 61; III. i. 7, iii. 13, xii. 30, xx. 12, xxii. 30; IV. i. 3, ii. 32, vi. 15, 27, 67, 76.

Phoenices, II. xxvii. 3.

Phoenix, II. i. 60. Phoenix was the tutor of Achilles. He was blinded by his father, but healed by Chiron, and became king of the Dolopes.

Phorcis, III. xxii. 8. A monster, the father of the Gorgon Medusa.

Phrygia, III. xiii. 63.

Phrygius, I. ii. 19; II. i. 42, xxx. 19, xxxiv. 35.

Phryne, II. vi. 6. A famous courtesan of Athens.

Phryx, II. xxii. 16, 30; IV. i. 2.

Phthius, II. xiii. 38. Adj. from Phthia, the home of Achilles.

Phylacides, I. xix. 7. Protesilaus, son of Phylacus, husband of Laodamia. He went to the siege of Troy immediately after his mar-

358

INDEX

riage, and was the first of the Greeks to be slain. He was permitted to leave Hades to visit his wife

Phyllis, II xxiv 44. Daughter of Lycurgus. *See* Demophoon

Phyllis, IV viii 29, 39, 57 A courtesan

Pierides, II x. 12

Pierius, II xiii 5 Adj from Mount Pierus, in Thessaly, sacred to the Muses

Pindaricus, III xvii 40

Pindus, III v. 33. A mountain on the borders of Macedonia and Epirus.

Piraeus, III xxi 23

Pirithous, II. vi 18 The husband of Ischomache, ravished from him by centaurs at his wedding feast *See also* Ixionides.

Pisces, IV i 85.

Plato, III xxi. 25

Pleias, II xvi. 51; III. v. 36.

Poenus, II. xxxi 3; IV iii. 51.

Pollux, I ii 16; III. xiv 17, xxii. 26.

Polydorus, III. xiii. 56. A son of Priam, sent for safety to Polymestor, King of Thrace, and murdered by his host for the sake of his gold

Polymestor, III. xiii. 55. *See above*.

Polyphemus, II xxiii 32; III ii. 7, xii 26

Pompeia Porticus, II xxxii 11 A colonnade built in 55 B C, and standing near Pompey's theatre on the Campus Martius

Pompeius, III xi. 35

Pompeius (adj), III xi 68; IV viii 75. The *Pompeia umbra* in the latter passage refers to the Porticus Pompeia.

Ponticus, I. vii. 1, 12, ix. 26. An epic poet and friend of Propertius

Postumus, III. xii. 1, 15, 23. A friend of Propertius, husband of Aelia Galla, perhaps identical with Lycotas.

Praeneste, II xxxii. 3 The modern Palestrina, some twenty miles east of Rome, famous for the oracle of Fortuna Primigenia

Praxiteles, III ix 16 A famous Athenian sculptor, flourished in the middle of the fourth century B C His most famous statue was the Venus of Cnidos, to which there is an allusion in *Triopos urbe*, Triops, or Triopas, being the legendary founder of Cnidos

Priamus, II. iii 40, xxviii 51; IV i. 52.

Prometheus (subst and adj), I. xii. 10; II i 69; III. v. 7

Propertius, II. viii. 17, xiv. 27, xxiv 35, xxxiv 93; III iii 17, x 15; IV i 71, vii 49

Propontiacus III xxii 2.

Ptolemaeus, II i 30

Pudicitia, II vi 25 There were two temples of Pudicitia at Rome, the one dedicated to Pudicitia patricia, the other to Pudicitia plebeia

Pulydamas, III. i. 29. A Trojan warrior.

Pyrrhus, III. xi. 60. King of Epirus; invaded Italy in the early years of the third century B C, and was only defeated by Rome with the greatest difficulty.

Pythius, II xxxi. 16; III xiii 52. An epithet of Apollo, = Delphian.

Python, IV. vi. 35 A gigantic snake slain by Apollo at Delphi

QUINTILIA, II xxxiv. 90 *See* Calvus

Quirinus, IV vi 21 Originally a title of Romulus, but here given to Augustus as second founder of the city.

Quirites, IV. i. 13, viii. 59.

INDEX

Ramnes, IV. i. 31. *See* Luceres
Remus, II. i. 23; III. ix. 50, IV. i. 9, 50, vi. 80. Frequently used *metri gratia* for Romulus
Rhenus, III. iii. 45; IV. x. 39, 41.
Rhipaeus, I. vi. 3. A mythical range of mountains in the North
Roma, I. viii. 31, xii. 2; II. v. 1, vi. 22, xv. 46, xvi. 19, xix. 1, xxxii. 43, xxxiii. 16; III. i. 15, 35, iii. 44, xi. 36, 49, 55, 66, xii. 18, xiii. 60, xiv. 34, xxii. 20; IV. i. 1, 67, 87, ii. 49, iv. 9, 35, 56, vi. 57, ix. 20, x. 10, xi. 37.
Romanus, I. vii. 22, xxii. 5; II. iii. 29, 30, x. 4, xviii. 26, xxviii. 55; III. iii. 11, iv. 10, ix. 23, 49, 55, xi. 31, 43, xxi. 15, xxii. 17; IV. i. 37, 64, ii. 6, 55, iii. 45, iv. 12, 35, vi. 3, x. 38.
Romulus, II. vi. 20; IV. i. 32, iv. 79, vi. 43, x. 5, 14.
Romulus (adj), III. xi. 52; IV. iv. 26.
Rubrum mare, I. xiv. 12; III. xiii. 6.

Sabinus, II. vi. 21, xxxii. 17; IV. ii. 52, iii. 58, iv. 12, 32, 57.
Sacra Via, II. i. 34, xxiii. 15, xxiv. 14; III. iv. 22. The Sacred Way was the road by which the triumphal procession passed to the Capitol. In II. xxiii. it is mentioned as the haunt of courtesans, in II. xxiv. as the street where lovers buy trinkets for their mistresses
Salmonis, I. xiii. 21; III. xix. 13. Tyro, daughter of Salmoneus, was ravished by Poseidon, disguised as the river-god Enipeus.
Sanctus, IV. ix. 71, 72, 74. A title of Hercules.
Saturnus, II. xxxii. 52; IV. i. 84.
Scaeae, III. ix. 39. A gate of Troy before which Achilles was slain.

Scamander, III. i. 27. A river in the plain of Troy
Scipiades, III. xi. 67. A Greeised version for Scipiones, used by Roman poets *metri gratia*
Sciron, III. xvi. 12. A robber dwelling where the road from Corinth to Megara and Athens ran along the edge of the cliff. He used to cast his victims down the precipice into the sea, but was at last himself destroyed by Theseus.
Scribonia, IV. xi. 55. The mother of Cornelia. She afterwards became the wife of Augustus
Scylla, II. xxvi. 53; III. xii. 28. A monster dwelling in a cave on the Italian shore of the Straits of Messina
Scylla, III. xix. 21; IV. iv. 39. *See* Nisus. In the latter passage she is identified with the above
Scyrius, II. ix. 16. *See* Deidamia
Scythia, IV. iii. 47.
Scythicus, III. xvi. 13.
Semela, II. xxviii. 27, xxx. 29. The mother of Bacchus. She besought her lover, Jupiter, to appear in all his majesty when he visited her. He did so, and she perished in the fire of his thunderbolts. Bacchus was born untimely, but saved by Jupiter, who cut open his own thigh and concealed the infant in it until the full time for his birth had come.
Semiramis, III. xi. 21. A Persian queen who founded Babylon
Sericus, IV. iii. 8, viii. 23. Adj from Seres, the Chinese
Sibylla, II. xxiv. 33; IV. i. 49.
Sicanus, I. xvi. 29.
Siculus, II. i. 28; III. xviii. 33.
Sidonius, II. xvi. 55, xxix. 15; IV. ix. 47.
Silenus, III. iii. 29.

INDEX

Silvanus, IV. iv 5

Simois, II ix 12; III. i 27 A river of Troy

Sinis, III xxii. 37 A robber who killed his victims by bending two pine-trees together and tying them between the two Then on the trees swinging back they were torn in two He was put to death by Theseus.

Sipylus, II xx. 8 A Phrygian mountain on which Niobe sat turned to stone. The rock, resembling a woman plunged in sorrow, is still to be seen

Sirenes, III. xii. 34

Sisyphus, II. xvii. 7, xx. 32. Sisyphus, IV. xi. 23. Sisyphus, King of Corinth, was condemned for his sins to roll a rock uphill to all eternity The moment the rock reached the top it rolled down again

Socraticus, II xxxiv 27.

Solonium, IV. i 31 A small town near Lanuvium, on the Appian Way

Spartanus, I iv 6; III xiv 21

Sparte, III xiv. 1

Strymonis, IV. iv 72. A woman of Strymon, a river in Thrace. = a Thracian Amazon.

Stygius, II. ix. 26, xxvii 13, xxxiv 53; III. xxiii 9; IV iii. 15, ix 41.

Subura, IV. vii 15. A quarter of Rome lying between the Esquiline, Viminal, and Quirinal, and a great haunt of courtesans

Suevus, III iii 45 The Suevi, a German tribe, crossed the Rhine in 29 B C, and were defeated by Gaius Carinas

Sycambri, IV vi. 77. The Sycambri defeated the Romans under Marcus Lollius in Gaul 16 B C, and Augustus went to Gaul to deal with the situation.

Syphax, III. xi 59 A Libyan king, deserted Rome and allied himself with Carthage in the second Punic war. He was defeated by Scipio and brought a captive to Rome 201 B.C

Syrius, II. xiii 30

Syrtes, II. ix. 33; III. xix. 7, xxiv. 16 The Syrtes were two gulfs on the North African coast, now Gulf of Cabes and Gulf of Sidra They were regarded with great terror owing to their shoals and shifting currents

TAENARIUS, (a) I. xiii 22; (b) III ii 11. (a) An epithet of Neptune (b) A reference to black marble quarried at Taenarum, in the south of the Peloponnese

Tanais, II xxx 2 The river Don.

Tantalis, II xxxi 14 Niobe, daughter of Tantalus

Tantaleus, II. i. 66, xvii 5, IV xi 24

Tarpeia, IV. iv 1, 15, 29, 81, 93

Tarpeius, I xvi 2; III xi 45; IV. i 7, iv 1, viii 31.

Tarquinius, III xi 47 Tarquin the Proud, King of Rome

Tatius (subst and adj), II xxxii 47; IV i 30, ii. 52, iv 7, 19, 26, 31, 34, 38, 89, ix 74 Titus Tatius, king of the Sabines, defeated Romulus, and became joint King of Rome.

Taygetus, III xiv 15 A range of mountains in Sparta.

Tegeaeus, III iii. 30 An epithet of Pan, who was worshipped at Tegea, in Arcadia

Teia, IV viii. 31, 58 A courtesan.

Telegonus, II xxxii. 4. Son of Ulysses and Circe, the founder of Tusculum

Teucer, IV. vi 21

Teuthras, I. xi. 11. Teuthras is a name associated with Cumae Who he was is not known.

361

INDEX

Teutonicus, III. iii 14. See Marius

Thais, II. vi. 3; IV v 43. A famous courtesan of Athens, the heroine of a play by Menander

Thamyras, II. xxii. 19. A legendary bard of Thrace who boasted that he could vanquish the Muses in a contest of song. They punished him for his boast by making him blind.

Thebae, I vii 1; II i. 21, vi 5, viii 10; III. ii 5, xvii. 33; IV v 25 In the last passage the reference is to Egyptian Thebes.

Thebanus, II. viii 24, ix. 50, III. xviii 6

Theiodamanteus, I. xx 6. Adj. from Theiodamas, father of Hylas.

Thermodon, IV. iv 71. Thermodontiacus, III xiv. 14. A river of Cappadocia

Theseus, II i. 37, xiv. 7, xxiv. 43

Theseus (adj), I iii 1, III. xxi 24.

Thesprotus, I xi 3 A King of Epirus; but he is also connected with the district round Cumae The connection is perhaps due to the fact that Acheron, Cocytus, and the Acherusian Lake were in Epirus, while there was an Acherusian Lake near Cumae, not to speak of Avernus

Thessalia, I v 6

Thessalicus, III. xix 13.

Thessalus, I. xix. 10; II xxii. 30, III xxiv. 10.

Thetis, III. vii 68. A sea-goddess, wife of Peleus and mother of Achilles.

Thrax, III xiii 55

Threicius, III. ii. 4

Thybris, III. iv. 4.

Thynias, I xx. 34 A nymph of Thynia, a district adjoining Bithynia

Thyrsis, II. xxxiv 68. A Vergilian shepherd.

Tiberinus (subst and adj.), I xiv 1; IV. ii 7

Tiberis, II xxxiii 20; III. xi 42. IV i 8, x 25.

Tibur, II xxxii. 5; III xvi 2 The modern Tivoli, a small town on the Anio in the Sabine hills.

Tiburnus, III xxii. 23.

Tiburtinus, IV. vii 85.

Tiresias, IV ix 57 A Theban who saw Pallas bathing. She in anger blinded him, but on the entreaty of his mother bestowed upon him powers of prophecy.

Tisiphone, III v 40. A Fury.

Titanes, II i 19.

Tithonus, II xviii 7, 15, xxv. 10. Tithonus when young was beloved by the Dawn, who gave him immortality She forgot, however, to give him eternal youth, and he grew old but could not die.

Titiens, IV. i. 31. See Lucenes.

Tityrus, II xxxiv 72 A Vergilian shepherd

Tityus, II. xx. 31; III. v 44. A giant, condemned to be eternally devoured by a vulture in Hades

Tolumnius, IV x 23, 37 King of Veii

Triops, III ix 16 Founder of Cnidos.

Triton, II. xxxii. 16; IV. vi 61

Trivia, II xxxii. 10. Diana

Troia, II. iii. 34, viii. 10, xviii 53, xxx 30; III i. 32, xviii. 3. IV i 39, 47, 87, 114.

Troianus, II. vi. 16, xxxiv 63

Troicus, IV. i. 87

Tullus, I i 9, vi. 2, xiv. 20, xxii 1; III xxii. 2, 6, 39. A friend of Propertius.

Tuscus, IV ii 3, 49, 50.

Tyndaridae, I xvii. 18. Castor and Pollux, sons of Tyndareus

INDEX

Tyndaris, II. xxxii 31, III. viii. 30. Clytemnestra, daughter of Tyndareus.

Tyrius, III. xiv 27; IV. iii 34, v 22

Tyro, II. xxviii 51 *See* Salmonis.

Tyros, II. xvi 18; III. xiii 7

Tyrrhenus, I. viii. 11, III. xvii 25. Etruscan.

VARRO, II. xxxiv. 85 86. A poet of the Alexandrian school, born at Atax. He translated the *Argonautica* of Apollonius Rhodius, and subsequently wrote elegies in honour of his mistress Leucadia.

Veii, IV. x 24, 27. An ancient town of Etruria

Veiens, IV. x 23.

Veius, IV. x 31.

Velabrum, IV. ix 5. The marshy land lying between the Vicus Tuscus and the Forum Boarium, beneath the Aventine. In early times it was flooded, and the Aventine could only be approached from the rest of the city by water

Venetus, I. xii 4

Venus, I. i. 33, ii. 30, xiv 16; II. x. 7, xiii. 56, xv 11, xvi 13, xix. 18, xxi 2, xxii 22, xxviii. 9, xxxii. 33; III. iii. 31, iv. 19, v. 23, vi 34, viii 12, ix 11, x 30, xiii 2, xvi 20, xvii. 3, xx 20, xxiv 13; IV. i. 46, 137, 138, iii 50, v. 5, 53, 65, vii. 19, viii. 16, 34, 45

Vergiliae, I. viii 10. The Pleiads.

Vergilius, II. xxxiv. 61.

Vertumnus, IV. ii. 2, 10, 12, 35 The "god of change," specially associated with the seasons and the fruits of the earth. His image stood in the Vicus Tuscus, leading from the Velabrum to the Forum Romanum

Vesta, II xxix. 27, III. iv 11; IV. i 21, iv. 18, 36, 69, xi 53 The goddess of the household also of flocks and herds.

Vicus Tuscus, IV. ii. 50 *See* Vertumnus

Virdomarus, IV. x 41. King of the Insubres, slain by M. Claudius Marcellus at Clastidium in 222 B C.

Vlixes, II vi. 23, ix. 7, xiv. 3 xxvi 37, III. vii 41, xii. 23.

Vmber, I. xx. 7; III. xxii. 23, IV. i 124.

Vmbria, I xxii. 9; IV. i. 63, 64, 121

Volsinii, IV ii 4 A town in Etruria, the modern Bolsena.

XERXES, II. i. 22 The allusion in this passage is to Xerxes' attempt to cut a canal across the promontory of Athos.

ZEPHYRUS, I. xvi. 34, xviii 2.

Zetes, I xx. 26. A winged son of the North Wind

Zethus, III xv. 29, 41 Son of Antiopa and Jupiter, brother of Amphion.

THE LOEB CLASSICAL LIBRARY

EDITED BY T. E. PAGE, M.A., AND W. H. D. ROUSE, LITT.D.

A SERIES OF GREEK AND LATIN TEXTS
WITH TRANSLATIONS INTO ENGLISH ON
THE OPPOSITE PAGE BY LEADING SCHOLARS

FCAP. 8VO.

Price 5s net in cloth, or 6s 6d net in leather

A LIST OF THE VOLUMES

FIRST TWENTY

Ready in September 1912

THE APOSTOLIC FATHERS, translated by Kirsopp Lake, of the University of Leyden. 2 volumes. Volume I, September. [Volume II, November.]

THE CONFESSIONS OF ST. AUGUSTINE, translated by W. Watts (1631). 2 volumes.

EURIPIDES, translated by A. S. Way, of the University of London. 4 volumes. Volume I, Iphigeneia at Aulis—Rhesus—Hecuba—The Daughters of Troy—Helen; Volume II, Electra—Orestes—Iphigeneia in Taurica—Andromache—Cyclops.

PHILOSTRATUS, THE LIFE OF APOLLONIUS OF TYANA, translated by F. C. Conybeare, of University College, Oxford. 2 volumes.

PROPERTIUS, translated by H. E. Butler, of the University of London. 1 volume.

TERENCE, translated by John Sargeaunt, of Westminster School. 2 volumes. Volume I, Lady of Andros—Self-Tormentor—Eunuch; Volume II, Phormio—Mother-in-Law—Brothers.

Ready in November 1912

APOLLONIUS RHODIUS, translated by R. C. Seaton, of Jesus College, Cambridge. 1 volume.

APPIAN'S ROMAN HISTORY, translated by Horace White, of New York. 4 volumes. Volumes I and II

CATULLUS, translated by F. W. Cornish, Vice-Provost of Eton College; TIBULLUS, translated by J P. Postgate, of Liverpool University; PERVIGILIUM VENERIS, translated by J. W. Mackail. 1 volume.

CICERO'S LETTERS TO ATTICUS, translated by E. O. Winstedt, of Magdalen College, Oxford. 3 volumes. Volume I.

JULIAN, translated by W. C. Wright, of Bryn Mawr College. 3 volumes. Volume I.

LUCIAN, translated by A. M. Harmon, of Princeton University. 8 volumes. Volume I

SOPHOCLES, translated by F. Storr, of Trinity College, Cambridge. 2 volumes. Volume I, Oedipus the King—Oedipus at Colonus—Antigone.

THEOCRITUS, BION AND MOSCHUS, translated by J. M. Edmonds, of Jesus College, Cambridge. 1 volume.

FURTHER VOLUMES PROJECTED IN THE LOEB CLASSICAL LIBRARY

GREEK AUTHORS

AESCHINES, translated by C. D. Adams, of Dartmouth College. 2 volumes.

APPIAN, translated by Horace White, of New York. Volumes III and IV.

ARISTOPHANES, translated by J. W. White, of Harvard University. 3 volumes.

ARISTOTLE, THE POLITICS AND THE ATHENIAN CONSTITUTION, translated by Edward Capps, of Princeton University. 1 volume.

LIST OF FURTHER VOLUMES—*continued*

DAPHNIS AND CHLOE, translated by J. M. Edmonds, of Jesus College, Cambridge. 1 volume.

DIO CASSIUS, translated by H. G. Foster (1906), revised by E. Cary, of Princeton University. 8 volumes.

EURIPIDES, translated by A. S. Way, of the University of London. Volumes III and IV.

GREEK LYRICS, translated by J. M. Edmonds, of Jesus College, Cambridge. 1 volume.

LUCIAN, translated by A. M. Harmon, of Princeton University. Volumes II–VIII.

MANETHO, translated by S. de Ricci. 1 volume.

MENANDER, translated by F. G. Allinson, of Brown University. 1 volume.

PAUSANIAS, translated by W. H. S. Jones, of St. Catharine's College, Cambridge. 5 volumes.

PLUTARCH, TWELVE LIVES, translated by B. Perrin, of Yale University. 2 volumes.

QUINTUS SMYRNAEUS, translated by A. S. Way, of the University of London. 1 volume.

STRABO, translated by J. R. S. Sterrett, of Cornell University. 8 volumes.

THUCYDIDES, translated by C. F. Smith, of the University of Wisconsin. 2 volumes.

XENOPHON, CYROPAEDIA, translated by Walter Miller, of the University of Missouri. 2 volumes.

LATIN AUTHORS

APULEIUS, GOLDEN ASS, translated by W. Addlington (1566), revised by S. Gaselee, of Magdalene College, Cambridge. 2 volumes.

CAESAR'S GALLIC WARS, translated by Lieut.-Col. H. J. Edwards, C.B., of Peterhouse, Cambridge. 1 volume.

LIST OF FURTHER VOLUMES—*continued*

CICERO, DE FINIBUS, translated by H. Rackham, of Christ's College, Cambridge. 1 volume.

DE OFFICIIS, translated by Walter Miller, of the University of Missouri. 1 volume.

FAMILIARES, translated by E. O. Winstedt, of Magdalen College, Oxford. 5 volumes.

LETTERS TO ATTICUS, translated by E. O. Winstedt, of Magdalen College, Oxford. Volume II.

HORACE, EPISTLES AND SATIRES, translated by W. G. Hale, of the University of Chicago, and G. L. Hendrickson, of Yale University. 1 volume.

ODES AND EPODES, translated by C. E. Bennett, of Cornell University. 1 volume.

PLAUTUS, translated by Paul Nixon, of Bowdoin College. 4 volumes.

PETRONIUS, translated by M. Heseltine, of New College, Oxford. 1 volume.

PLINY'S LETTERS, Mellmott's translation, revised.

SENECA'S TRAGEDIES, translated by F. J. Miller, of the University of Chicago. 2 volumes

SUETONIUS, translated by J. C. Rolfe, of the University of Pennsylvania. 2 volumes.

TACITUS, DIALOGUS, translated by Wm. Peterson, of McGill University; GERMANIA AND AGRICOLA, translated by Maurice Hutton, of the University of Toronto. 1 volume.

VIRGIL, translated by H. R. Fairclough, of Stamford University. 2 volumes.

Full Prospectus on application.

NOTE: Under the title *Machines or Mind*, Dr. Rouse has written an essay on the advantages to be gained by study of the Classics. It will be forwarded post-free on application.

LONDON: WILLIAM HEINEMANN, 21 BEDFORD ST. W.C.